In the Back Country

A Journey in the Back Country

In the Winter of 1853-4

By

Frederick Law Olmsted

Author of " A Journey in the Seaboard Slave States," " A Journey in Texas,"
" Walks and Talks of an American Farmer in England," etc.

[Originally Issued in 1860]

In Two Volumes

Volume I

G. P. Putnam's Sons

New York   London

27 and 29 W. 23d Street   24 Bedford Street, Strand

The Knickerbocker Press

1907

The Knickerbocker Press, New York

PREFACE

THE narrative presented in this volume, containing the record of certain journeys through the Slave States, is devoted in the main to the hill-country people and to those who are engaged in, or are most directly affected by, the great business of the South—the production of cotton.

The record of facts, except as regards the domestic life of the people, is less elaborate than that undertaken in the *Journey in the Seaboard Slave States*, because, reference being made to previous observations, less detail is needed to give a full statement of that which was seen by the writer. Facts of general observations and conclusions of judgment form a larger part of this volume than of the preceding volume, because these are appropriately deduced from the details before given. The book was prepared for the press nearly in its present form, and was announced for publication in 1857. A chapter was then intended to be added upon the natural history of Southern politics, before preparing which I was interrupted by unanticipated duties. Upon recent examination, it was found that the facts recorded had not lost significance, and that the volume might be published without revision or addition. As the topic of slave insurrection is considerably discussed,

I will here observe that all of the narrative portion had been printed, and that all the matter of the last chapter bearing upon that subject had been written, some time before the John Brown plot is supposed to have been formed.

The controlling considerations which now induce the publication of this volume are, first, that after the publication of the *Seaboard Slave States* and the *Journey in Texas* to leave untold what is reported in this, would be to leave my story untrue through incompleteness; secondly, that the agitation growing out of the condition of the South is now graver, and the truth more important to be known than ever before. Before preparing this volume, I had given more than two years' careful study simply to the matter of fact of the condition of the people, especially the white people, living under a great variety of circumstances where slavery is not prohibited. There has been no publication of observations made with similar advantages, and extended over so large a field. I may add that few men could have been so little inclined to establish previously formed opinions as I was when I began my journey in the South. I left a farm in New York to examine farms in Virginia. The Fillmore compromises had just been accomplished; a reaction from a state of suspicion and unwholesome excitement was obvious in the public mind. Looking upon slavery as an unfortunate circumstance, for which the people of the South were in no wise to blame, and the abolition of which was no more immediately practicable than the abrogation of hospitals, penitentiaries, and boarding-schools, it was with the distinct hope of aiding in this reaction, and of aiding those disposed to consider the subject of slavery in a rational, philosophical, and conciliatory spirit, that I undertook, at the suggestion of the editor of the *New York Times*, to make a personal study of the ordinary condition and habits of the people of the South. I believed that much mischief had resulted from statements and descriptions of occurrences which were exceptional, as if they were ordinary phenomena attending slavery. I had the most unquestioning faith that while the fact of slavery imposed much unenviable duty upon the people of the South, and occasioned much inconvenience, the clear knowledge of which would lead to a disposition of forbearance, and encourage a respectful purpose of assistance (such as soon after this found an expression in the organization of the Southern Aid Society), there was at the same time a moral condition of the human race, in connection with slavery—that there was an expression of peculiar virtues in the South, too little known or considered, the setting forth of which would do good.

I will not here conceal for a moment that I was disappointed in the actual condition of the people of the South, citizen and slave; that the more thoroughly and the longer I was acquainted with that which is ordinary and general, the greater was my disappointment. In the present aspect of affairs, it would be an affectation of moderation if I refrained from expressing my conviction that the larger part of the people of the South are in a condition which cannot be too much deplored, the extension and aggravation of the causes of which cannot be too firmly and persistently guarded against.

The subjection of the negroes of the South to the mastership of the whites, I still consider justifiable and necessary, and I fully share the general ill-will of the people of the North toward any suggestion of their interfering politically to accomplish an immediate abolition of slavery. This is not from idolatry of a parchment, or from a romantic attachment to the word Union ; it certainly is not from a low estimation of the misfortune of slavery, or of the flagrant wrong of the laws and customs of the Slave States. It is from a fair consideration of the excellence of our confederate constitution when compared with other instruments of human association, and from a calculation of the chances of getting a better, after any sort of revolution at this time, together with the chances of thereby accomplishing a radical and satisfactory remedy for the evils which must result from slavery. I do not see that a mere setting free of the blacks, if it could be accomplished, would surely remedy these evils. An extraction of the bullet does not at once remedy the injury of a gun-shot wound ; it sometimes aggravates it.

It does not follow, however, that the evils of slavery must continue to be as great as at present. Nor does it follow that consideration of these evils at the North must be either futile or impertinent, for they are by no means limited in their action to the people of the Slave States, and there are matters in the discussion of which the people of the North have a constitutional right to be heard, the decision of which may greatly help to perpetuate or to limit them.

The emancipation of the negroes is evidently not a matter to be accomplished by this generation, but, again, it does not follow that even emancipation cannot be anticipated, or the way of accomplishing it in some degree prepared. The determination that it shall not be, is much more impracticable, fanatical, and dangerous than argument for immediate abolition. The present agitation of the country results less from the labors of abolitionists than from the conceit, avarice, and folly of wealthy owners of slaves. These constantly, and by organized action, endeavor to reverse the only line of policy by which safety and peace can, in the nature of things, be secured to the people of the South ; for there are moral forces, as well as material, in nature, and there is the same folly in expecting to overcome the one as the other.

It would be presumptuous in any man to predict when, or in what manner, slavery is to end, but, if the owners of slaves were so disposed, it appears to me that there would be no difficulty whatever, politically, financially, or socially, in diminishing the evil of slavery, and in preparing the way for an end to it. It is to be hoped that elements will, by-and-by, come into play, the nature of which we cannot now imagine, which will make a peaceful end more practicable than it now appears. Whitney's invention has, to all appearance, strengthened the hold of slavery a thousand

times more than all labors directly intended for
that purpose A botanical discovery, a new motive
power, the decease of some popular fallacy, a physical,
or mental, or moral epidemic, a theological reformation, a religious revival, a war, or a great man fortunately placed, may, in a single year, do more to remove
difficulties than has thus far been done in this century.

Popular prejudice, if not popular instinct, points to a
separation of black from white as a condition of the
abolition of slavery. It may be hoped that something
will occur which will force, or encourage and facilitate,
a voluntary and spontaneous separation. If this is to
be considered as a contingency of emancipation, it is
equally to be anticipated that an important emigration
of whites to the slave districts will precede it.[1] I do
not now say that it is, or is not, right or desirable that
this should be so, but, taking men as they are, I think
a happy and peaceful association of a large negro with
a large white population cannot at present be calculated on as a permanent thing. I think that the
emancipation from slavery of such part of the existing
actual negro population as shall remain in the country
until the white population is sufficiently Christianized,
and civilized, and properly educated to understand

---

[1] If gold fields as attractive as those of California should, for
instance, be discovered and opened to adventurers in Mississippi, slavery would be practically abolished in that State within
two years. Cotton culture would be more profitable work than
gold digging, but not until something else had once drawn free
laborers to a cotton district in large numbers.

that its interests are identical with its duty, will take place gradually, and only after an intermediate period of systematic pupilage, restraint, and encouragement, of such a nature as is suggested in this volume.

To be more explicit: it seems to me to be possible that a method of finally emancipating the slaves and of immediately remedying many of the evils of slavery, without an annihilation of that which the State has made property, or conceded to be held as property, may be eventually based on these accepted facts : That a negro's capacities, like a horse's, or a dog's, or a white man's, for all industrial purposes, including cotton-growing and cotton-picking, must be enlarged by a voluntary, self-restrained, self-urged, and self-directed exercise of those capacities; that a safely conducted cultivation and education of the capacities of the slaves will, of necessity, increase the value of the slaves, and that the slaves may thus be made to pay, year by year, for their own gradual emancipation.

I do not suppose that in one generation or two the effects of centuries of barbarism and slavery are to be extinguished. I do not think negroes are ever to become Teutons or Celts, but I do suppose that negroes may become thoroughly civilized, thoroughly independent individuals, and thus of tenfold more value in the commonwealth than they are. I, know, for a certainty, that the most dogged have a capacity for some improvement, even within their own lives ; that the most valuable cotton-pickers are capable of being made yet more valuable ; and I do not believe that

even ten years of careful, judicious, and economical
cultivation of this capacity, with all the negroes of a
large plantation, would fail to earn some pecuniary as
well as moral reward.

But a vain delusion possesses the South that slavery
carries with it certain defined advantages for the
master class. (I do believe, after a careful study,
that there are no such advantages.) Owing to this
delusion, moral forces in nature, as irresistible as the
laws of climate, are blindly disregarded, or held in
contempt,-and the hope lives that a power, found paramount within the South itself, must yet control the
continent. This hope makes light of all present evils,
growing out of slavery, or attributes them to causes
which it purposes to remove. Not till it is deci-
sively and finally dispelled, can any general policy
for remedying the evils of slavery be initiated, or even
an individual slaveholder be permitted to govern his
property in a manner consistent with what would
otherwise be the requirements of Christianity, civilization, and a sound and far-seeing economy.

In the preparation of this book, my conscious first
purpose has been to obtain and report facts of ordinary
life at the South, not to supply arguments. Lest it
should be thought I had some concealed purpose
to advocate by my selection of facts, I have here
frankly set forth the inner plans and theories for which
it might have been agreeable to me to have gained the
approval of its readers. The facts of my personal
observation fill the greater part of the book, though

I have not neglected others obtained at second hand in the South. There are various theories and purposes for which these facts may be turned to account. Their influence need not be, and should not be, the same with all that it has been with me, but I believe that there are few who will chance to read to whom they will not afford some entertainment and instruction.

CONTENTS

IN
THE BACK COUNTRY

CHAPTER I

THE VALLEY OF THE LOWER MISSISSIPPI

A COTTON MAN

A DEEP notch of sadness marks in my memory the morning of the May day on which I rode out of the chattering little town of Bayou Sara, and I recollect little of its suburbs but the sympathetic cloud-shadows slowing going before me over the hill of St. Francis. At the top is an old French hamlet, and a very American tavern.

One from among the gloomy, staring loungers at the door, as I pass, throws himself upon a horse, and overtaking me, checks his pace to keep by my side. I turn toward him, and full of aversion for the companionship of a stranger, nod, in such a manner as to say, " Your equality is acknowledged; go on " Not a nod; not the slightest deflection of a single line in the austere countenance; not a ripple of radiance in the sullen eyes, which wander slowly over, and, at distinct intervals, examine my horse, my saddle-bags, my spurs, lariat, gloves, finally my face, with such stern deliberation that at last I should not be sorry if he would speak. But he does not ; does not make the smallest response to a further turning of my head, which acknowledges the reflex interest excited in my own mind; his eyes remained fixed upon me, as if they were dead. I can no longer endure it in silence, so I ask, in a voice attuned to his apparent humor, "How far to Woodville ? "

The only reply is a slight grunt, with an elevation of the chin

"You don't know ? "

" No."

" Never been there ? "

" No."

" I can ride there before night, I suppose ? "

No reply.

" Good walker, your horse ? "

Not a nod.

" I thought mine pretty good."

Not a sneer, or a gleam of vanity, and Belshazzar and I warmed up together. Scott's man of leather occurred to my mind, and I felt sure that I could guess my man's chord. I touched it, and in a moment he became animated, civil ; hospitable even   I was immediately informed that this was a famous cotton region ; "when it was first settled up by 'Mericans, used to be reckoned the gardying of the world, the almightiest

rich sile God Almighty ever shuck down; gettin'
thinned down powerful fast now, though; nothin' to
what it was. All on't owned by big-bugs.'' Finally
he confided to me that he was an overseer for one of
them, "one of the biggest sort.'' This greatest of the
local hemipteras was not now on his plantation, but
had "gone North to Paris or Saratogy, or some of
them places.''

Wearing no waistcoat, the overseer carried a pistol,
without a thought of concealment, in the fob of his
trousers. The distance to Woodville, which, after he
had exhausted his subject of cotton, I again tried to
ascertain, he did not know, and would not attempt to
guess. The ignorance of the more brutalized slaves is
often described by saying of them that they cannot
count above twenty. I find many of the whites but
little more intelligent. At all events, it is rarely that
you meet, in the plantation districts, a man, whether
white or black, who can give you any clear information about the roads, or the distances between places
in his own vicinity. While in or near Bayou Sara
and St. Francisville, I asked, at different times, ten
men, black and white, the distance to Woodville
(the next town to the northward on the map.) None
answered with any appearance of certainty, and
those who ventured to give an opinion differed in
their estimates as much as ten miles. I found the actual distance to be, I think, about twenty-four miles.
After riding by my side for a mile or two, the overseer
suddenly parted from me at a fork in the road, with

hardly more ceremony than he had used in joining
me.

For some miles about St. Francisville the landscape
has an open, suburban character, with residences in-
dicative of rapidly accumulating wealth, and advance-
ment in luxury among the proprietors. For twenty
miles to the north of the town, there is on both sides a
succession of large sugar and cotton plantations Much
land still remains uncultivated, however. The roadside fences are generally hedges of roses—Cherokee
and sweetbrier. These are planted first by the side of
a common rail fence, which, while they are young,
supports them in the manner of a trellis ; as they grow
older they fall each way, and mat together, finally
forming a confused, sprawling, slovenly thicket, often
ten feet in breadth and four to six feet high. Trum-
pet creepers, grape-vines, greenbriers, and in very rich
soil, cane, grow up through the mat of roses, and
add to its strength. It is not as pretty as a trimmed
hedge, yet very agreeable, and the road being sometimes narrow, deep, and lane-like, delightful memo-
ries of England were often brought to mind .

There were frequent groves of *Magnolia grandiflora*
large trees, and every one in the glory of full blossom.
The magnolia does not, however, show well in masses,
and those groves, not unfrequently met, were much
finer where the beech, elm, and liquidamber formed
the body, and the magnolias stood singly out, magnifi-

cent chandeliers of fragrance. The large-leafed magnolia, extremely beautiful at this season of the year,
was more rarely seen.

THE PLANTATIONS.

The soil seems generally rich, though much washed
off the higher ground. The cultivation is directed
with some care to prevent this. Young pine trees,
however, and other indications of impoverishing agriculture, are seen on many plantations.

The soil is a sandy loam, so friable that the negroes,
always working in large gangs, superintended by a
driver with a whip, continued their hoeing in the midst
of quite smart showers, and when the road had become
a poaching mud.

Only once did I see a gang which had been allowed
to discontinue its work on account of the rain. This
was after a very heavy thunder-shower, and the appearance of the negroes whom I met crossing the
road in returning to the field, from the gin-house to
which they had retreated, was remarkable.

First came, led by an old driver carrying a whip,
forty of the largest and strongest women I ever saw
together; they were all in a simple uniform dress of a
bluish check stuff, the skirts reaching little below the
knee; their legs and feet were bare; they carried
themselves loftily, each having a hoe over the shoulder,
and walking with a free, powerful swing, like *chasseurs*
on the march. Behind them came the cavalry, thirty
strong, mostly men, but a few of them women, two of

whom rode astride on the plow mules. A lean and
vigilant white overseer, on a brisk pony, brought up
the rear. The men wore small blue Scotch bonnets;
many of the women, handkerchiefs, turban fashion, and
a few nothing at all on their heads.

The slaves generally of this district appear uncommonly well—doubtless, chiefly, because the wealth of
their owners has enabled them to select the best from
the yearly exportations of Virginia and Kentucky, but
also because they are systematically well fed.

The plantation residences were of a cottage class, sometimes with extensive and tasteful grounds about them.

An old gentleman, sensible, polite, and communicative, and a favorable sample of the wealthy planters,
who rode a short distance with me, said that many of
the proprietors were absentees—some of the plantations
had dwellings only for the negroes and the overseer. He
called my attention to a field of cotton which, he said,
had been ruined by his overseer's laziness. The
negroes had been permitted at a critical time to be too
careless in their hoeing, and it was now impossible to
recover the ground thus lost. Grass grew so rampantly
in this black soil, that if it once got a good start ahead,
you could never overtake it. That was the devil of a
rainy season. Cotton could stand drouth better than it
could grass. [1]

[1] "FINE PROSPECT FOR HAY.—While riding by a field the
other day, which looked as rich and green as a New England
meadow, we observed to a man sitting on the fence, 'You have
a fine prospect for hay, neighbor.' 'Hay! that's *cotton, sir,*'
said he, with an emotion that betrayed an excitement which we

The inclosures are not often of less area than a hundred acres. Fewer than fifty negroes are seldom found on a plantation; many muster by the hundred. In general the fields are remarkably free from weeds and well tilled.

I arrived shortly after dusk at Woodville, a well-built and pleasant court-town, with a small but pretentious hotel. Court was in session, I fancy, for the house was filled with guests of somewhat remarkable character. The landlord was inattentive, and, when followed up, inclined to be uncivil. At the ordinary—supper and breakfast alike—there were twelve men beside myself, all of them wearing black cloth coats,

---

cared to provoke no further; for we had as soon sport with a rattlesnake in the blind days of August as a farmer at this season of the year, badly in the grass. * * *

"All jesting aside, we have never known so poor a prospect for cotton in this region. In some instances the fields are clean and well worked, but the cotton is diminutive in size and sickly in appearance. We have seen some fields so foul that it was almost impossible to tell what had been planted

"All this backwardness is attributable to the cold, wet weather that we have had almost constantly since the planting season commenced. When there was a warm spell, it was raining so that plows could not run to any advantage; so, between the cold and the rain, the cotton crop is very unpromising. * * *

"The low, flat lands this year have suffered particularly. Thoroughly saturated all the time, and often overflowed, the crops on them are small and sickly, while the weeds and grass are luxurious and rank.

"A week or two of dry weather will make a wonderful change in our agricultural prospects, but we have no idea that any sort of seasons could bring the cotton to more than an average crop."—*Hernando (Miss.) Advance,* June 22, 1854.

black cravats, and satin or embroidered silk waistcoats ; all, too, sleek as if just from a barber's hands, and redolent of perfumes, which really had the best of it with the exhalations of the kitchen. Perhaps it was because I was not in the regulation dress that I found no one ready to converse with me, and could obtain not the slightest information about my road, even from the landlord.

I might have left Woodville with more respect for this decorum if I had not, when shown by a servant to my room, found two beds in it, each of which proved to be furnished with soiled sheets and greasy pillows, nor was it without reiterated demands and bribery of the servant, that I succeeded in getting them changed on the one I selected. A gentleman of embroidered waistcoat took the other bed as it was, with no apparent reluctance, soon after I had effected my arrangements. One wash-bowl, and a towel which had already been used, was expected to answer for both of us, and would have done so but that I carried a private towel in my saddle-bags. Another requirement of a civilized household was wanting, and its only substitute unavailable with decency.

The bill was excessive, and the hostler, who had left the mud of yesterday hanging all along the inside of Belshazzar's legs, and who had put the saddle on so awkwardly that I resaddled him myself after he had brought him to the door, grumbled, in presence of the landlord, at the smallness of the gratuity which I saw fit to give him.

The country, for some distance north of Woodville,
is the most uneven, for a non-mountainous region, I
ever saw. The road seems well engineered, yet you
are nearly all the time mounting or descending the sides
of protuberances or basins, ribs or dikes. In one place
it follows along the top of a crooked ridge, as steep-
sided and regular for nearly a quarter of a mile as a
high railroad embankment. A man might jump off
anywhere and land thirty feet below. The ground
being too rough here for cultivation, the dense native
forest remains intact.

"IMPORTANT TO BUSINESS MEN"

This ridge, a man told me, had been a famous place
for robberies. It is not far from the Mississippi bottoms.

"Thar could n't be," said he, "a better location for
a feller that wanted to foller that business. There was
one chap there a spell ago, who built himself a cabin
t' other side the river. He used to come over in a
dug-out. He could paddle his dug-out up the swamp,
you see, to within two mile of the ridge ; then, when he
stopped a man, he'd run through the woods to his dug-
out, and before the man could get help, he'd be t' other
side the Mississippi, a sittin' in his housen as honest as
you be."

The same man had another story of the ridge.

"Mr. Allen up here caught a runaway once, and
started to take him down to Woodville to the jail. He
put him in irons and carried him along in his waggin.

The nigger was peaceable and submissive till they got along onto that yer ridge place. When they got thar, all of a sudden he gin a whop like, and over he went twenty foot plum down the side of the ridge. 'Fore Allen could stop his hoss he'd tumbled and rolled himself 'way out of sight. He started right away arter him, but he never cotched a sight on him again."

HILL-SIDE COTTON CULTURE

Not far north of the ridge, plantations are found again, though the character of the surface changes but little. The hill-sides are so plowed that each furrow forms a narrow terrace. After the first plowing, thus scientifically directed, the lines are followed in subsequent cultivation, year in and year out, so long as enough soil remains to grow cotton with profit. On the hills recently brought into cultivation, broad, serpentine ditches, having a fall of from two to four inches in a rod, have been frequently constructed : these are intended to prevent the formation of more direct gullies, during heavy rains. Of course, these precautions are not perfectly successful, the cultivated hills in spite of them losing soil every year in a melancholy manner.

ABANDONED PLANTATIONS

I passed during the day four or five large plantations, the hill-sides gullied like icebergs, stables and negro quarters all abandoned, and given up to decay.

The virgin soil is in its natural state as rich as possible. At first it is expected to bear a bale and a half of cotton to the acre, making eight or ten bales for each able field-hand.   But from the cause described its productiveness rapidly decreases.

Originally, much of this country was covered by a natural growth of cane, and by various nutritious grasses. A good Northern farmer would deem it a crying shame and sin to attempt to grow any crops upon such steep slopes, except grasses or shrubs which do not require tillage. The waste of soil which attends the practice is much greater than it would be at the North, and, notwithstanding the unappeasable demand of the world for cotton, its bad economy, considering the subject nationally, can not be doubted.

If these slopes were thrown into permanent terraces, with turfed or stone-faced escarpments, the fertility of the soil might be preserved, even with constant tillage. In this way the hills would continue for ages to produce annual crops of greater value than those which are at present obtained from them at such destructive expense—from ten to twenty crops of cotton rendering them absolute deserts.   But with negroes at one thousand dollars a head and fresh land in Texas at one dollar an acre, nothing of this sort can be thought of The time will probably come when the soil now washing into the adjoining swamps will be brought back by our descendants, perhaps on their heads, in pots and baskets, in the manner Huc describes in China, which may be seen also in the Rhenish vineyards, to be relaid on the sunny slopes, to grow the luxurious cotton in.

The plantations are all large, but, except in their size and rather unusually good tillage, display few signs of wealthy proprietorship. The greater number have but small and mean residences upon them. No poor white people live upon the road, nor in all this country of rich soils are they seen, except *en voyage*. In a distance of seventy-five miles I saw no houses without negro-cabins attached, and I calculated that there were fifty slaves, on an average, to every white family resident in the country under my view. There is a small sandy region about Woodville, which I passed through after nightfall, and which of course my note does not include.

I called in the afternoon, at a house, almost the only one I had seen during the day which did not appear to be the residence of a planter or overseer, to obtain lodging. No one was at home but a negro woman and children. The woman said that her master never took in strangers; there was a man a few miles further on who did; it was the only place she knew of where I was likely to be entertained.

I found the place: probably the proprietor was the poorest white man whose house I had passed during the day, but he had several slaves; one of them, at least, a first-class man, worth two thousand dollars.

Just before me, another traveller, a Mr. S, from beyond Natchez, had arrived. Learning that I was from Texas, he immediately addressed me with volubility:

"Ah! then you can tell us something about it, and I would be obliged to you if you would. Have you been out west about Antonio? Ranchering's a good

business, eh, out west there, isn't it? Can a man
make thirty per cent. by it, eh? I hear so; should
think that would be a good business. But how much
capital ought a man to have to go into ranchering,
good, eh? so as to make it a good business?"

He was a middle-aged, well-dressed man, devouring
tobacco prodigiously; nervous and wavering in his
manner; asking questions, a dozen at a breath, and
paying no heed to the answers. He owned a plantation in the bottoms, and another on the upland; the
latter was getting worn out, it was too unhealthy for
him to live in the bottoms, and so, as he said, he had
had "a good notion to go into ranchering, just for ease
and pleasure."

"Fact is, though, I've got a family, and this is no
country for children to be raised in. All the children
get such foolish notions. I don't want my children
to be brought up here—ruins everybody; does, sir,
sure—spoils 'em; too bad; 'tis so, too bad; can't
make anything of children here, sir—can't, sir;
fact."

He had been nearly persuaded to purchase a large
tract of land at a point upon a certain creek where, he
had been told, was a large court-house, an excellent school, etc. The waters of the creek he named
are brackish, the neighboring country is a desert, and
the only inhabitants savages. Some knavish speculator had nearly got a customer, but could not quite
prevail on him to purchase until he examined the
country personally. He gave me no time to tell him

how false was the account he had had, but went on, after describing its beauties and advantages:

"But negro property is n't very secure there I 'm told. How is 't? Know?"

"Not at all secure, sir; if it is disposed to go, it will go—the only way you could keep it would be to make it always contented to remain. The road would always be open to Mexico; it would go when it liked."

"So I hear. Only way is, to have young ones there and keep their mothers here, eh? negroes have such attachments, you know; don't you think that would fix 'em, eh? No? No, I suppose not; if they got mad at anything, they 'd forget their mothers, eh? Yes, I suppose they would; can't depend on niggers; but I reckon they 'd come back; only be worse off in Mexico—eh?"

"Nothing but——"

"Being free, eh? get tired of that, I should think—nobody to take care of them. No, I suppose not; learn to take care of themselves."

Then he turned to our host and began to ask him about the neighbors, many of whom he had known when he was a boy, and been at school with. A sorry account he got of nearly all. Generally they had run through their property; their lands had passed into new hands; their negroes had been disposed of; two were now, he thought, "strikers" for gamblers in Natchez.

"What is a striker?" I asked the landlord at the first opportunity.

"Oh ! to rope in fat fellows for the gamblers ; they don't do that themselves, but get somebody else.   I don't know as it is so ; all I know is, they don't have no business, not till late at night ; they never stir out till late at night, and nobody knows how they live, and that 's what I expect they do.   Fellows that come into town flush, you know—sold out their cotton and are flush—they always think they must see everything, and try their hands at everything—these fellows bring 'em in to the gamblers, and get 'em tight for 'em, you know."

"How 's —— got along since his father died ? " asked Mr. S.

"Well, ——'s been 'unfortunate.   Got mad with his overseer ; thought he was lazy and packed him off ; then he undertook to oversee for himself, and he was unfortunate.   Had two bad crops.   Finally the sheriff took about half his niggers.   He tried to work the plantation with the rest, but they was old, used-up hands, and he got mad that they would not work more, and tired o' seein' 'em, and 'fore the end of the year he sold 'em all."

A MISSISSIPPI FAST MAN

Another young man, of whom he spoke, had had his property managed for him by a relative till he came of age, and had been sent North to college.   Two years previously he returned and got it into his own hands, and the first year he ran it in debt sixteen thousand dollars.   He had now put it back into the hands of his relative to manage, but continued to live upon it. "I see," continued our host, "every time any of their teams are coming back from town they fetch a barrel or a demijohn. There is a parcel of fellows, who, when they can't liquor anywhere else, always go to him."

"But how did he manage to spend so much the first year,—in gambling?"

"Well, he gambled some and he run horses. He don't know anything about a horse, and of course he thinks he knows everything Those fellows up at Natchez would sell him any kind of a tacky for four or five hundred dollars, and then after he'd had him a month, they'd ride out another and make a bet of five or six hundred dollars they'd beat him. Then he'd run with 'em, and of course he'd lose it."

"But sixteen thousand dollars is a large sum of money to be worked off even in that way in a year," I observed.

"Oh, he had plenty of other ways. He'd go into a bar-room, and get tight and commence to break things. They'd let him go on, and the next morning hand him a bill for a hundred dollars. He thinks that's a smart thing, and just laughs and pays it, and then treats all around again "

By one and the other, many stories were then told of similar follies of young men. Among the rest, this:

A certain man had, as was said to be the custom when running for office, given an order at a grocery for all to be "treated" who applied in his name. The grocer, after the election, which resulted in the defeat of the treater, presented what was thought an exorbitant bill. He refused to pay it, and a lawsuit ensued. A gentleman in the witness box being asked if he thought it possible for the whole number of people taking part in the election to have consumed the quantity of liquor alleged, answered .

" Moy Goad ! Judge " (reproachfully). " Yes, sir ! Why, I 've been charged for a hundred and fifty drinks *'fore breakfast*, when I 've stood treat, and I never thought o' disputin' it."

EDUCATION

At supper, Mr. S., looking at the daughter of our host, said :

" What a pretty girl that is. My dear, do you find any schools to go to out here—eh ? I reckon not. This isn't the country for schools. There 'll not be a school in Mississippi 'fore long, I reckon ; nothing but Institutes, eh ? Ha ! ha ! ha ! Institutes, humph ! Don't believe there 's a school between this and Natchez, is there ? "

" No, sir."

" Of course there isn't." [1]

---

[1] " Sectional excitement " has given a great impetus to educational projects in the South, and the Mississippi newspapers about this time contained numerous advertisements of a similar character to the following :

" CALHOUN INSTITUTE—FOR YOUNG LADIES ; MACON, NOXUBEE COUNTY, MISSISSIPPI — W. R POINDEXTER, A M., Principal and Proprietor.—The above School, formerly known as the ' Macon Female Institute,' will be reopened on the first of October, 1855, with an entirely new corps of teachers from

"What sort of a country is it, then, between here and Natchez?" I asked. "I should suppose it would be well settled."

"SWELL-HEADS"

"Big plantations, sir, nothing else—aristocrats; swell-heads I call them, sir—nothing but swell-heads, and you can't get a night's lodging, sir. Beyond the ferry, I 'll be bound, a man might die on the road 'fore he 'd get a lodging with one of them, eh, Mr. N.? so, is n't it? 'Take a stranger in, and I 'll clear you out!' That 's the rule. That 's what they tell their overseers, eh? Yes, sir; just so inhospitable as that—swell-heads? swell-heads, sir, every plantation—can't get a meal of vituals or a night's lodging from one of them, I don't suppose, not if your life depended on it. Can you, Mr. N.?"

"Well, I believe Mr. ——, his place is right on the road, and it 's half way to the ferry, and I believe he tells his overseer if a man comes and wants something to eat, he must give it to him, but he must not take any pay for it, because strangers must have something to eat. They start out of Natchez, thinking it 's as 't is in other countries; that there 's houses along, where they can get a meal, and so they don't provide for themselves,

Principal down. Having purchased the property at public sale, and thus become *sole proprietor*, the Principal has determined to use all means he can now command, as well as he may realize for several years yet to come, in building, refitting, and procuring such appurtenances as shall enable him to contribute his full quota, as a professional man, to the progress of the great cause of ' SOUTHERN EDUCATION.' "

and when they get along about there, they are sometimes desperate hungry. Had to be something done.''

" Do the planters not live themselves on their plantations? "

" Why, a good many of them has two or three plantations, but they don't often 'live on any of them ''

" Must have ice for their wine, you see," said Mr. S.,
"or they 'd die ; and so they have to live in Natchez or
New Orleans ; a good many of them live in New
Orleans.''

" And in summer they go up into Kentucky, do they
not ? I have seen country houses there which were
said to belong to cotton-planters from Mississippi.''

" No, sir ; they go North, to New York, and New-
port, and Saratoga, and Cape May, and Seneca Lake—
somewhere that they can display themselves worse than
they do here ; Kentucky is no place for that. That 's
the sort of people, sir, all the way from here to Natchez,
and all round Natchez, too, and in all this section of
country where there 's good land. Good God ! I
would n't have my children educated, sir, among them,
not to have them as rich as Dr. ——, every one of them.
You can know their children as far off as you can see
them—young swell-heads ! You 'll take note of 'em
in Natchez. Why, you can tell them by their walk ; I
noticed it yesterday at the Mansion House. They sort
o' throw out their legs as if they had n't got strength
enough to lift 'em and put them down in any particular
place. They do want so bad to look as if they were n't
made of the same clay as the rest of God's creation.''

Some allowance is of course to be made for the splenetic temperament of this gentleman, but facts evidently afford a justification of his sarcasms. And this is easily accounted for. The farce of the vulgar-rich has its foundation in Mississippi, as in New York and in Manchester, in the rapidity with which certain values have advanced, especially that of cotton, and, simultaneously, that of cotton lands and negroes.[1] Of course, there are men of refinement and cultivation among the rich planters of Mississippi, and many highly estimable and intelligent persons outside of the wealthy class, but the number of such is smaller in proportion to that of the immoral, vulgar, and ignorant newly-rich, than in any other part of the United States. And herein is a radical difference between the social condition of this region and that of the seaboard Slave States, where there are fewer wealthy families, but where, among the people wealth, refinement and education are much more general.

I asked how rich the sort of men were of whom he spoke.

[1] As "a Southern lawyer," writing for *Harper's Weekly* (February, 1859), observes: "The sudden acquisition of wealth in the cotton-growing region of the United States, in many instances by planters commencing with very limited means, is almost miraculous. Patient, industrious, frugal, and self-denying, nearly the entire amount of their cotton-crops is devoted to the increase of their capital. The result is, in a few years large estates, as if by magic, are accumulated. The fortunate proprietors then build fine houses, and surround themselves with comforts and luxuries to which they were strangers in their earlier years of care and toil."

"Why, sir, from a hundred thousand to ten million."

"Do you mean that between here and Natchez there are none worth less than a hundred thousand dollars?"

"No, sir, not beyond the ferry. Why, any sort of a plantation is worth a hundred thousand dollars; the niggers would sell for that."

"How many negroes are there on these plantations?"

"From fifty to a hundred."

"Never over one hundred?"

"No; when they've increased to a hundred they always divide them; stock another plantation. There are sometimes three or four plantations adjoining one another, with an overseer for each, belonging to the same man; but that is n't general—in general, they have to strike off for new land."

"How many acres will a hand tend here?"

"About fifteen—ten of cotton, and five of corn; some pretend to make them tend twenty."

"And what is the usual crop?"

"A bale and a half to the acre on fresh land and in the bottom. From four to eight bales to a hand they generally get; sometimes ten and better, when they are lucky."

"A bale and a half on fresh land? How much on old?"

"Well, you can't tell—depends on how much it's worn and what the season is, so much. Old land, after a while, is n't worth bothering with."

"Do most of these large planters who live so freely, anticipate their crops as the sugar planters are said to—

spend the money, I mean, before the crop is sold?"

"Yes, sir, and three and four crops ahead generally."

"Are most of them the sons of rich men? are they old estates?"

"No, sir; many of them were overseers themselves once."

"Well, have you noticed whether it is a fact that these large properties seldom continue long in the same family? Do the grandsons of wealthy planters often become poor men?"

"Generally the sons do; almost always their sons are fools, and soon go through with it."

"If they don't kill themselves before their fathers die," said the other.

"Yes; they drink hard and gamble, and of course that brings them into fights."

This was while they were smoking on the gallery after supper. I walked to the stable to see how my horse was provided for; when I returned they were talking of negroes who had died of yellow fever while confined in the jail at Natchez. Two of them were spoken of as having been thus "happily released," being under sentence of death, and unjustly so, in their opinion.

THE LOWER LAW

A man living in this vicinity having taken a runaway while the fever was raging in the jail, a physician advised him not to send him there. He did not, and the negro escaped; was sometime afterward recaptured, and the owner learned from him that he had been once taken and not detained according to law. Being a patriotic man, he made a journey to inquire into the matter, and was very angry. He said, "Whenever you catch a nigger again, you send him to jail, no matter what 's to be feared. If he dies in the jail, you are not responsible. You 've done your duty, and you can leave the rest to Providence."

"That was right, too," said Mr. P. "Yes, he ought to a' minded the law ; then if he 'd died in jail, he 'd know 't was n't his fault "

Next morning, near the ferry house, I noticed a set of stocks, having holes for the head as well as the ankles ; they stood unsheltered and unshaded in the open road.

I asked an old negro what it was.

"Dat ting, massa?" grinning; "well, sah, we calls dat a ting to put black people, niggers in, when dey misbehaves bad, and to put runaways in, sah. Heaps o' runaways, dis country, sah. Yes, sah, heaps on 'em round here."

Mr. S. and I slept in the same room. I went to bed some time before him ; he sat up late, to smoke, he said. He woke me when he came in, by his efforts to barricade the door with our rather limited furniture. The room being small, and without a window, I expostulated. He acknowledged it would probably make us rather too warm, but he should n't feel safe if the door were left open. "You don't know," said he ; "there may be runaways around."

He then drew two small revolvers, hitherto concealed under his clothing, and began to examine the caps. He was certainly a nervous man, perhaps a madman. I suppose he saw some expression of this in my face, for he said, placing them so they could be easily taken up as he lay in bed, "Sometimes a man has a use for them when he least expects it. There was a gentleman on this road a few days ago ; he was going to Natchez He overtook a runaway, and he says to him, 'bad company 's better n' none, boy, and I reckon I 'll keep you along with me into Natchez.' The nigger appeared to be pleased to have company, and went along, talking with him, very well, till they came to a thicket place about six miles from Natchez, and then he told him he reckoned he would not go any further with him. 'What ! you black rascal,' says he ; 'you mean you won't go in with me ; you step out and go straight ahead, and if you turn your face till you get into Natchez, I'll shoot you.' 'Aha ! massa,' says the nigger, mighty good-natured, 'I reckon you haint got no shootin' irons,' and he bolted off into the thicket, and got away from him."   .

The carpentry of the house, as usual, was so bad that we did not suffer at all perceptibly, for ventilation.

At breakfast, Mr. S. came rather late. He bowed his head as he took his seat, and closed his eyes for a second or two ; then, withdrawing his quid of tobacco and throwing it in the fire-place, he looked round with a smile, and said :

"I always think it a good plan to thank the Lord for

His mercies.   I'm afraid some people'll think I'm a
member of the church.   I aint, and never was.   Wish
I was.   I am a Son, though [of Temperance?].   Give
me some water, girl; coffee first—never too soon for
coffee.   And never too late, I say.   Wait for anything
but coffee.   These swell-heads drink their coffee after
they've eaten all their dinner.   I want it with dinner,
eh?   Don't nothing taste good without coffee, I
reckon.''

Before he left, he invited me to visit his plantations,
giving me careful directions to find them, and saying
that if he should not have returned before I reached
them, his wife and his overseer would give me every
attention if I would tell them he told me to visit them.
He said again, and in this connection, that he believed
this was the most inhospitable country in the world and
asked, "as I had been a good deal of a traveler, did n't
I think so myself?"   I answered that my experience
was much too small to permit me to form an opinion so
contrary to that generally held.

If they had a reputation for hospitality, he said, it
could only be among their own sort.   They made great
swell-head parties; and when they were on their plantation places, they made it a point to have a great deal
of company; they would not have anything to do if
they did n't.   But they were all swell-heads, I might
be sure; they'd never ask anybody but a regular swell-
head to see them.

His own family, however, seemed not to be excluded
from the swell-head society.

Among numerous ancedotes illustrative of the folly of his neighbors, or his own prejudices and jealousy, I remember none which it would be proper to publish but the following :

REFUSING A NOBLE TITLE

"Do you remember a place you passed [describing the locality]?"

"Yes," said I ; "a nice house, with a large garden, and a lawn with some statues or vases in it "

"I think it likely ; got a foreign gardener, I expect ; that's all the fashion with them ; a nigger is n't good enough for them. Well, that belongs to Mr A. J. Clayborn. [?] He 's got to be a very rich man ; I suppose he's got as many as five hundred people on all his places. He went out to Europe a few years ago, and some time after he came back, he came up to Natchez. I was there with my wife at the same time, and as she and Mrs. Clayborn came from the same section of country, and used to know each other when they were girls, she thought she must go and see her. Mrs. Clayborn could not talk about anything but the great people they had seen in Europe. She was telling of some great nobleman's castle they went to, and the splendid park there was to it, and how grandly they lived. For her part, she admired it so much, and they made so many friends among the people of quality, she said, she did n't care if they always staid there ; in fact, she really wanted Mr. Clayborn to buy one of the castles, and be a nobleman himself ; 'but he would n't,' says

she; 'he's such a strong Democrat, you know.' Ha!
ha! ha! I wonder what old Tom Jeff. would have
said to these swell-head Democrats."

WHERE ARE ALL THE POOR PEOPLE?

I asked him if there were no poor people in this country. I could see no houses which seemed to belong to
poor people.

"Of course not, sir—every inch of the land bought
up by the swell-heads on purpose to keep them away.
But you go back on to the pine ridge. Good Lord!
I've heard a heap about the poor folks at the North,
but if you ever saw any poorer people than them, I
should like to know what they live on. Must be a
miracle if they live at all. I don't see how these people live, and I've wondered how they do a great many
times. Don't raise corn enough, great many of them,
to keep a shoat alive through the winter. There's no
way they can live, 'less they steal."

EXPERIENCE OF A FOREIGN TOURIST

At the ferry of the Homochitto I fell in with a German, originally from Dusseldorf, whence he came
seventeen years ago, first to New York; afterward he
had resided successively in Baltimore, Cincinnati, New
Orleans, Pensacola, Mobile, and Natchez. By the time
he reached the last place he had lost all his money.
Going to work as a laborer in the town, he soon earned
enough again to set him up as a trinket peddler; and a
few months afterward he was able to buy "a leetle

coach-dray." Then, he said, he made money fast ; for he would go back into the country, among the poor people, and sell them trinkets, and calico, and handkerchiefs, and patent medicines. They never had any money. "All poor folks," he said ; "dam poor ; got no money ; oh, no ; but I say, dat too bad, I don't like to balk you, my friend ; may be so, you got some egg, some fedder, some cheeken, some rag, some sass, or some skin vot you kill. I takes dem dings vot they have, and ven I gets my load I cums to Natchez back and sells dem, alvays dwo or dree times so much as dey coss me ; and den I buys some more goods. Not bad beesnes—no. Oh, dese poor people dey deenk me is von fool ven I buy some dime deir rag vat dey bin vear ; dey calls me de ole Dutch cuss. But dey don't know nottin' vot it is vorth. I deenk dey neever see no money ; may be so dey geev all de cheeken vot dey been got for a leetle breastpin vot cost me not so much as von beet. Sometime dey be dam crazy fool , dey know not how do make de count at all. Yees, I makes some money, a heap."

NATCHEZ

From the Homochitto to the suburbs of Natchez, a good half day's ride, I found the country beautiful ; fewer hills than before, the soil very rich, and the land almost all inclosed in plantations, the roadside boundaries of which are old rose-hedges. The road is well constructed ; often, in passing through the hills, with high banks on each side, coped with thick and dark, but free and sportive hedges, out of which avenues of trees grow carelessly and bend angel-like over the traveler, the sentiment of the most charming Herefordshire lanes is reproduced. There are also frequent woods, of a park-like character in their openness; the trees chiefly oak, and of great height. Sometimes these have been inclosed with neat palings, and slightly and tastily thinned out, so as to form noble grounds around the residences of the planters, which are always cottages or very simple and unostentatious mansions. Near two of these are unusually good ranges of negro-houses. On many of the plantations, perhaps most, no residence is visible from the road, and the negro-quarters, when seen, are the usual comfortless cabins.

Within three miles of the town the country is entirely occupied by houses and grounds of a villa character; the grounds usually exhibiting a paltry taste, with miniature terraces, and trees and shrubs planted and trimmed with no regard to architectural and landscape considerations. There is, however, an abundance of good trees, much beautiful shrubbery, and the best hedges and screens of evergreen shrubs that I have seen in America. The houses are not remarkable.

I was amused to recognize specimens of the "swell-head" fraternity, as described by my nervous friend, as soon as I got into the villa district. First came two boys in a skeleton wagon, pitching along with a racking pony, which ran over Jude; she yelped, I wheeled round, and they pulled up and looked apologetic. She was only slightly hurt, but thereafter gave a quicker

and broader sheer to approaching vehicles than her
Texas experience had taught her to do.

Then came four indistinct beards and two old, roué-
looking men, all trotting horses, the young fellows
screaming, breaking up, and swearing. After them
cantered a mulatto groom, white-gloved and neatly
dressed, who, I noticed, bowed politely, lifting his hat
and smiling to a ragged old negro with a wheelbarrow
and shovel, on the footpath.

Next came—and it was a swelteringly hot afternoon—
an open carriage with two ladies taking an airing.
Mr. S. had said the swell-heads had "got to think that
their old mammy niggers were not good enough for
their young ones"; and here, on the front seat of the
carriage, was a white and veritable French bonne,
holding a richly-belaced baby. The ladies sat back,
good-looking women enough, and prettily dressed, but
marble-like in propriety, looking stealthily from the
corners of their eyes without turning their heads. But
the dignity of the turn-out chiefly reposed in the coachman, an obese old black man, who should have been a
manufacturer of iced root-beer in a cool cellar, but who
had by some means been set high up in the sun's face
on the bed-like cushion of the box, to display a great
livery top-coat, with the wonted capes and velvet, but-
toned brightly and tightly to the chin, of course, and
crowned by the proper narrow-brimmed hat, with broad
band and buckle; his elbows squared, the reins and
whip in his hands, the sweat in globules all over his
ruefully-decorous face, and his eyes fast closed in sleep.

The houses and shops within the town itself are generally small, and always inelegant. A majority of the names on the signs are German ; the hotel is unusually clean, and the servants attentive ; and the stable at which I left Belshazzar is excellent, and contains several fine horses. Indeed, I never saw such a large number of fine horses as there are here, in any other town of the size. In the stable and the hotel there are a remarkable number of young men, extraordinarily dressed, like New York clerks on their Sunday excursions, all lounging or sauntering, and often calling at the bar ; all smoking, all twisting lithe walking-sticks, all "talking horse."

THE BLUFF.

But the grand feature of Natchez is the bluff, terminating in an abrupt precipice over the river, with the public garden upon it. Of this I never had heard, and when, after seeing my horse dried off and eating his oats with great satisfaction—the first time he had ever tasted oats, I suppose,—I strolled off to see the town, I came upon it by surprise. I entered a gate and walked up a slope, supposing that I was approaching the ridge or summit of a hill, and expecting to see beyond it a corresponding slope and the town again, continuing in terraced streets to the river. I found myself, almost at the moment I discovered that it was not so, on the very edge of a stupendous cliff, and before me an indescribably vast expanse of forest, extending on every hand to a hazy horizon, in which, directly in front of me, swung the round, red, setting sun.

Through the otherwise unbroken forest, the Mississippi had opened a passage for itself, forming a perfect arc, the hither shore of the middle of the curve being hidden under the crest of the cliff, and the two ends lost in the vast obscurity of the Great West. Overlooked from such an eminence, the size of the Mississippi can be realized—a thing difficult under ordinary circumstances; but though the fret of a swelling torrent is not wanting, it is perceptible only as the most delicate chasing upon the broad, gleaming expanse of polished steel, which at once shamed all my previous conceptions of the appearance of the greatest of rivers. Coming closer to the edge and looking downward, you see the lower town, its roofs with water flowing all around them, and its pigmy people wading, and laboring to carry upward their goods and furniture, in danger from a rising movement of the great water. Poor people, emigrants and niggers only.

I lay down, and would have reposed my mind in the infinite vision westward, but was presently disturbed by a hog which came grunting near me, rooting in the poor turf of this wonderful garden. I rose and walked its length. Little more has been done than to inclose a space along the edge, which would have been dangerous to build upon, to cut out some curving alleys now recaptured by the grass and weeds, and to plant a few succulent trees. A road to the lower town, cutting through it, is crossed by slight wooden foot-bridges, and there are some rough plank benches, adorned with stenciled " medical " advertisements.

Some shrubs are planted on the crumbling face of the cliff, so near the top that the swine can obtain access to them. A man, bearded and smoking, and a woman with him, sitting at the extreme end, were the only visitors except myself and the swine.

As I am writing there is a bustle in the street. A young man is being lifted up and carried into the bar-room. He is insensible. A beautiful mare, from which he has evidently been thrown, is led back from around the corner quivering with excitement.

I could find no reading-room ; no recent newspapers, except *The Natchez Free Trader*, which has nothing but cotton and river news, and steamboat puffs ; no magazines but aged *Harper's* ; and no recent publications of any sort are for sale or to be seen at the booksellers' ; so, after supper, I went to the cliff again, and most exquisite and solemn was the scene : the young moon shining through rents in the clouds, the great gleaming crescent of water below, the dim, ungapped horizon—the earth sensibly a mere swinging globe.

Of all the town, only five Germans, sitting together, but smoking in silence, had gathered here for evening worship.

As I returned up the main street, I stopped opposite a house from which there came the sound of excellent music—a violin and piano. I had heard no music since I was in Western Texas, and I leaned upon a lamp-post for an hour, listening. Many stopped near me

for a few minutes, and went on.   At length, a man
who had remained some time addressed me, speaking in
a foreign tongue.   " Can't you speak English ? " said I.

" You are not an American ? "

" Yes."

" I should tzink it not."

" I am ; I am a New Yorker."

" So ?—O yes, perhaps, but not zis country."

" What are you ? "

" Italian."

" Do you live here ? "

" Yes."

" Are there many Italians in Natchez ? "

" Yes—some many—seven. All big dam rascaal.
Yes. Ha ! ha ! ha ! True. Dam rascaal all of us."

" What do you do for a living here ? "

" For me it is a cigar-store ; fruit ; confectionery."

" And the rest ? "

" Oh, everytzing.   I don't expect dem here so much
long now "

" Why—what will they do ? "

" Dey all go to Cuba   Be vawr zair soon now. All
go. All dam rascaal go, can go, ven ze vawr is.
Good ting dat for Natchez, eh ?   Yes, I tzink."

He told me the names of the players ; the violinist,
an Italian, he asserted to be the best in America.   He
resided in Natchez, I understood, as a teacher ; and, I
presume, the town has metropolitan advantages for
instruction in all fashionable accomplishments.   Yet,
with a population of 18,601, the number of children

registered for the public schools and academies, or
"Institutes," of the county seat, is but 1015 ; and
among these must be included many sent from
other parts of the State, and from Arkansas and Louisiana ; the public libraries contain but 2000 volumes,
and the churches seat but 7700.[1]

Franklin, the next county in the rear of the county
in which Natchez is situated (Adams), has a population of 6000, and but 132 children attending school.

Mr. Russell[2] states that he had been led to believe that "as refined society was to be found at
Natchez as in any other part of the United States,"
but his personal observation was, that "the chief
frequenters of the best hotel were low, drunken
fellows."

LABOR AND WAGES.—TOWN AND COUNTRY

The first night after leaving Natchez I found lodging
with a German, who, when I inquired if he could
accommodate me, at once said, "Yes, sir, I make it a
business to lodge travelers."

He had a little farm, and owned four strong negro
men and a woman and children. All his men, however, he hired out as porters or servants in Natchez,

---

[1] This may be compared with the town of Springfield,
county of Sangamon, Illinois, in which, with a population of
19,228 (nearer to that of Natchez than any other town I observe
in the free States), the number of registered school children is
3300, the public libraries contain 20,000 volumes, and the
churches can accommodate 28,000 sitters.

[2] *North America: its Agriculture and Climate*, page 258.

employing a white man, a native of the country, to work with him on his farm.

To explain the economy of this arrangement, he said that one of his men earned in Natchez $30 a month clear of all expenses, and the others much more than he could ever make their labor worth to him. A negro of moderate intelligence would hire, as a house-servant, for $200 a year and his board, which was worth $8 a month; whereas he hired this white fellow, who was strong and able, for $10 a month; and he believed he got as much work out of him as he could out of a negro. If labor were worth so much as he got for that of his negroes, why did the white man not demand more? Well—he kept him in whiskey and tobacco beside his wages, and he was content. Most folks here do not like white laborers. They had only been used to have niggers do their work, and they did not know how to manage with white laborers; but he had no difficulty.

FOOD OF THE SLAVES

I asked if $8 would cover the cost of a man's board. He supposed it might cost him rather more than that to keep the white man; $8 was what it was generally reckoned in town to cost to keep a negro; niggers living in town or near it were expected to have "extras"; out on the plantations, where they did not get anything but bacon and meal, of course it did not cost so much. Did he know what it cost to keep a negro generally upon the plantations? It was generally reckoned, he said, that a nigger ought to have a peck of meal and three pounds of bacon a week; some did n't give so much meat, but he thought it would be better to give them more.

"You are getting rich," I said. "Are the Germans generally, hereabouts, doing well? I see there are a good many in Natchez."

"Oh yes; anybody who is not too proud to work can get rich here."

The next day, having ridden thirty tedious miles, about six o'clock I called at the first house standing upon or near the road which I had seen for some time, and solicited a lodging. It was refused, by a woman. How far was it to the next house? I asked her. Two miles and a half. So I found it to be, but it was a deserted house, falling to decay, on an abandoned plantation. I rode several miles further, and it was growing dark and threatening rain before I came in sight of another. It was a short distance off the road, and approached by a private lane, from which it was separated by a grass plat. A well-dressed man stood between the gate and the house. I stopped and bowed to him, but he turned his back upon me and walked to the house. I opened a gate and rode in. Two men were upon the gallery, but as they paid no attention to my presence when I stopped near them, I doubted if either were the master of the house. I asked, "Could I obtain a lodging here to-night, gentlemen?" One of them answered, surlily and decidedly, "No." I paused a moment that they might observe me—evidently a stranger benighted, with a fatigued horse—and then asked, "Can you tell me, sir, how far it is to a public house?" "I don't know," answered the same man. I again remained silent a moment. "No public houses in this section of the country, I reckon, sir," said the other. "Do you know how far it is to the next house on the road, north of this?" "No," answered one. "You'll find one about two miles or two miles and a half from here," said the other. "Is it a house in which I shall be likely to get a lodging, do you know?" "I don't know, I'm sure"

"Good-night, gentlemen; you'll excuse me for troubling you. I am entirely a stranger in this region."

A grunt, or inarticulate monosyllable, from one of them, was the only reply, and I rode away, glad that I had not been fated to spend an evening in such company.

Soon afterward I came to a house and stables close upon the road. There was a man on the gallery playing the fiddle. I asked, "Could you accommodate me here to-night, sir?" He stopped fiddling, and turned his head toward an open door, asking, "Wants to know if you can accommodate him?" "Accommodate him with what?" demanded a harsh-toned woman's voice. "With a bed, of course—what do you s'pose?—ho! ho! ho!" and he went on fiddling again. I had, during this conversation, observed ranges of negro huts behind the stables, and perceived that it must be the overseer's house of the plantation at which I had previously called. "Like master, like man," I thought, and rode on, my inquiry not having been even answered.

I met a negro boy on the road, who told me it was about two miles to the next house, but he did not reckon that I would get in there. "How far to the next house beyond that?" "About four miles, sir, and I reckon you can get in there, master; I've heerd they did take in travelers to that place."

Soon after this it began to rain and grow dark; so dark that I could not keep the road, for soon finding Belshazzar in difficulty, I got off and discovered that we were following up the dry bed of a small stream. In trying to get back I probably crossed the road, as I did not find it again, and wandered cautiously among trees for nearly an hour, at length coming to open country and a fence. Keeping this in sight, I rode on until I found a gate, entering at which, I followed a nearly straight and tolerably good road full an hour, at last coming to a large negro "settlement."

AN OVERSEER AT HOME

I passed through it to the end of the rows, where was a cabin larger than the rest, facing on the space between the two lines of huts. A shout here brought out the overseer. I begged for a night's lodging; he was silent; I said that I had traveled far, was much fatigued and hungry; my horse was nearly knocked up; and I was a stranger in the country; I had lost my road, and only by good fortune had found my way here. At length, as I continued urging my need, he said:

"Well, I suppose you must stop. Ho, Byron!

Here, Byron, take this man's horse, and put him in *my* stable. 'Light, sir, and come in.''

Within I found his wife, a young woman, showily dressed—a caricature of the fashions of the day. Apparently, they had both been making a visit to neighbors, and but just come home. I was not received very kindly, but at the request of her husband she brought out and set before me some cold corn-bread and fat bacon.

Before I had finished eating my supper, however, they both quite changed their manner, and the woman apologized for not having made coffee. The cook had gone to bed and the fire was out, she said. She presently ordered Byron, as he brought my saddle in, to get some " light-wood " and make a fire; said she was afraid I had made a poor supper, and set a chair by the fire-place for me as I drew away from the table.

I plied the man with inquiries about his business, got him interested in points of difference between Northern and Southern agriculture, and soon had him in a very sociable and communicative humor. He gave me much overseer's lore about cotton culture, nigger and cattle maladies, the proper mode of keeping sweet potatoes, etc.; and when I proposed to ride over the plantation with him in the morning, he said he " would be very thankful of my company. "

I think they gave up their own bed to me, for it was double, and had been slept in since the sheets were last changed; the room was garnished with pistols and other arms and ammunition, rolls of negro-cloth, shoes and hats, handcuffs, a large medicine chest and several books on medical and surgical subjects and farriery ; while articles of both men's and women's wearing apparel hung against the walls, which were also decorated with some large patent-medicine posters.   One of them is characteristic of the place and the times.[1]

REVIEW OF A FIRST-RATE COTTON PLANTATION

We had a good breakfast in the morning, and immediately afterward mounted and rode to a very large cotton-field, where the whole field-force of the plantation was engaged.

[1] THE WASHINGTON REMEDIES — TO PLANTERS AND OTHERS —These Remedies, now offered to the public under the title of the Washington Remedies, are composed of ingredients, many of which are not even known to Botany.   No apothecary has them for sale ; they are supplied to the subscriber by the native red-men of Louisiana.   The recipes by which they are compounded have descended to the present possessor, M. A. MICKLEJOHN, from ancestors who obtained them from the friendly Indian tribes, prior to and during the Revolution, and they are now offered to the public with that confidence which has been gained from a knowledge of the fact that during so long a series of years there has never been known an instance in which they have failed to perform a speedy and permanent cure.   The subscribers do not profess these remedies will cure *every* disarrangement of the human system, but in such as are enumerated below they feel they can not fail.   The directions for use have only to be strictly followed, and however despairing the patient may have been, he will find cause for blissful *hope* and renewed *life*.

These preparations are no Northern patent humbug, but are manufactured in New Orleans by a Creole, who has long used them in private practice, rescuing many unfortunate victims of disease from the grave, after they have been given up by their physicians as incurable, or have been tortured beyond endurance by laceration and painful operations.

It was a first-rate plantation. On the highest ground stood a large and handsome mansion, but it had not been occupied for several years, and it was more than two years since the overseer had seen the owner. He lived several hundred miles away, and the overseer would not believe that I did not know him, for he was a rich man and an honorable, and had several times been where I came from—New York.

The whole plantation, including the swamp land around it, and owned with it, covered several square miles. It was four miles from the settlement to the nearest neighbor's house. There were between thirteen and fourteen hundred acres under cultivation with cotton, corn, and other hoed crops, and two hundred hogs running at large in the swamp. It was the intention that corn and pork enough should be raised to keep the slaves and cattle. This year, however, it has been found necessary to purchase largely, and such was probably usually the case,[1] though the overseer intimated the owner had been displeased, and he "did not mean to be caught so bad again."

[1] "The bacon is almost entirely imported from the Northern States, as well as a considerable quantity of Indian corn. This is reckoned bad management by intelligent planters. * * * On this plantation as much Indian corn was raised as was needed, but little bacon, which was mostly imported from Ohio. The sum annually paid for this article was upward of eight hundred pounds Large plantations are not suited to the rearing of hogs; for it is found almost impossible to prevent the negroes from stealing and roasting the young pigs." Mr. Russell, visiting the plantation of a friend near Natchez.—*North America : its Agriculture*, etc., p. 265.

There were 135 slaves, big and little, of which 67 went to field regularly—equal, the overseer thought, to 60 able-bodied hands.   Beside the field-hands, there were 3 mechanics (blacksmith, carpenter, and wheelwright), 2 seamstresses, 1 cook, 1 stable servant, 1 cattle-tender, 1 hog-tender, 1 teamster, 1 house servant (overseer's cook), and one midwife and nurse.   These were all first-class hands; most of them would be worth more, if they were for sale, the overseer said, than the best field-hands.   There was also a driver of the hoe-gang who did not labor personally, and a foreman of the plow-gang   These two acted as petty officers in the field, and alternately in the quarters.

There was a nursery for sucklings at the quarters, and twenty women at this time who left their work four times each day, for half an hour, to nurse their young ones, and whom the overseer counted as half-hands—that is, expected to do half an ordinary day's work.

DESERTERS AND DETECTIVES

He had no runaways out at this time, but had just sold a bad one to go to Texas.   He was whipping the fellow, when he turned and tried to stab him—then broke from him and ran away.   He had him caught almost immediately by the dogs.   After catching him, he kept him in irons till he had a chance to sell him. His niggers did not very often run away, he said, because they were almost sure to be caught.   As soon as

he saw that one was gone he put the dogs on, and if
rain had not just fallen, they would soon find him.
Sometimes, though, they would outwit the dogs, but if
they did they almost always kept in the neighborhood,
because they did not like to go where they could not
sometimes get back and see their families, and he would
soon get wind of where they had been; they would
come round their quarters to see their families and to
get food, and as soon as he knew it, he would find
their tracks and put the dogs on again. Two months
was the longest time any of them ever kept out. They
had dogs trained on purpose to run after niggers, and
never let out for anything else.

DRIVING

We found in the field thirty plows, moving together,
turning the earth from the cotton plants, and from
thirty to forty hoers, the latter mainly women, with a
black driver walking about among them with a whip,
which he often cracked at them, sometimes allowing
the lash to fall lightly upon their shoulders. He was
constantly urging them also with his voice. All
worked very steadily, and though the presence of a
stranger on the plantation must have been rare, I saw
none raise or turn their heads to look at me. Each
gang was attended by a "water-toter," that of the hoe-
gang being a straight, sprightly, plump little black
girl, whose picture, as she stood balancing the bucket
upon her head, shading her bright eyes with one hand,
and holding out a calabash with the other to maintain

her poise, would have been a worthy study for Murillo.

DAYS AND HOURS OF LABOR

I asked at what time they began to work in the morning. "Well," said the overseer, "I do better by my niggers than most. I keep 'em right smart at their work while they do work, but I generally knock 'em off at 8 o'clock in the morning Saturdays, and give 'em all the rest of the day to themselves, and I always gives 'em Sundays, the whole day. Pickin' time, and when the crap's bad in grass, I sometimes keep 'em to it till about sunset, Saturdays, but I never work 'em Sundays."

"How early do you start them out in the morning, usually?"

"Well, I don't never start my niggers 'fore daylight except 't is in pickin' time, then maybe I get 'em out a quarter of an hour before. But I keep 'em right smart to work through the day." He showed an evident pride in the vigilance of his driver, and called my attention to the large area of ground already hoed over that morning; well hoed, too, as he said.

"At what time do they eat?" I asked. They ate "their snacks" in their cabins, he said, before they came out in the morning (that is before daylight—the sun rising at this time at a little before five, and the day dawning, probably, an hour earlier); then at 12 o'clock their dinner was brought to them in a cart—one cart for the plow-gang and one for the hoe-gang. The hoe-gang ate its dinner in the field, and only stopped work long enough to eat it. The plow-gang drove its teams to the "weather houses"—open sheds erected for the purpose in different parts of the plantation, under which were cisterns filled with rain water, from which the water-toters carried drink to those at work. The mules were fed as much oats (in straw), corn, and fodder as they would eat in two hours; this forage having been brought to the weather houses by another cart. The plowmen had nothing to do but eat their dinner in all this time. All worked as late as they could see to work well, and had no more food nor rest until they returned to their cabins.[1] At half past nine o'clock the drivers, each on an alternate night, blew a horn, and at ten visited every cabin to see that its occupants were at rest, and not lurking about and spending their strength in fooleries, and that the fires were safe—a very unusual precaution; the negroes are generally at liberty after their day's work is done till they are called in the morning. When washing and patching were done, wood hauled and cut for the fires, corn ground, etc., I

[1] This would give at this season hardly less than sixteen hours of plodding labor, relieved by but one short interval of rest, during the daylight, for the hoe-gang. It is not improbable. I was accustomed to rise early and ride late, resting during the heat of the day, while in the cotton district, but I always found the negroes in the field when I first looked out, and generally had to wait for the negroes to come from the field to have my horse fed when I stopped for the night. (See *Journey in Texas*, p. 82) I am told, however, and I believe, that it is usual in the hottest weather, to give a rest of an hour or two to all hands at noon. I never happened to see it done. The legal limit of a slave's day's work in South Carolina is 15 hours.

did not learn : probably all chores, not of daily necessity, were reserved for Saturday.   Custom varies in this
respect.   In general, with regard to fuel for the cabins,
the negroes are left to look out for themselves, and
they often have to go to "the swamp" for it, or at
least, if it has been hauled, to cut it to a convenient
size, after their day's work is done.   The allowance of
food was a peck of corn and four pounds of pork per
week, each.   When they could not get "greens"
(any vegetables) he generally gave them five pounds of
pork.   They had gardens, and raised a good deal for
themselves ; they also had fowls, and usually plenty of
eggs.   He added, "the man who owns this plantation
does more for his niggers than any other man I know.
Every Christmas he sends me up a thousand or fifteen
hundred dollars' [equal to eight or ten dollars each]
worth of molasses and coffee, and tobacco, and calico,
and Sunday tricks for 'em.   Every family on this plantation gets a barrel of molasses at Christmas."   (Not
an uncommon practice in Mississippi, though the quantity is very rarely so generous.   It is usually made
somewhat proportionate to the value of the last crop
sold.) [1]

Besides which, the overseer added, they are able, if
they choose, to buy certain comforts for themselves—
tobacco for instance—with money earned by Saturday
and Sunday work.   Some of them went into the swamps

[1] I was told by a gentleman in North Carolina, that the custom of supplying molasses to negroes in Mississippi was usually mentioned to those sold away from his part of the country,
to reconcile them to going thither.

on Sunday and made boards—"puncheons" made with the ax. One man sold last year as much as fifty dollars' worth.

Finding myself nearer the outer gate than the "quarters," when at length my curiosity was satisfied, I did not return to the house After getting a clear direction how to find my way back to the road I had been upon the previous day, I said to the overseer, with some hesitation lest it should offend him, "You will allow me to pay you for the trouble I have given you?" He looked a little disconcerted by my putting the question in this way, but answered in a matter-of-course tone, "It will be a dollar and a quarter, sir."

This was the only large plantation that I had an opportunity of seeing at all closely, over which I was not chiefly conducted by an educated gentleman and slave owner, by whose habitual impressions and sentiments my own were probably somewhat influenced. From what I saw in passing, and from what I heard by chance of others, I suppose it to have been in no respect an unfavorable specimen of those plantations on which the owners do not reside. A merchant of the vicinity recently in New York tells me that he supposes it to be a fair enough sample of plantations of its class. There is nothing remarkable in its management that he had heard. When I asked about molasses and Christmas presents, he said he reckoned the overseer rather stretched that story, but the owner was a very good man. A magistrate of the district, who had often been on the plantation, said in answer to an inquiry from me, that the negroes were very well treated upon it, though not extraordinarily so. His comparison was with plantations in general.[1] He also spoke well of the overseer. He had been a long time on this plantation—I think he said, ever since it had begun to be cultivated. This is very rare ; it was the only case I met with in which an overseer had kept the same place ten years, and it was a strong evidence of his comparative excellence, that his employer had been so long satisfied with him Perhaps it was a stronger evidence that the owner of the negroes was a man of good temper, systematic and thorough in the management of his property.[2]

The condition of the fences, of the mules and tools,

[1] In Debow's *Resources of the South*, vol. i., p. 150, a table is furnished by a cotton planter to show that the expenses of raising cotton are "generally greatly underrated." It is to be inferred that they certainly are not underrated in the table. On "a well improved and properly organized plantation," the expense of feeding one hundred negroes, "as deduced from fifteen years' experience" of the writer, is asserted in this table to be $750 per annum, or seven dollars and a half each ; in this sum is included, however, the expenses of the "hospital and the overseer's table." This is much less than the expense for the same purposes, if the overseer's account was true, of the plantation above described. Clothing, shoes, bedding, *sacks for gathering cotton, and so forth*, are estimated by the same authority to cost an equal sum—$7.50 for each slave. I have just paid on account of a day laborer on a farm in New York, his board bill, he being a bachelor living at the house of another Irish laborer with a family. The charge is twenty-one times as large as that set down for the slave.

[2] "I was informed that some successful planters, who held several estates in this neighborhood [Natchez], made it a rule to *change their overseers every year*, on the principle that the

and tillage, which would have been considered admirable in the best farming district of New York—the dress of the negroes and the neatness and spaciousness of their "quarters," which were superior to those of most of the better class of plantations on which the owners reside, all bore strong testimony to a very unusually prudent and provident policy.

I made no special inquiries about the advantages for education or means of religious instruction provided for the slaves. As there seems to be much public desire for definite information upon that point, I regret that I did not. I did not need to put questions to the overseer to satisfy my own mind, however. It was obvious that all natural incitements to self-advancement had been studiously removed or obstructed, in subordination to the general purpose of making the plantation profitable The machinery of labor was ungeared during a day and a half a week, for cleaning and repairs ; experience having proved here, as it has in Manchester and New York, that operatives do very much better work if thus privileged. During this interval, a limited play to individual qualities and impulses was permitted in the culture of such luxuries as potatoes and pumpkins, the repair of garments, and in other sordid recreations involving the

---

two years' service system is sure to spoil them."—Russell's *North America : its Agriculture*, etc., p. 258.

"Overseers are changed every year ; a few remain four or five years, but the average time they remain on the same plantation does not exceed two years."—*Southern Agriculturist*, vol. iv., p. 351.

least possible intellectual friction. Regarding only
the balance sheet of the owner's ledger, it was admirable management.   I am sorry to think that it is rare,
where this is the uppermost object of the cotton-
planter, that an equally frugal economy is maintained ;
and as the general character of the district along the
Mississippi, which is especially noticeable for the number of large and very productive plantations which
it contains, has perhaps been sufficiently drawn in
my narrative, I will now present, in a collective form,
before entering a different region, certain observations
which I wish to make upon the peculiar aspect of
slavery in that and similar parts of the Southern
States.

CHAPTER II

IN a hilly part of Alabama, fifty miles north of the principal cotton-growing districts of that State, I happened to have a tradesman of the vicinity for a traveling companion, when we passed a rather large plantation. Calling my attention to the unusually large cluster of negro cabins, he observed that a rugged range of hills behind them was a favorite lurking-ground for runaway negroes. It afforded them numerous coverts for concealment during the day, and at night the slaves of this plantation would help them to find the necessaries of existence. He had seen folks who had come here to look after niggers from plantations two hundred miles to the southward. "I suppose," said he, "'t would seem kind o' barbarous to you to see a pack of hounds after a human being?"

"Yes, it would."

"Some fellows take just as much delight in it as in runnin' a fox. Always seemed to me a kind o' barbarous sport. [A pause.] It 's necessary, though."

"I suppose it is. Slavery is a custom of society which has come to us from a barbarous people, and naturally, barbarous practices have to be employed to maintain it."

"Yes, I s'pose that 's so. But niggers is generally

52

pretty well treated, considering   Some people work their niggers too hard, that's a fact.   I know a man at —— ; he's a merchant there, and I have had dealings with him ; he 's got three plantations, and he puts the hardest overseers he can get on them.   He is all the time a-buying niggers, and they say around there he works 'em to death.   On these small plantations, niggers ain't very often whipped bad ; but on them big plantations, they 've got to use 'em hard to keep any sort o' control over 'em.   The overseers have to always go about armed ; their life would n't be safe, if they did n't.   As 't is, they very often get cut pretty bad." (Cutting is knifing—it may be stabbing, in south-western parlance.)

" In such cases, what is done with the negro ? "

" Oh, he gets hung for that—if he cuts a white man. that's the law ; 'intent to kill,' they call it ; and the State pays the owner what he 's worth, to hang him."

He went on to describe what he had seen on some large plantations which he had visited for business purposes—indications, as he thought, in the appearance of " the people," that they were being " worked to death." " These rich men," he said, " were always bidding for the overseer who would make the most cotton ; and a great many of the overseers did not care for anything but to be able to say they had made so many bales in a year.   If they made plenty of cotton, the owners never asked how many niggers they killed."

I suggested that this did not seem quite credible ; a

negro was a valuable piece of property. It would be
foolish to use him in such a way

"Seems they don't think so," he answered. "They
are always bragging—you must have heard them—how
many bales their overseer has made, or how many their
plantation has made to a hand. They never think of
anything else. You see, if a man did like to have his
niggers taken care of, he could n't bear to be always hearing that all the plantations round had beat his. He 'd
think the fault was in his overseer. The fellow who
can make the most cotton always gets paid the best." [1]

Overseers' wages were ordinarily from $200 to $600,
but a real driving overseer would very often get $1000.
Sometimes they'd get $1200 or $1500. He heard of
$2000 being paid one fellow.[2] A determined and per-

[1] Another person in this vicinity observed to me, that it was
one of the effects of the increasing demand for cotton, that
planters who would formerly have discharged an overseer for
cruel usage of his slave, now thought it right to let him have
his own way. "If he makes cotton enough, they don't think
they ought to interfere with him."

[2] "Editors of *Delta* : Under the head of ' Home Reforms,' in
your paper of the 19th ultimo, I find views and opinions in regard to the institution of slavery identical with those long
entertained by myself, and embodied, some years ago, in a communication to your predecessors.

"I hold, sirs, that no gentleman will intentionally injure or
oppress a poor slave or others under his authority or protection ;
and I insist upon the justice and propriety of a rigid enforce-
ment of our humane laws, no matter by whom violated, or how
high the offender. * * *

"The defective education and consequent habits of the overseers of the South, with a few exceptions, disqualify them for
the high and sacred trust confided to them ; and yet the ex-

fectly relentless man—I can't recall his words, which were very expressive—a real devil of an overseer, would get almost any wages he'd ask ; because when it was told round that such a man had made so many bales to the hand, everybody would be trying to get him.

The man who talked in this way was a native Alabamian, ignorant, but apparently of more than ordinarily reflective habits, and so situated as to have unusually good opportunities for observation. In character, if not in detail, I must say that his information was entirely in accordance with the opinions I should have been led to form from the conversations I heard by chance, from time to time, in the richest cotton districts. That his statements as to the bad management of large plantations, in respect to the waste of negro property, were not much exaggerated, I find frequent evidence in Southern agricultural journals. The following is an extract from one of a series of essays published in *The Cotton Planter*, the object of which is to present the economical advantages of a more mixed system of agriculture than is usually followed in the cotton region. The writer, Mr. M. W. Phillips, is a well-known, intelligent, and benevolent planter, who resides constantly on his estate, near Jackson, Mississippi .

"I have known many in the rich planting portion of Mississippi especially, and others elsewhere, who, acting on the policy

travagant salaries which they receive (from one to three thousand dollars) [*i. e.*, on sugar plantations] should command the services of men of exemplary character and distinguished abilities."—*New Orleans Delta*, Dec., 1856.

of the boy in the fable, who 'killed the goose for the golden egg,' accumulated property, yet among those who have relied solely on their product in land and negroes, I doubt if this be the true policy of plantation economy. With the former everything has to bend, give way to large crops of cotton, land has to be cultivated wet or dry, negroes to work, cold or hot, large crops planted, and they must be cultivated, or done so after a manner. When disease comes about as, for instance, cholera, pneumonia, flux, and other violent diseases, these are more subject, it seemeth to me, than others, or even if not, there is less vitality to work on, and, therefore, in like situations and similar in severity, they must sink with more certainty; or even should the animal economy rally under all these trials, the neglect consequent upon this 'cut and cover' policy must result in greater mortality. Another objection, not one fourth of the children born are raised, and perhaps not over two-thirds are born on the place, which, under a different policy, might be expected. And this is not all : hands, and teams, and land must wear out sooner ; admitting this to be only one year sooner in twenty years, or that lands and negroes are less productive at forty than at forty-two, we see a heavy loss. Is this not so? I am told of negroes not over thirty-five to forty-five who look older than others at forty-five to fifty-five. I know a man now, not short of sixty, who might readily be taken for forty-five ; another on the same place full fifty (for I have known both for twenty-eight years, and the last one for thirty-two years), who could be sold for thirty-five, and these negroes are very leniently dealt with. Others, many others, I know and have known twenty-five to thirty years, of whom I can speak as above. As to rearing children, I can point to equally as strong cases ; aye, men who are, 'as it were,' of one family, differing as much as four and eight bales in cropping, and equally as much in raising young negroes. The one scarcely paying expenses by his crop, yet in the past twenty-five years raising over seventy-five to a hundred negroes, the other buying more than raised, and yet not as many as the first.

"I regard the 'just medium' to be the correct point. Labor is conducive to health ; a healthy woman will rear most children. I favor good and fair work, yet not overworked so as to tax the animal economy, that the woman can not rear healthy children, nor should the father be over-wrought, that his vital powers be at all infringed upon.

"If the policy be adopted, to make an improvement in land visible, to raise the greatest number of healthy children, to make an abundance of provision, to rear a portion at least of work horses, rely on it we will soon find by our tax list that our country is improving. * * *

"Brethren of the South, we must change our policy. *Overseers are not interested in raising children, or meat, in improving land, or improving productive qualities of seed, or animals. Many of them do not care whether property has depreciated or improved, so they have made a crop to boast of.*

"As to myself, I care not who has the credit of making crops at Log Hall, and I would prefer that an overseer, who has been one of my family for a year or two, or more, should be benefited ; but this thing is to be known and well understood. I plant such fields in such crops as I see fit; I plant acres in corn, cotton, oats, potatoes, etc., as I select, and the general policy of rest, cultivation, etc., must be preserved which I lay down. A self-willed overseer may fraudulently change somewhat in the latter, by not carrying out orders—that I can not help. What I have written, I have written, and think I can substantiate."

From the *Southern Agriculturist*, vol. iv., page 317 :

OVERSEERS

"* * * When they seek a place, they rest their claims entirely on the number of bags they have heretofore made to the hand, and generally the employer unfortunately recognizes the justice of such claims.

"No wonder, then, that the overseer desires to have entire control of the plantation. No wonder he opposes all experiments, or, if they are persisted in, neglects them ; *presses everything at the end of the lash ; pays no attention to the sick, except to keep them in the field as long as possible ; and drives them out again at the first moment and forces sucklers and breeders to the utmost.* He has no other interest than to make a big cotton crop. And if this does not please you, and induce you to increase his wages, he knows men it will please, and secure him a situation with."

From the Columbia *South Carolinian :*

"* * * Planters may be divided into two great classes, viz., those who attend to their business, and those who do not. And this creates corresponding classes of overseers. The planter who does not manage his own business must, of course, surrender everything into the hands of his overseer. Such a planter usually rates the merits of the overseer exactly in proportion to the number of bags of cotton he makes, and of course the overseer cares for nothing but to make a large crop To him it is of no consequence that the old hands are worked down, or the young ones overstrained ; that the breeding women miscarry, and the sucklers lose their children ; that the mules are broken down, the plantation tools destroyed, the stock neglected, and the lands ruined · *so that he has the requisite number of cotton bags, all is overlooked ;* he is re-employed at an advanced salary ; and his reputation increased. Everybody knows that by such a course, a crop may be increased by the most inferior overseer, in any given year, unless his predecessors have so entirely exhausted the resources of the plantation, that there is no part of the capital left which can be wrought up into current income. * * * Having once had the sole management of a plantation, and imbibed the idea that the only test of good planting is to make a large crop of cotton, an overseer becomes worthless. He will no longer obey orders ; he will not stoop to details ; he scorns all improvements, and *will not* adopt any other plan of planting than simply to work lands, negroes, and mules to the top of their bent, which necessarily proves fatal to every employer who will allow it.

" It seems scarcely credible, that any man owning a plantation will so abandon it and his people on it entirely to a hireling, no matter what his confidence in him is. Yet there are numbers who do it habitually ; and I have even known overseers to stipulate that their employers should not give any order, nor interfere in any way with their management of the plantation. There are also some proprietors of considerable property and pretention to being planters, who give their overseer a proportion of the crop for his wages ; thus bribing him by the strongest inducements of self-interest, to overstrain and work down everything committed to his charge.

" No planter, who attends to his own business, can dispense

with agents and sub-agents. It is impossible, on a plantation of any size, for the proprietor to attend to all the details, many of which are irksome and laborious, and he requires more intelligence to assist him than slaves usually possess. To him, therefore, a good overseer is a blessing. But an overseer who would answer the views of such a planter is most difficult to find. The men engaged in that occupation who combine the most intelligence, industry, and character, are allured into the service of those who place all power in their hands, and are ultimately spoiled."

An English traveler writes to the London *Daily News* from Mississippi (1857):

" On crossing the Big Block river, I left the sand hills and began to find myself in the rich loam of the valley of the Mississippi. The plantations became larger, the clearings more numerous and extensive, and the roads less hilly, but worse. Along the Yazoo river one meets with some of the richest soil in the world, and some of the largest crops of cotton in the Union. My first night in that region was passed at the house of a planter who worked but few hands, was a fast friend of slavery, and yet drew for my benefit one of the most mournful pictures of a slave's life I have ever met with   He said, and I believe truly, that the negroes of small planters are, on the whole, well treated, or at least as well as the owners can afford to treat them. Their master not unfrequently works side by side with them in the fields. * * * But on the large plantations, where the business is carried on by an overseer, and everything is conducted with military strictness and discipline, he described matters as being widely different *The future of the overseer depends altogether on the quantity of cotton he is able to make up for the market.* Whether the owner be resident or non-resident, if the plantation be large, and a great number of hands be employed upon it, the overseer gets credit for a large crop, and blame for a small one. His professional reputation depends in a great measure upon the number of bales or hogsheads he is able to produce, and neither his education nor his habits are such as to render it likely that he would allow any consideration for the negroes to stand in the way of his advancing it. His interest is to get as much

work out of them as they can possibly perform. His skill consists in knowing exactly how hard they may be driven without
incapacitating them for future exertion. The larger the plantation the less chance there is, of course, of the owner's soften-
ing the rigor of the overseer, or the sternness of discipline by
personal interference. So, as Mr. H—— said, a vast mass of
the slaves pass their lives, from the moment they are able to go
afield in the picking season till they drop worn out into the grave,
in incessant labor, in all sorts of weather, at all seasons of the
year, without any other change or relaxation than is furnished
by sickness, without the smallest hope of any improvement
either in their condition, in their food, or in their clothing,
which are of the plainest and coarsest kind, and indebted
solely to the forbearance or good temper of the overseer for ex-
emption from terrible physical suffering. They are rung to
bed at nine o'clock, almost immediately after bolting the food
which they often have to cook after coming home from their
day's labor, and are rung out of bed at four or five in the morning. The interval is one long round of toil. Life has no sunny
spots for them. Their only refuge or consolation in this world
is in their own stupidity and grossness. The nearer they are to
the beast, the happier they are likely to be. Any mental or
moral rise is nearly sure to bring unhappiness with it."

The same gentleman writes from Columbus :

" One gets better glimpses of the real condition of the negroes
from conversations one happens to overhear than from what is
told to one's self—above all, when one is known to be a
stranger, and particularly an Englishman. The cool way in
which you hear the hanging of niggers, the shooting of niggers, and the necessity for severe discipline among niggers
talked of in bar-rooms, speaks volumes as to the exact state
of the case. A negro was shot when running away, near
Greensboro', a small town on my road, the day before I passed
through, by a man who had received instructions from the
owner to take him alive, and shoot him if he resisted. I heard
the subject discussed by some 'loafers' in the bar, while getting my horse fed, and I found, to my no small—I do not know
whether to say horror or amusement—that the point in dispute
was not the degree of moral guilt incurred by the murderer,

but the degree of loss and damage for which he had rendered himself liable to the owner of the slave in departing from the letter of his commission.   One of the group summed up the arguments on both sides, by exclaiming, 'Well, this shootin' of niggers should be put a stop to, that's a fact.'   The obvious inference to be deduced from this observation was, that 'nigger shootin'' was a slight contravention of police regulations—a little of which might be winked at, but which, in this locality, had been carried to such an extent as to call for the interference of the law.''

At Jackson, Mississippi, the door of my room at the hotel, opened upon a gallery where, late at night, a number of servants had been conversing together in an animated manner.   After some time, a white man joined them, and they immediately became quiet, reserved, and respectful.   He was evidently a coarse, vulgar man, in a gossiping humor.   Talking of a recent sale of negroes in town, led him to boast to these slaves of his own attractive qualities as a slaveowner. He had got, he said, a parcel of likely gals which he could sell any day for a great deal more'n they were worth to him.   He had been on the pint of doing it several times, but he could n't, because they was of his own raisin', and every time they heard he was talking of it, they'd come and cry so they'd make him change his mind.   He expected he was a kind of a soft-hearted man, and he could not part with them gals more'n he could with his own children.   He always carried shootin'-irons with him, but he never yet shot a nigger—never shot a nigger.   Some folks was mighty quick to shoot a nigger, but nary one of his niggers ever got shot, and he did n't expect they ever would— long as they behaved themselves.

This was said and repeated in a tone which would indicate that he thought such moderation quite laudable, and that it would highly recommend him to the niggers whom he was then addressing. They answered him in a manner which showed their sense of his condescension in thus talking to them, if not of his forbearance in the use of shootin'-irons.

I do not think that I have ever seen the sudden death of a negro noticed in a Southern newspaper, or heard it referred to in conversation, that the loss of property, rather than the extinction of life, was not the evident occasion of interest The following paragraphs are examples coming first in a search therefor

"We are informed that a negro man, the property of Mr. William Mays of this city, was killed last Thursday by a youth, the son of Mr. William Payne, of Campbell county. The following are the circumstances, as we have received them. Two sons of Mr. Payne were shooting pigeons on the plantation of Mr. Mays, about twenty miles from this place, and went to the tobacco-house, where the overseer and hands were housing tobacco ; one of the boys had a string of pigeons and the other had none.   On reaching the house, the negro who was killed asked the boy who had no pigeons, 'where his were' He replied that he killed none, but could kill him (the negro), and raised his gun and fired.   The load took effect in the head, and caused death in a few hours.   The negro was a valuable one. Mr. Mays had refused $1,200 *for him.*"—*Lynchburg Virginian.*

"A valuable negro boy, the property of W. A. Phipps, living in the upper end of this county, was accidentally drowned in the Holston river a few days ago."—*Rogersville Times.*

"Mr. Tilghman Cobb's barn at Bedford, Va , was set fire to by lightning on Friday, the 11th, and consumed Two negroes and three horses perished in the flames."—*New Orleans Daily Crescent.*

I have repeated these accounts, not to convey to the reader's mind the impression that slaves are frequently shot by their masters, which would be, no doubt, a mistaken inference, but to show in what manner I was made to feel, as I was very strongly in my journey, that what we call the sacredness of human life, together with a great range of kindred instincts, scarcely attaches at all, with most white men, to the slaves, and also in order to justify the following observation :—that I found the lives, and the comfort of negroes, in the great cotton-planting districts especially, habitually regarded, by all classes, much more from a pecuniary point of view, than I had ever before supposed they could be ; and yet, that, as property, negro life and negro vigor were generally much less carefully economized than I had always before imagined them to be.

As I became familiar with the circumstances, I saw reasons for this, which, in looking from a distance, or through the eyes of travelers, I had not been able adequately to appreciate. I will endeavor to explain :

It is difficult to handle simply as property, a creature possessing human passions and human feelings, however debased and torpid the condition of that creature may be ; while, on the other hand, the absolute necessity of dealing with property, as a thing, greatly embarrasses a man in any attempt to treat it as a person. And it is the natural result of this complicated state of things, that the system, of slave-management, is irregular, ambiguous, and contradictory—that it is never either consistently humane or consistently economical.

As a general rule, the larger the body of negroes on a plantation or estate, the more completely are they treated as mere property, and in accordance with a policy calculated to insure the largest pecuniary returns. Hence, in part, the greater proportionate profit of such plantations, and the tendency which everywhere prevails in the planting districts to the absorption of small, and the augmentation of large estates. It may be true, that among the wealthier slaveowners, there is oftener a humane disposition, a better judgment, and a greater ability to deal with their dependents indulgently and bountifully, but the effects of this disposition are chiefly felt, even on those plantations where the proprietor resides permanently, among the slaves employed about the house and stables, and perhaps a few old favorites in the quarters. It is more than balanced by the difficulty of acquiring a personal interest in the units of a large body of slaves, and an acquaintance with the individual characteristics of each. The treatment of the mass must be reduced to a system, the ruling idea of which will be, to enable one man to force into the same channel of labor the muscles of a large number of men, of various, and often conflicting wills.

The chief difficulty is to overcome their great aversion to labor. They have no objection to eating, drinking, and resting, when necessary, and no general disinclination to receive instruction. If a man own many slaves, therefore, the faculty which he values highest, and pays most for, in an overseer, is that of making them work. Any fool could see that they were properly supplied with food, clothing, rest, and religious instruction.

SLAVERY AS A MISSIONARY SYSTEM

In the county of Liberty, in Georgia, a Presbyterian minister has been for many years employed exclusively in laboring for the moral enlightenment of the slaves, being engaged and paid for this especial duty by their owners. From this circumstance, almost unparalleled as it is, it may be inferred that the planters of that county are, as a body, remarkably intelligent, liberal, and thoughtful for the moral welfare of the childlike wards Providence has placed under their care and tutorship. According to my private information, there is no body of slaveowners more, if as much so, in the United States. I heard them spoken of even as far away as Virginia and Kentucky. I believe, that in no other district has there been displayed as general and long-continued an interest in the spiritual well-being of the negroes. It must be supposed that nowhere else are their circumstances more happy and favorable to Christian nurture.[1]

[1] In White's *Statistics of Georgia* (page 377), the citizens of Liberty county, are characterized as "unsurpassed for the great attention paid to the duties of religion." Dr. Stevens, in his *History of Georgia*, describes them as "worthy of their sires," who were "the moral and intellectual nobility of the province," "whose accession was an honor to Georgia, and has ever proved one of its richest blessings." In the biography of General

After laboring thirteen years with a zeal and judgment which had made him famous, this apostle to the slaves of Liberty was called to the professorship of theology in the University of South Carolina. On retiring from his field of labor as a missionary, he addressed a valedictory sermon to his patrons, which has been published. While there is no unbecoming despondency or absence of proper gratitude for such results as have rewarded his protracted labor, visible in this document, the summing up is not such as would draw unusual cheers if given in the report of an African missionary at the Tabernacle or Exeter Hall. Without a word on which the most vigilant suspicion could raise a doubt of his entire loyalty to the uttermost rights of property which might be claimed by those whom he addressed, he could not avoid indicating, in the following passages, what he had been obliged to see to be the insurmountable difficulty in the way of any vital elevation of character among those to whom he had been especially charged to preach the gospel wherewith Christ blessed mankind :

Scrivens, the county of Liberty is designated "proud spot of Georgia's soil!" Dr. J. M. B. Harden, in a medical report of the county, says, "the use of intoxicating drinks has been almost entirely given up" by its people. White says (*Statistics*, 373), "the people of Liberty, from their earliest settlement, have paid much attention to the subject of education. Excellent schools are found in different portions of the county, and it is believed a greater number of young men from Liberty graduate at our colleges than from any [other] section of Georgia. Indeed, it has been proverbial for furnishing able ministers and instructors."

"They are [his pastoral charge], in the language of Scripture, *'your money.'* They are the source, the means of your wealth; by their labor do you obtain the necessaries, the conveniences, and comforts of life. The increase of them is the general standard of your worldly prosperity, without them you would be comparatively poor. *They are consequently sought after and desired as property, and when possessed, must be so taken care of and managed as to be made profitable.*

"Now, it is exceedingly difficult to use them as money ; to treat them as property, and at the same time render to them that which is just and equal as immortal and accountable beings, and as heirs of the grace of life, equally with ourselves. They are associated in our business, and thoughts, and feelings with labor, and interest, and gain, and wealth. Under the influence of the powerful feeling of self-interest, there is a tendency to view and to treat them as instruments of labor, as a means of wealth, and to forget, or pass over lightly, the fact that they are what they are, under the eye and government of God. There is a tendency to rest satisfied with very small and miserable efforts for their moral improvement, and to give one's self but little trouble to correct immoralities and reform wicked practices and habits, should they do their work quietly and profitably, and enjoy health, and go on to multiply and increase upon the earth."

This is addressed to a body of "professing Evangelical Christians," in a district in which more is done for the elevation of the slaves than in any other of the South. What they are called to witness from their own experience, as the tendency of a system which recognizes slaves as absolute property, mere instruments of labor and means of wealth, "exceedingly difficult" for them to resist, is the *entirely irresistible effect* upon the mass of slaveholders. Fearing that moral and intellectual culture may injure their value as property, they oftener interfere to prevent than they endeavor to assist their

slaves from using the poor opportunities that chance
may throw in their way

Moreover, the missionary adds:

"The current of the conversation and of business in society,
in respect to negroes, runs in the channel of interest, and thus
increases the blindness and insensibility of owners. * * *
And this custom of society acts also on the negroes, who, seeing, and more than seeing, *feeling and knowing, that their
owners regard and treat them as their money—as property only*
—are inclined to lose sight of their better character and higher
interests, and, in their ignorance and depravity, to estimate
themselves, and religion, and virtue, no higher than their owners do."

Again, from the paramount interest of owners in the
property quality of these beings, they provide them
only such accommodations for spending the time in
which they are not actively employed, as shall be
favorable to their bodily health, and enable them to
comply with the commandment, to "increase and
multiply upon the earth," without regard to their
moral health, without caring much for their obedience to the more pure and spiritual commands of the
Scriptures.

"The consequent mingling up of husbands and wives, children and youths, banishes the privacy and modesty essential to
domestic peace and purity, and opens wide the door to dishon-
esty, oppression, violence, and profligacy. The owner may see,
or hear, or know little of it. His servants may appear cheerful,
and go on in their usual way, and enjoy health and do his will,
yet their actual moral state may be miserable. * * * *If
family relations are not preserved and protected, we cannot
look for any considerable degree of moral and religious improvement.*"

It must be acknowledged of slavery, as a system, not only in Liberty county, but as that system finds the expression of the theory on which it is based in the laws of every Southern State, that family relations are not preserved and protected under it. As we should therefore expect, the missionary finds that

"one of the chief causes of the immorality of negroes arises from the indifference both of themselves and of their owners to their family relations."

Large planters generally do not allow their negroes to marry off the plantation to which they belong, conceiving "that their own convenience and interest, and," says the missionary, "comfort and *real* happiness of their people" are thereby promoted. Upon this point, however, it is but just to quote the views of the editor of the *Southern Agriculturist*, who, in urging planters to adopt and strictly maintain such a regulation, says: "If a master has a servant, and no suitable one of the other sex for a companion, he had better give an extra price for such an one as his would be willing to marry, than to have one man owning the husband, and the other the wife."

But this mode of arranging the difficulty seems not to have occurred to the Liberty county missionary; and while arguing against the course usually pursued, he puts the following, as a pertinent suggestion :

" Admitting that they are people having their preferences as well as others, *and there be a supply*, can that love which is the foundation and essence of the marriage state, be forced?"

Touching honesty and thrift among the negroes, he says:

"While some discipline their people for every act of theft committed against their interests, they have no care whatever what amount of pilfering and stealing the people carry on *among themselves.* Hence, in some places, thieves thrive and honest men suffer, until it becomes a practice 'to keep if you can what is your own, and get all you can besides that is your neighbor's.' Things come to such a pass, that the saying of the negroes is literally true, 'The people live upon one another ' "

Referring to the evil of intemperance, it is observed:

"Whatever toleration masters use toward ardent spirits in others, they are generally inclined to use none in respect to their servants; and in effecting this reformation, masters and mistresses should set the example; for without example, precepts and persuasions are powerless. Nor can force effect this reformation as surely and perfectly as persuasion—appealing to the character and happiness of the servant himself, the appeal recognizes him in such a manner as to produce self-respect, and it tends to give elevation of conduct and character. I will not dwell upon this point."

He will not dwell on this point; yet, is it not evident that until this point can be dwelt upon, all effort for the genuine Christianization of the negro race in the South must be puerile?

SLAVERY AS AN EDUCATIVE SYSTEM

"The mental faculties will be most developed where they are most exercised, and what gives them more exercise than the having a multitude of interests, none of which can be neglected, and which can be provided for only by varied efforts of the will and intelligence? * * *

" It is precisely these cares and anxieties which tend to make the independent proprietor a superior being to an English day-laborer. * * *

"If there is a first principle in intellectual education, it is this, that the discipline which does good to the mind is that in which the mind is active, not in that in which it is passive."— *Principles of Political Economy*, by J. Stuart Mill.

The benefit to the African which is supposed to be incidental to American slavery, is confessedly proportionate to the degree in which he is forced into intercourse with a superior race and made subject to its example. Before I visited the South, I had believed that the advantages accruing from slavery, in this way, far outweighed the occasional cruelties, and other evils incidental to the system. I found, however, the mental and moral condition of the negroes, even in Virginia, and in those towns and districts containing the largest proportion of whites, much lower than I had anticipated, and as soon as I had an opportunity to examine one of the extensive plantations of the interior, although one inherited by its owner, and the home of a large and virtuous white family, I was satisfied that the advantages arising to the blacks from association with their white masters were very trifling, scarcely appreciable indeed, for the great majority of the field-hands. Even the overseer had barely acquaintance enough with the slaves individually, to call them by name; the owner could not determine with confidence if he were addressing one of his own chattels, by its features. Much less did the slaves have an opportunity to cultivate their minds by intercourse with other white people. Whatever of civilization, and of the forms, customs and shibboleths of Christianity they were acquiring by example, and through police restraints might, it occurred to me, after all, but poorly compensate the effect of the systematic withdrawal from them of all the usual influences which tend to nourish the moral nature and develop the intellectual faculties, in savages as well as in civilized free men.

This doubt, as my Northern friends well know, for I had habitually assumed the opposite, in all previous discussions of the slavery question, was unexpected and painful to me. I resisted it long, and it was not till I had been more than twelve months in the South with my attention constantly fixed upon the point that I ceased to suspect that the circumstances which brought me to it were exceptional and deceptive. I grew constantly stronger with every opportunity I had of observing the condition, habits, and character of slaves whom I could believe to present fair examples of the working of the system with the majority of those subject to it upon the large plantations.

The laborers we see in towns, at work on railroads and steamboats, about stations and landings; the menials of our houses and hotels, are less respectable, moral, and intelligent than the great majority of the whole laboring class of the North. The traveller at the South has to learn that there the reverse is the case to a degree which can hardly be sufficiently estimated. I have been obliged to think that many amiable travellers who have received impressions with regard to the condition of the slaves very different from mine, have failed to make a sufficient allowance for this.

The rank-and-file plantation negroes are not to be readily made acquaintance with by chance or through letters of introduction.

SLAVE MANAGEMENT ON THE LARGEST SCALE

The estate I am now about to describe, was situated upon a tributary of the Mississippi, and accessible only by occasional steamboats; even this mode of communication being frequently interrupted at the low stages of the rivers. The slaves upon it formed about one twentieth of the whole population of the county, in which the blacks considerably out-number the whites. At the time of my visit, the owner was sojourning upon it, with his family and several invited guests, but his usual residence was upon a small plantation, of little productive value, situated in a neighborhood somewhat noted for the luxury and hospitality of its citizens, and having a daily mail, and direct railroad and telegraphic communication with New York. This was, if I am not mistaken, his second visit in five years.

The property consisted of four adjoining plantations, each with its own negro-cabins, stables, and overseer, and each worked to a great extent independently of the others, but all contributing their crop to one gin-house and warehouse, and all under the general superintendence of a bailiff or manager, who constantly resided upon the estate, and in the absence of the owner, had vice-regal power over the overseers, controlling, so far as he saw fit, the economy of all the plantations.

The manager was himself a gentleman of good education, generous and poetic in temperament, and pos-

sessing a capacity for the enjoyment of nature and a
happiness in the bucolic life, unfortunately rare with
Americans. I found him a delightful companion, and
I have known no man with whose natural tastes and
feelings I have felt, on so short acquaintance, a more
hearty sympathy   The gang of toiling negroes to him,
however, was as essential an element of the poetry of
nature as flocks of peaceful sheep and herds of lowing
kine, and he would no more appreciate the aspect in
which an Abolitionist would see them than would VIR-
GIL have honored the feelings of a vegetarian, who could
only sigh at the sight of flocks and herds destined to
feed the depraved appetite of the carnivorous savage of
modern civilization. The overseers were superior to
most of their class, and, with one exception, frank, honest, temperate, and industrious, but their feelings toward
negroes were such as naturally result from their occupation. They were all married, and lived with their
families, each in a cabin or cottage, in the hamlet of the
slaves of which he had especial charge. Their wages
varied from $500 to $1000 a year each.

These five men, each living more than a mile distant
from any of the others, were the only white men on
the estate, and the only others within several miles of
them were a few skulking vagabonds. Of course, to
secure their own personal safety and to efficiently direct
the labor of such a large number of ignorant, indolent,
and vicious negroes, rules, or rather habits and customs,
of discipline, were necessary, which would in particular
cases, be liable to operate unjustly and cruelly. It is

apparent, also, that, as the testimony of negroes against them would not be received as evidence in court, that there was very little probability that any excessive severity would be restrained by fear of the law. A provision of the law intended to secure a certain privilege to slaves, was indeed disregarded under my own observation, and such infraction of the law was confessedly customary with one of the overseers, and was permitted by the manager, for the reason that it seemed to him to be, in a certain degree, justifiable and expedient under the circumstances, and because he did not like to interfere unnecessarily in such matters.

In the main, the negroes appeared to be well taken care of and abundantly supplied with the necessaries of vigorous physical existence. A large part of them lived in commodious and well-built cottages, with broad galleries in front, so that each family of five had two rooms on the lower floor, and a loft. The remainder lived in log-huts, small and mean in appearance, but those of their overseers were little better, and preparations were being made to replace all of these by neat boarded cottages. Each family had a fowl-house and a hog-sty (constructed by the negroes themselves), and kept fowls and swine, feeding the latter during the summer on weeds and fattening them in the autumn on corn *stolen* (this was mentioned to me by the overseers as if it were a matter of course) from their master's corn-fields. I several times saw gangs of them eating the dinner which they had brought, each for himself, to the field, and observed that they generally had plenty,

often more than they could eat, of bacon, corn-bread,
and molasses. The allowance of food is weighed and
measured under the eye of the manager by the drivers,
and distributed to the head of each family weekly :
consisting of, for each person, 3 pounds of pork, 1
peck of meal ; and from January to July, 1 quart of
molasses. Monthly, in addition, 1 pound tobacco, and
4 pints salt. No drink is ever served but water, except
after unusual exposure, or to ditchers working in
water, who get a glass of whisky at night. All hands
cook for themselves after work at night, or whenever
they please between night-fall and daybreak, each
family in its own cabin. Each family had a garden,
the products of which, together with eggs, fowls, and
bacon, they frequently sold, or used in addition to their
regular allowance of food. Most of the families bought
a barrel of flour every year. The manager endeavored
to encourage this practice, and that they might spend
their money for flour instead of liquor, he furnished it
to them at rather less than what it cost him at wholesale. There were many poor whites within a few
miles who would always sell liquor to the negroes, and
encourage them to steal, to obtain the means to buy it
of them. These poor whites were always spoken of with
anger by the overseers, and they each had a standing
offer of much more than the intrinsic value of their
land, from the manager, to induce them to move
away.

The negroes also obtain a good deal of game. They
set traps for raccoons, rabbits, and turkeys, and I once

heard the stock-tender complaining that he had detected one of the vagabond whites stealing a turkey which had been caught in his pen. I several times partook of game while on the plantation, that had been purchased of the negroes. The stock-tender, an old negro, whose business it was to ride about in the woods and keep an eye on the stock cattle that were pastured in them, and who was thus likely to know where the deer ran, had an ingenious way of supplying himself with venison. He lashed a scythe blade or butcher's knife to the end of a pole so that it formed a lance; this he set near a fence or fallen tree which obstructed a path in which the deer habitually ran, and the deer in leaping over the obstacle would leap directly on the knife. In this manner he had killed two deer the week before my visit.

The manager sent to him for some of this venison for his own use, and justified himself to me for not paying for it on the ground that the stock-tender had undoubtedly taken time which really belonged to his owner to set his spear. Game taken by the field-hands was not looked upon in the same light, because it must have been got at night when they were excused from labor for their owner.

The first morning I was on the estate, while at breakfast with the manager, an old negro woman came into the room and said to him, "Dat gal's been bleedin' agin dis mornin'."

"How much did she bleed?"

"About a pint, sir."

" Very well ; I 'll call and see her after breakfast."

" I come up for some sugar of lead, master; I gin her some powdered alum 'fore I come away."

" Very well ; you can have some."

After breakfast the manager invited me to ride with him on his usual daily round of inspection through the plantations.

PLANTATION WORK-HOUSE

On reaching the nearest "quarters," we stopped at a house, a little larger than the ordinary cabins, which was called the loom-house, in which a dozen negroes were at work making shoes, and manufacturing coarse cotton stuff for negro clothing. One of the hands so employed was insane, and most of the others were cripples, invalids with chronic complaints, or unfitted by age, or some infirmity, for field-work.

MEDICAL SURVEY

From this we went to one of the cabins, where we found the sick woman who had been bleeding at the lungs, with the old nurse in attendance upon her. The manager examined and prescribed for her in a kind manner. When we came out he asked the nurse if any one else was sick.

" Oney dat woman Carline."

" What do you think is the matter with her ? "

" Well, I don't tink dere's anyting de matter wid her, masser ; I mus' answer you for true, I don't tink anyting de matter wid her, oney she's a little sore from dat whippin' she got."

We went to another cabin and entered a room where a woman lay on a bed, groaning. It was a very dingy, comfortless room, but a musquito bar, much patched and very dirty, covered the bed. The manager asked the woman several times what was the matter, but could get no distinct reply. She appeared to be suffering great pain. The manager felt her pulse and looked at her tongue, and after making a few more inquiries, to which no intelligible reply was given, told her he did not believe she was ill at all. At this the woman's groans redoubled. "I have heard of your tricks," continued the manager; "you had a chill when I came to see you yesterday morning; you had a chill when the mistress came here, and you had a chill when the master came. I never knew a chill to last the whole day. So you'll just get up now and go to the field, and if you don't work smart, you'll get a dressing; do you hear?"

We then left. The manager said that he rarely—almost never—had occasion to employ a physician for the people   Never for accouchements; the women, from their labor in the field, were not subject to the difficulty, danger, and pain which attended women of the better classes in giving birth to their offspring.

Near the first quarters we visited there was a large blacksmith's and wheelwright's shop, in which a number of mechanics were at work. Most of them, as we rode up, were eating their breakfast, which they warmed at their fires. Within and around the shop there were some fifty plows which they were putting in order. The manager inspected the work, found some of it faulty, sharply reprimanded the workmen for not getting on faster, and threatened one of them with a whipping for not paying closer attention to the directions which had been given him. He told me that he once employed a white man from the North, who professed to be a first-class workman, but he soon found he could not do nearly as good work as the negro mechanics on the estate, and the latter despised him so much, and got such high opinions of themselves in consequence of his inferiority, that he had been obliged to discharge him in the midst of his engagement.

The overseer of this plantation rode up while we were at the shop, and reported to the manager how all his hands were employed. There were so many at this and so many at that, and they had done so much since yesterday. "There's that girl, Caroline," said the manager; "she's not sick, and I told her she must go to work; put her to the hoeing; there's nothing the matter with her, except she's sore with the whipping she got. You must go and get her out" A woman was passing at the time, and the manager told her to go and tell Caroline she must get up and go to work, or the overseer would come and start her. She returned in a few minutes, and reported that Caroline said she could not get up. The overseer and manager rode toward the cabin, but before they reached it, the girl, who had probably been watching us from the window, came out and went to the field with her hoe. They then returned to me and continued their conversation. Just before we left the overseer, he said, "I think that girl

who ran away last week was in her cabin last night."
The manager told me, as we rode on, that the people
often ran away after they had been whipped, or something else had happened to make them angry. They
hide in the swamp, and come in to the cabins at night
to get food. They seldom remain away more than a
fortnight, and when they come in they are whipped.
The woman, Caroline, he said, had been delivered of a
dead child about six weeks before, and had been complaining and getting rid of work ever since. She was
the laziest woman on the estate. This shamming illness
gave him the most disagreeable duty he had to perform.
Negroes were famous for it. "If it was not for her bad
character," he continued, "I should fear to make her
go to work to-day; but her pulse is steady, and her
tongue perfectly smooth. *We have to be sharp with
them; if we were not, every negro on the estate would be
abed.*"

CLOTHES AND CLEANLINESS

We rode on to where the different gangs of laborers
were at work, and inspected them one after another. I
observed, as we were looking at one of the gangs, that
they were very dirty. "Negroes are the filthiest people in the world," said the manager; "there are some
of them who would not keep clean twenty-four hours at
a time if you gave them thirty suits a year." I asked
him if there were any rules to maintain cleanliness.
There were not, but sometimes the negroes were told at
night that any one who came into the field the next

morning without being clean would be whipped. This gave no trouble to those who were habitually clean, while it was in itself a punishment to those who were not, as they were obliged to spend the night in washing.

They were furnished with two suits of summer, and one of winter clothing each year. Besides which, most of them got presents of some holiday finery (calico dresses, handkerchiefs, etc.), and purchased more for themselves, at Christmas. One of the drivers now in the field had on a splendid uniform coat of an officer of the flying artillery. After the Mexican war, a great deal of military clothing was sold at auction in New Orleans, and much of it was bought by planters at a low price, and given to their negroes, who were greatly pleased with it.

HOURS OF LABOR

Each overseer regulated the hours of work on his own plantation. I saw the negroes at work before sunrise and after sunset. At about eight o'clock they were allowed to stop for breakfast, and again at noon, to dine. The length of these rests was at the discretion of the overseer or drivers, usually, I should say, from half an hour to an hour. There was no rule.

OVERSEERS

The number of hands directed by each overseer was considerably over one hundred. The manager thought it would be better economy to have a white man over every fifty hands, but the difficulty of obtaining trustworthy overseers prevented it.   Three of those he then had were the best he had ever known.   He described the great majority as being passionate, careless, inefficient men, generally intemperate, and totally unfitted for the duties of the position   The best overseers, ordinarily, are young men, the sons of small planters, who take up the business temporarily, as a means of acquiring a little capital with which to purchase negroes for themselves.

PLOW-GIRLS

The plowing, both with single and double mule teams, was generally performed by women, and very well performed too.   I watched with some interest for any indication that their sex unfitted them for the occupation.   Twenty of them were plowing together, with double teams and heavy plows.   They were superintended by a male negro driver, who carried a whip, which he frequently cracked at them, permitting no dawdling or delay at the turning ; and they twitched their plows around on the head-land, jerking their reins, and yelling to their mules, with apparent ease, energy, and rapidity.   Throughout the Southwest the negroes, as a rule, appear to be worked much harder than in the eastern and northern Slave States.   I do not think they accomplish as much daily, as agricultural laborers at the North usually do, but they certainly labor much harder, and more unremittingly. They are constantly and steadily driven up to their work, and the stupid, plodding, machine-like manner in which they labor, is painful to witness. This was especially the case with the hoe-gangs. One of them numbered nearly two hundred hands (for the force of two plantations was working together), moving across the field in parallel lines, with a considerable degree of precision. I repeatedly rode through the lines at a canter, with other horsemen, often coming upon them suddenly, without producing the smallest change or interruption in the dogged action of the laborers, or causing one of them to lift an eye from the ground. A very tall and powerful negro walked to and fro in the rear of the line, frequently cracking his whip, and calling out, in the surliest manner, to one and another, "Shove your hoe, there! shove your hoe!" But I never saw him strike any one with the whip.

DISCIPLINE

The whip was evidently in constant use, however. There were no rules on the subject, that I learned; the overseers and drivers punished the negroes whenever they deemed it necessary, and in such manner, and with such severity as they thought fit. "If you don't work faster," or "If you don't work better," or "If you don't recollect what I tell you, I will have you flogged," are threats which I have often heard. I said to one of the overseers, "It must be very disagreeable to have to punish them as much as you do?" "Yes, it would be to those who are not used to it—but it's my business, and I think nothing of it. Why, sir, I wouldn't mind killing a nigger more than I would a dog." I asked if he had ever killed a negro? "Not quite," he said, but overseers were often obliged to. Some negroes are determined never to let a white man whip them, and will resist you, when you attempt it; of course you must kill them in that case. Once a negro, whom he was about to whip in the field, struck at his head with a hoe. He parried the blow with his whip, and drawing a pistol tried to shoot him, but the pistol missing fire he rushed in and knocked him down with the butt of it. At another time a negro whom he was punishing, insulted and threatened him. He went to the house for his gun, and as he was returning, the negro, thinking he would be afraid of spoiling so valuable a piece of property by firing, broke for the woods. He fired at once, and put six buck-shot into his hips. He always carried a bowie-knife, but not a pistol, unless he anticipated some unusual act of insubordination. [1] He always kept a pair of pistols ready loaded over the mantel-piece, however, in case they should be needed. It was only when he first came upon a plantation that he ever had much trouble   A great many overseers were unfit for their business, and too easy

[1] "On Monday last, as James Allen (overseer on Prothro's plantation at St. Maurice), was punishing a negro boy named Jack, for stealing hogs, the boy ran off before the overseer had chastised him sufficiently for the offense. He was immediately pursued by the overseer, who succeeded in catching him, when the negro drew a knife and inflicted a terrible gash in his abdomen. The wounds of the overseer were dressed by Dr. Stephens, who pronounces it a very critical case, but still entertains hope of his recovery "—*Nachitoches Chronicle.*

and slack with the negroes.   When he succeeded such
a man, he had hard work for a time to break the
negroes in, but it did not take long to teach them their
place.   His conversation on this subject was exactly
like what I have heard said, again and again, by
Northern shipmasters and officers, with regard to
seamen.

PUNISHMENT

The severest corporal punishment of a negro that I
witnessed at the South, occurred while I was visiting
this estate.   I suppose, however, that punishment
equally severe is common—in fact, it must be necessary
to the maintenance of adequate discipline on every large
plantation.   It is much more necessary than on ship-
board, because the opportunities of hiding away and
shirking labor, and of wasting and injuring the owner's
property without danger to themselves, are far greater
in the case of the slaves than in that of the sailors, but
above all, because there is no real moral obligation on
the part of the negro to do what is demanded of him.
The sailor performs his duty in obedience to a voluntary contract ; the slave is in an involuntary servitude.
The manner of the overseer who inflicted the punishment, and his subsequent conversation with me about
it, indicated that it was by no means an unusual occur-
rence with him.   I had accidentally encountered him,
and he was showing me his plantation.   In going from
one side of it to the other, we had twice crossed a deep
gully, at the bottom of which was a thick covert of
brushwood.   We were crossing it a third time, and had

nearly passed through the brush, when the overseer
suddenly stopped his horse, exclaiming, "What 's that?
Hallo ! who are you there ?"

It was a girl lying at full length on the ground at the
bottom of the gully, evidently intending to hide herself
from us in the bushes.

"Who are you there ?"

"Sam's Sall, sir."

"What are you skulking there for ?"

The girl half rose, but gave no answer.

"Have you been here all day ?"

"No, sir."

"How did you get here ?"

The girl made no reply.

"Where have you been all day ? "

The answer was unintelligible

After some further questioning, she said her father
accidentally locked her in, when he went out in the
morning

"How did you manage to get out ?"

"Pushed a plank off, sir, and crawled out."

The overseer was silent for a moment, looking at the
girl, and then said, "That won't do—come out here "
The girl arose at once, and walked towards him ; she
was about eighteen years of age   A bunch of keys
hung at her waist, which the overseer espied, and he
said, "Ah, your father locked you in ; but you have
got the keys."   After a little hesitation, the girl replied
that these were the keys of some other locks ; her father
had the door-key.

Whether her story were true or false, could have been ascertained in two minutes by riding on to the gang with which her father was at work, but the overseer had made up his mind as to the facts of the case.

"That won't do," said he, "get down on your knees." The girl knelt on the ground ; he got off his horse, and holding him with his left hand, struck her thirty or forty blows across the shoulders with his tough, flexible, "raw-hide" whip. They were well laid on, as a boatswain would thrash a skulking sailor, or as some people flog a balking horse, but with no appearance of angry excitement on the part of the overseer. At every stroke the girl winced, and exclaimed, "Yes, sir !" or "Ah, sir !" or "Please, sir !" not groaning or screaming. At length he stopped and said, "Now tell me the truth." The girl repeated the same story. "You have not got enough yet," said he, "pull up your clothes —lie down." The girl without any hesitation, without a word or look of remonstrance or entreaty, drew closely all her garments under her shoulders, and lay down upon the ground with her face toward the overseer, who continued to flog her with the raw-hide, across her naked loins and thigh, with as much strength as before. She now shrunk away from him, not rising, but writhing, groveling, and screaming, "Oh, don't, sir ! oh, please stop, master ! please, sir ! please, sir ! oh, that's enough, master ! oh, Lord ! oh, master, master ! oh, God, master, do stop ! oh, God, master ! oh, God, master !"

A young gentleman of fifteen was with us ; he had

ridden in front, and now, turning on his horse looked back with an expression only of impatience at the delay.   It was the first time I had ever seen a woman flogged.   I had seen a man cudgeled and beaten, in the heat of passion, before, but never flogged with a hundredth part of the severity used in this case.   I glanced again at the perfectly passionless but rather grim business-like face of the overseer, and again at the young gentleman, who had turned away ; if not indifferent he had evidently not the faintest sympathy with my emotion.   Only my horse chafed with excitement.   I gave him rein and spur and we plunged into the bushes and scrambled fiercely up the steep acclivity. The screaming yells and the whip strokes had ceased when I reached the top of the bank.   Choking, sobbing, spasmodic groans only were heard.   I rode on to where the road coming diagonally up the ravine ran out upon the cotton-field.   My young companion met me there, and immediately afterward the overseer.   He laughed as he joined us, and said,

"She meant to cheat me out of a day's work—and she has done it, too."

"Did you succeed in getting another story from her?"

"No; she stuck to it."

"Was it not perhaps true?"

"Oh no, sir, she slipped out of the gang when they were going to work, and she's been dodging about all day, going from one place to another as she saw me coming.   She saw us crossing there a little while ago, and thought we had gone to the quarters, but we turned back so quick, we came into the gully before she knew it, and she could do nothing but lie down in the bushes."

"I suppose they often slip off so."

"No, sir; I never had one to do so before—not like this, they often run away to the woods and are gone some time, but I never had a dodge-off like this before."

"Was it necessary to punish her so severely?"

"Oh yes, sir," (laughing again.) "If I had n't punished her so hard she would have done the same thing again to-morrow, and half the people on the plantation would have followed her example. Oh, you 've no idea how lazy these niggers are; you Northern people don't know anything about it. They 'd never do any work at all if they were not afraid of being whipped."

We soon afterward met an old man, who, on being closely questioned, said that he had seen the girl leave the gang as they went to work after dinner. It appeared that she had been at work during the forenoon, but at dinner-time the gang was moved and as it passed through the gully she slipped out. The driver had not missed her. The overseer said that when he first took charge of this plantation, the negroes ran away a great deal—they disliked him so much They used to say 't was hell to be on his place; but after a few months they got used to his ways, and liked him better than any of the rest. He had not had any run away now in some time. When they ran away they would generally return within a fortnight. If many of them went off, or if they staid out long, he would make the rest of the force work Sundays, or deprive them of some of their usual privileges until they returned. The negroes on the plantation could always bring them in if they chose to. They depended on them for their food, and they had only to stop the supplies to oblige them to surrender.

NAMES

Afterward, as I was sitting near a gang with an overseer and the manager, the former would occasionally call out to one and another by name, in directing or urging their labor. I asked if he knew them all by name He did, but the manager did not know one fifth of them. The overseer said he generally could call most of the negroes on a plantation by their names in two weeks after he came to it, but it was rather difficult to learn them on account of there being so many of the same name, distinguished from each other by a prefix. "There's a Big Jim here, and a Little Jim, and Eliza's Jim, and there's Jim Bob, and Jim Clarisy."

" What's Jim Clarisy?—how does he get that name?"

" He's Clarisy's child, and Bob is Jim Bob's father. That fellow ahead there, with the blue rag on his head, his name is Swamp; he always goes by that name, but his real name is Abraham, I believe; is it not, Mr. [Manager]? "

"His name is Swamp on the plantation register—
that's all I know of him."

"I believe his name is Abraham," said the overseer;
"he told me so. He was bought of Judge ——, he
says, and he told me his master called him Swamp because he ran away so much. He is the worst runaway
on the place."

MORAL EDUCATION OF THE NEGROES

I inquired about the increase of the negroes on the
estate, and the manager having told me the number of
deaths and births the previous year, which gave a net
increase of four per cent.—on Virginia estates it is often
twenty per cent.—I asked if the negroes began to have
children at a very early age. "Sometimes at sixteen,"
said the manager "Yes, and at fourteen," said the
overseer; "that girl's had a child"—pointing to a girl
that did not appear older than fourteen. "Is she married?" "No." "You see," said the manager, "negro
girls are not remarkable for chastity, their habits
indeed rather hinder them from having children.
They'd have them younger than they do, if they would
marry or live with but one man, sooner than they do.¹
They often do not have children till they are twenty-
five years old." "Are those who are married true to
each other?" I asked. The overseer laughed heartily
at the idea, and described a disgustingly "Free Love"
state of things. "Do you not try to discourage this?"

¹ Mr. Russell makes an observation to the same effect with
regard to the Cuba plantations, p 230.

" No, not unless they quarrel." " They get jealous and quarrel among themselves sometimes about it," the manager explained, " or come to the overseer and complain, and he has them punished." " Give all hands a damned good hiding," said the overseer. " You punish for adultery, then, but not for fornication ? " " Yes," answered the manager, but " No," replied the overseer, " we punish them for quarreling ; if they don't quarrel I don't mind anything about it, but if it makes a muss, I give all four of 'em a warming."

BLACK, WHITE, AND YELLOW

Riding through a large gang of hoers, with two of the overseers, I observed that a large proportion of them appeared to be thorough-bred Africans. Both of them thought that the " real black niggers " were about three fourths of the whole number, and that this would hold as an average on Mississippi and Louisiana plantations One of them pointed out a girl—" That one is pure white ; you see her hair ? " (It was straight and sandy.) " She is the only one we have got." It was not uncommon, he said, to see slaves so white that they could not be easily distinguished from pure-blooded whites. He had never been on a plantation before, that had not more than one on it. [1] " Now,"

---

[1] " A woman, calling herself Violet Ludlow, was arrested a few days ago, and committed to jail, on the supposition that she was a runaway slave belonging to A. M. Mobley, of Upshur county, Texas, who had offered through our columns a reward of fifty dollars for her apprehension On being brought before a justice of the peace, she stated that she was a white woman,

said I, "if that girl should dress herself well, and run away, would she be suspected of being a slave?"

"Oh, yes; you might not know her if she got to the North, but any of us would know her."

"How?"

"By her language and manners."

"But if she had been brought up as a house-servant?"

"Perhaps not in that case."

The other thought there would be no difficulty; a

---

and claimed her liberty. She states that she is a daughter of Jeremiah Ludlow, of Pike county, Alabama, and was brought from that country in 1853, by George Cope, who emigrated to Texas. After arriving in Texas, she was sold by George Cope to a Dr. Terry, in Upshur county, Texas, and was soon after sold by him to a Mrs. Hagen, or Hagens, of the same county Violet says that she protested against each sale made of her, declaring herself a free woman. She names George Gilmer, Thomas Rogers, John Garret, and others, residents of Pike county, Alabama, as persons who have known her from infancy as the daughter of one Jeremiah Ludlow and Rene Martin, a widow at the time of her birth, and as being a free white woman, and her father a free white man. Violet is about instituting legal proceedings for her freedom."—*Shreveport Southwestern*

"Some days since, a woman named Pelasgie was arrested as a fugitive slave, who has lived for more than twelve years in this city as a free woman. She was so nearly white that few could detect any traces of her African descent. She was arrested at the instance of a man named Raby, who claimed her as belonging to an estate of which he is heir-at-law. She was conveyed to the First District guard-house for safe keeping, and while there she stated to Acting Recorder Filleul that she was free, had never belonged to Raby, and had been in full and unquestioned enjoyment of her freedom in this city for the above mentioned period. She also stated that she had a house, well furnished, which she was in the habit of letting out in rooms."— *New Orleans Picayune.*

slave girl would always quail when you looked in her eyes.

I asked if they thought the mulattoes or white slaves were weaker or less valuable than the pure negroes.

"Oh, no; I'd rather have them a great deal," said one. "Well, I had not," said the other; "the blacker the better for me" "The white ones," added the first, "are more active, and know more, and I think do a good deal the most work." "Are they more subject to illness, or do they appear to be of weaker constitutions?" One said they were not, the other that they did not seem to bear the heat as well. The first thought that this might be so, but that, nevertheless, they would do more work. I afterwards asked the manager's opinion. He thought they did not stand excessive heat as well as the pure negroes, but that, from their greater activity and willingness, they would do more work. He believed they were equally strong, and no more liable to illness; had never had reason to think them of weaker constitution. They often had large families, and he had not noticed that their children were weaker or more subject to disease than others. He thought that perhaps they did not have so many children as the pure negroes, but he had supposed the reason to be that they did not begin bearing so young as the others, and this was because they were more attentive to the men, and perhaps more amorous themselves He knew a great many mulattoes living together, and they generally had large and healthy families.

Afterwards, at one of the plantation nurseries, where there were some twenty or thirty infants and young children, a number of whom were evidently the off-spring of white fathers, I asked the nurse to point out the healthiest children to me, and of those she indicated, more were of the pure, than of the mixed breed. I then asked her to show me which were the sickliest, and she did not point to any of the latter. I then asked if she noticed any difference in this respect between the black and the yellow children. "Well, dey do say, master, dat de yellow ones is de sickliest, but I can't tell for true dat I ever see as dey was."

RELIGION

Being with the proprietor and the manager together, I asked about the religious condition of the slaves. There were "preachers" on the plantations, and they had some religious observances on a Sunday; but the preachers were the worst characters among them, and, they thought, only made their religion a cloak for habits of especial depravity.[1] They were, at all events, the most deceitful and dishonest slaves on the plantation, and oftenest required punishment. The negroes of all denominations, and even those who ordinarily made no religious pretensions, would join together in excit-

[1] The bad character of slave preachers in general, I have often heard assumed in conversation, as if it were notorious, and it seems always to have been so. On the records of the Superior Court of Augusta, Georgia, in 1790 "the number of negroes calling themselves parsons, going about the country," is presented as a nuisance —White's *Statistics of Georgia*

ing religious observances. These gentlemen considered the religious exercises of the negroes to be similar, in their intellectual and moral character, to the Indian feasts and war-dances, and did not encourage them. Neither did they like to have white men preach on the estate ; and in future they did not intend to permit them to do so. It excited the negroes so much as to greatly interfere with the subordination and order which were necessary to obtain the profitable use of their labor. They would be singing and dancing every night in their cabins, till dawn of day, and utterly unfit themselves for work.

I remarked that I had been told that a religious negro was considered to be worth a third more, because of his greater honesty and steadiness.   ·

" Quite the contrary," they both assured me, for a religious negro generally made trouble, and they were glad to get rid of him.

I have no doubt these opinions were sincere. Probably these gentlemen held different views of the intellectual and moral capabilities of the African race from those entertained by the Liberty planters. I did not infer, however, that they shared the most advanced views of Southern philosophers on this subject. Perhaps I should briefly indicate to what point these have reached, before pursuing the subject further.

Cotemporaneously with the anatomico-metaphysical studies of Dr. Wilkinson and of Dr Doherty, in London, Doctors Nott and Gliddon of Mobile, and Professor Cartwright of the University of Louisiana, have been laboring in a similar field with different purposes and to much more practical ends.

The general character of the results with which they are rewarded will be sufficiently shown by a few extracts from a profound discourse delivered by the latter gentleman, before a convocation of the University of Mississippi :

"Is he a son of Adam ? Does his peculiar physical conformation stand in opposition to the BIBLE, *or does it prove its truth ?* * * * Anatomy and physiology have been interrogated, and the response is that the Ethiopian or Canaanite is unfitted, from his organization and the physiological laws predicated in that organization, for the responsible duties of a free man. * * * When the original Hebrew of the Bible is interrogated, we find in the significant meaning of the original name of the negro, the identical fact set forth, which the knife of the anatomist at the dissecting table, has made appear : as if the revelations of anatomy, physiology, and history were a mere re-writing of what Moses wrote. * * * A knowledge of THE GREAT PRIMARY TRUTH that the negro is a slave by nature, and can never be happy, industrious, moral or religious, in any other condition than the one he was intended to fill, is of great importance to the theologian and the statesman, and to all those who are at heart seeking to promote his temporal and future welfare. * * * It is this defective hematosis, or atmosperization of the blood conjoined with a deficiency of cerebral matter in the cranium and an excess of nervous matter distributed to the organs of sensation and assimilation, that is the true cause of that debasement of mind which has rendered the people of Africa unable to take care of themselves."

Dr. Cartwright dwells with such pardonable enthusiasm upon the inestimable value of these researches in the positive proof they afford of what was so long suspected by the students of the Middle Ages—the truth of the Bible—that he omits any consideration

of them in another aspect, in which they will appear
still more interesting to the earnest Christian souls
to whom he addresses himself.   Let us, for instance,
passing from the sacred record and the pages of ancient
history, interrogate the explorers of Africa, and see to
what practical conclusions we are at once irresistibly
led.   Did Mungo Park, or Lardner, or Anderson, or
Robertson, or Livingstone, or Bayard Taylor, or Captain
Canot in all their various wanderings, ever find existing in a single tribe of the true Negro, Ethiopian, or
Canaanitish race, a true Christian church, of indigenous
origin and growth?   If not, what are we to infer?
Certainly not that we are to oppose the evident will
of divine Providence, by preaching the religion of white
men to this race.   No, the proper and only divinely
designated duty of a Canaanite's soul has been for
countless ages, fetish worship, devotion, that is, to
some person, animal, thing, or things—cotton, corn-
bread, hog, pumpkins and Sunday-tricks, for instance.

Let no whining fanatic say that the whole race is
not thus condemned to fetishism, that many tribes
have been found to recognize a supreme Spirit, to
look forward to a happy existence after death, etc.
So there are known to be legislative assemblies among
some tribes, and elective kings who hold office only
during good behavior—there is, in fact, every thing
among the Africans which Professor Cartwright says
there is not, but the question yet remains, are these
true Canaanites?—a question the superficial observer
is not likely to answer.   For after all, mere blackness

of the skin no more authorizes a being otherwise in the likeness of a man, to be detained as a slave, or to be forbidden the Bible, than mere whiteness of the skin shows an entire fitness for the responsible duties of a freeman, or proves a clean heart to be within.

Real, God-ordained, unchangeable Canaanites and fetish-worshippers, Professor Cartwright has proved, can only be surely known by a careful analysis of the "mental functions," and a close scrutiny of "the membranes, muscles, and tendons of all the fluids and secretions, and of the brain, the nerves, the chyle, and all the humors." You must examine the bones of the alleged Canaanite; if he be a genuine specimen, they contain + phosphate of lime, and — gelatine: and as for his eyes, they will be furnished with "something like the membrana nictitans formed by a preternatural enlargement of the plica lunaris in the inner canthus."[1]

It is fortunate that this, the surest test of the true Canaanite, is the most readily applied, and involves no use of the dissecting-knife. Let a man's color be what it may, if an examination of the eye discloses the preternatural enlargement of the plica lunaris in the

[1] Was my friend the overseer a disciple of science and of Cartwright, and did he therefore look in the white woman's eyes, to see if she were a slave? There are "secrets of the craft" among overseers, I have been told. Was this among them—"to detect a white-skinned slave, pretending to be free, see if there be not a preternatural enlargement of the plica lunaris, in the inner canthus, having the semblance of a membrana nictitans?"

inner canthus there can be no danger in treating him as a slave, a Canaanite ; a fore-ordained goat.[1]

Thus are these great discoveries immediately applied to further the ends of human justice. The North boasts of the greater speed of its railroads, and the celerity of its printing-presses, pin-making and hog-chopping machines, but true to its higher instincts, the South brings its discoveries to bear upon the administration of criminal jurisprudence, and thus furnishes the crowning glory of the genius of the nineteenth century.

Unfortunately a knowledge of these grand and harmonious truths is as yet but imperfectly disseminated in the South itself, and all kinds of explanations and defences of slavery are made by simple men who are uninstructed in the beautiful and satisfactory theories based upon them.

If I had asked my friends on the estate last described, for instance, by what right they held their people in subjection, and on what principle they governed them, they would probably have answered somewhat thus :

[1] "However zealously," says that true conservative journal, the *Richmond Whig* "however zealously a negro seeks to affect innocence, the eye always betrays guilt and a great evil capacity Bill, the slave of Mrs Elizabeth Johnson, who stole the coat and five dollars from Richard, a slave of T Cauthorn, who works on board the canal boat *Glazebrook*, was ordered thirty lashes by the Mayor on yesterday, in disregard of the most solemn protestation of innocence on the part of Bill. There was an amount of villainy reflected in his eyes that could well contradict all the protestation he could utter for a month."

"We have been brought up in slavery; it has always existed around us unquestioned and unquestionable. Perhaps it is wrong in a comprehensive view, but if so, habit prevents us from realizing it. It seems to us as much the natural relation of the white and the black, and of those who come of the black, as marriage is of the man and the woman. To see a negro free from the special government of some one of our superior race seems to us a phenomenon as exceptional and as much in need of investigation and reform as it does to you to see him held to involuntary servitude. We are not disposed to argue the matter —the negroes are a chief part of our property, inherited of our fathers and improved by us. If you undertake to destroy that property we will stand on its defence with arms.

"As for religion, we respect it, but we do not respect cant or fanatical superstition under the name of religion. Perhaps the negro might be trained and educated, if we began with him young, to a capacity for better things; certainly our household servants seem in general much superior in character to the fieldhands. But to give him such an education would not be safe, nor could it at present be afforded. We need his whole force to supply the demand for cotton, we can not therefore try dangerous experiments with him. As to the effect of this on ourselves you must remember that the negro is in our eyes, not a man, as he is in yours, but simply a negro; therefore our sympathies for those of our own race are not blunted, as it seems

to you they must be, by the severities we have to employ with our unruly and disobedient slaves.''

Possibly, after all, in the present state of science,
such an explanation would have quite as favorable an
influence on the mind of the majority of honest anti-
slavery men, would do quite as much to lessen the
disgust with which some persons view the whole business, as the medico-theological treatises to which so
much importance is attached by the more advanced
minds of the South.

And here I must observe, that after taking no little
pains to obtain the views of the enlightened admirers
and defenders of the institution of slavery, I have failed
to find a single writer among the hosts with whom the
religious bearings of the system form a favorite topic,
who even makes an attempt to assault the real position
occupied with regard to it by the advocates of emancipation. This position, as I understand it, does not
involve a denial that the descendants of a certain number of savages, dispersed and incorporated socially in a
previously civilized and educated community of Christians, will acquire habits of life more in accordance
with the moral standard of that community than they
would possess had they never emerged from the primi-
tive barbarism of their ancestors, but only maintains
that after having been so incorporated during several
generations, their spiritual development is at length
likely to be more rapid if they are allowed to regulate
the disposition of their own time and labor, and to
freely enjoy the returns of that labor, than if they

continued to be held in a state of complete vassalage in these and other respects ; and that this is still more true, if for the purpose of keeping them in such vassalage, the ordinary facilities for intellectual improvement, so essential to civilization and religion, are carefully withheld from them.

Nor can I refrain from remarking here on the folly of that disdainful temper, so habitual with Southern controversialists (and which so few of them attempt even rhetorically to disguise), toward those whom they deem their enemies in the matter of slavery. They fire so wide of their opponents' position that their books and speeches often serve only as arguments against themselves, in the minds of honest inquirers. This Asiatic policy of supreme contempt may still answer in the South, but except with the recent immigrants, it is no longer successful in hindering the growth of anti-slavery principles at the North, yet the only other weapon generally employed, even by the ablest of its advocates, is a shallow pretence of resorting for testimony to the results of scientific investigations, and to statistical inductions

"It is fortunate for slavery that the controversy with abolition is reduced to an issue of fact and argument. The plausible fallacies of the abolitionists will disappear before the revelations of the census. Casuists may dispute over the nice distinctions of ethical science until all just perceptions of right and wrong are confounded, but statistics will speedily and conclusively determine the effect of slavery as an economic and social institution. Already has it been shown by irresistible argument, that the proportion of wealth to the individual in a slaveholding community, greatly exceeds that in the free States. Even in the

North, candid men concede that their liberty is rapidly degenerating into license and anarchy. The following statistics, exhibiting a comparative view of Northern and Southern society in respect to two most important elements, are pregnant with instruction and encouragement to the slaveholding community .

FROM THE CENSUS OF 1850

States	Population	No of Churches	No. of Criminals
Maine............ ...	583,169	945	62
Massachusetts...... . .	994,514	1,475	301
New Hampshire	317,976	626	77
Vermont.......	314,120	599	39
Connecticut	370,792	734	145
Rhode Island.......	147,545	228	24
New York................3,097,394		4,134	1,080
New Jersey..	489,555	813	135
Pennsylvania.............2,311,786		3,566	302
Delaware..................	91,532	180	6
Total.............8,718,383		13,300	2,171
Maryland......	583,034	909	200
Virginia........ 1,421,661		2,383	188
North Carolina	869,039	1,795	14
South Carolina....	668,507	1,182	19
Georgia	906,185	1,862	85
Alabama......... ..	771,623	1,373	23
Mississippi..... .	606,526	1,016	81
Louisiana	517,762	306	160
Tennessee.... 1,002,717		2,014	187
Kentucky	982,405	1,845	141
Total.............8,329,459		14,685	1,098

"With a less population by half a million, the ten Southern States have above a thousand more churches than the ten Northern States, which boast loudest of their morality and enlightenment. With an excess of only half a million in population, the ten free States have double the number of criminals which are found in ten corresponding slave States Such revelations will complete the revolution of public opinion in respect to slavery."

This imposing array of figures was originaly marshaled, with the comments attached, by the *Richmond Enquirer*, but has since been repeatedly used to point a similar moral by the journals and orators of the North who are allied with that respectable "Democratic" organ. The folly of such a display is precisely like that of the Chinese generals who draw up their warriors in a position from which they are expected to throw terror into the ranks of their advancing adversaries, by frightful grimaces and menacing gestures, but in which they are quite unnecessarily exposed to the fire of their deadliest artillery. The Commissioner of the Census himself, a most careful, though sincerely loyal partisan of slavery, is at once seized and made to serve the guns of the anti-slavery partisan whenever his attention is called to this buggaboo of figures. In a work entitled *A Statistical View of the United States*, published and extensively given away in the Free as well as the Slave States, by Congress, Mr. DeBow observes, commenting upon the census returns of churches (p.133) that they do not undertake to show the number of members of the churches or the number of attendants on their worship ; that in the rural districts there are "thousands of buildings—rude sheds or log houses "—which are enumerated as church edifices, and which are used both as schoolhouses and places of worship. The Northern man knows that there can be but an extremely small proportion of the Northern churches which have no better accommodation for their meetings than a rude shed or log school house. On turning over a few pages he finds the information set out by Mr DeBow again that while the average value of the church edifices in New England and the Middle States is over $4000 each, in the Southern Seaboard and Central it is less than $1000; that in the Northwestern it is $1200 and in the Southwestern $900, (p. 139); that in the ten States above mentioned (of which it is to be noted that one of the so-called Northern is a Slave State,) the amount of church accommodation for each square mile of territory is, in the Northern, equal to one hundred and three; in the Southern, to thirty-seven; while in the Northern States there are on an average four hundred and thirty-seven church edifices to every thousand square miles, and in the Slave States but one hundred and thirty-six. By a very simple calculation he ascertains from the figures furnished by Mr. DeBow, that in the ten Northern States mentioned, the people have paid for their churches more than three times as much as those of the ten Southern, and the former unitedly will accommodate seven hundred and fifty thousand more worshippers than the latter. A little inquiry of travellers, or an examination of the reports of the Southern Aid Society, will satisfy him that while there are few Northern churches in which religious instruction is not regularly given at least once a week, and in the great majority of cases much more frequently, and that by an educated man, engaged and paid for this purpose, this is by no means the case with those edifices in the Slave States returned as churches. This indeed might be inferred from the marked absence of comfort in a large proportion of the houses of worship at the South, as also from their remoteness and inaccessibility to a great part of the inhabitants of the district to which they belong.

Then as to the "number of criminals," he finds in the census only returns of such as are confined in the prisons, jails, etc., of the different States. Under these heads he will look in vain for figures corresponding to those arranged by the Virginia Commissioner Lin.   At page 166, however, Mr. DeBow furnishes the following statement respecting the inmates of the prisons of the United States:

	Native Whites.	Foreign Whites.	Colored, including slaves
Slaveholding States, . .	988	370	323
Free States, ...	2271	1129	565

	In every 10,000 native whites	In every 10,000 foreign whites.	In every 10,000 colored
Slaveholding States, . .	$1\frac{673}{1000}$	$11\frac{634}{1000}$	$0\frac{938}{1000}$
Free States, ...	$1\frac{091}{1000}$	$51\frac{368}{1000}$	$28\frac{440}{1000}$

The defence of Lynch law which is so commonly made at the South has made it notorious that the administration of criminal justice in that portion of our country is very imperfect, and that comparatively a small fraction of those offending against the laws can be brought to a regular trial , and it is also well known to many that in several of the Slaves States but a small proportion of the criminals convicted in courts of justice are sentenced to confinement in jails or penitentiaries, but that they are punished by whipping, exposure in the pillory, and branding with a hot iron, modes of correction long ago abandoned in all the Free States. And as to the number of colored persons in the jails of the North, as compared with the South, we turn again to Mr. DeBow (*Industrial Resources of the*

South,) and under the head of "Negroes" (vol. ii., page 249) we find this explanation of the remarkable disproportion between the amount of valuable labor—capital under lock and key in the former and in the latter part of the country.

> "On our estates we dispense with the whole machinery of public police, and public courts of justice. Thus we try, decide, and execute the sentences in *thousands of cases*, which, in other countries, would go into courts."

To what effect, then, have those tables been arranged, except to awaken suspicions in the mind of the careful student, of the solidity of all the foundations of the recent, hastily constructed "Southern Democratic" philosophy? Suspicions which will be abundantly confirmed, as my experience would indicate, if he will observe and investigate honestly, its alleged premises, whether psychological or ethnological, in a sufficient number of instances to warrant any safe and confident deductions.

What Southern writer has investigated with impartiality the subject of emancipation in the British West Indies? We have in our Democratic journals on the one side, and in the Abolition journals on the other, abundant *ex parte* statements of the results of that Act, but I have yet to see an attempt made by an American to form an honest judicial conclusion upon the subject, resulting from any respectable study of evidence, except by persons whom Southern writers assume to be unworthy of their attention. Southern writers and their Northern allies utterly ignore the position, statements and arguments of their opponents on this subject, and content themselves with repeated displays of evidence which they appear to regard as incontrovertible, when in reality it entirely overshoots the position of those who defend the Emancipation Act.   I am not at all willing to be classed with these defenders myself, yet it is my impression that wherever they get the ear of the public in this country, they are having it all their own way, because their opponents disdain to cope with them.   But there is also another class, to which I profess to belong myself, and which numbers in its ranks, I suspect, most of the thinking men at the North, which holds the opinion that however untimely and perhaps injudicious and rash in method the act of negro emancipation in the British West Indies may have been, the original design was both right in itself, and reasonable in its anticipations, both philanthropic and economical, and is thus justified in the results.   I certainly have seen no evidence drawn from West India emancipation, cited by any of those writers who so delight in parliamentary returns of exports and imports, value of estates, etc., which are not satisfactorily replied to by temperately written books (such as Mr. Bigelow's little volume of personal observations in Jamaica,) which are in every tolerable library at the North.   On the other hand, I know of no attempt to refute much respectable evidence derived from the English islands, that is favorable to this view, and before the public.   Is such evidence unknown and unconsidered at the South? If so, the alleged success on the part of the latter in an issue of fact and argument, will prove fallacious, for the Abolitionists will not fail to put it within reach of every candid, thoughtful mind in the Free States.

RELIGIOUS CHARACTERISTICS OF THE SLAVES

The frequency with which the slaves use religious phrases of all kinds, the readiness with which they engage in what are deemed religious exercises, and fall into religious ecstacies, with the crazy, jocular manner in which they often talk of them, are striking and general characteristics. It is not at all uncommon to hear them refer to conversations which they allege, and apparently believe themselves to have had with Christ, the Apostles, or the prophets of old, or to account for some of their actions by attributing them to the direct influence of the Holy Spirit, or of the devil. It seems to me that this state of mind is fraught with more danger to their masters than any to which they could possibly have been brought by general and systematic education, and by the unrestricted study of the Bible, even though this involved what is so much dreaded, but which is, I suspect, an inevitable accompaniment of moral elevation, the birth of an ambition to take care of themselves. Grossly ignorant and degraded in mind, with a crude, undefined, and incomplete system of theology and ethics, credulous and excitable, intensely superstitious and fanatical, what better field could a cunning monomaniac or a sagacious zealot desire in which to set on foot an appalling crusade?

The negro races, compared with the white, at least

with the Teutonic, have greater vanity or love of approbation, a stronger dramatic and demonstrative character, more excitability, less exact or analytic minds, and a nature more sensuous, though (perhaps from want of cultivation, less refined. They take a real pleasure, for instance, such as it is a rare thing for a white man to be able to feel, in bright and strongly contrasting colors, and in music, in which nearly all are proficient to some extent   They are far less adapted for steady, uninterrupted labor than we are, but excel us in feats demanding agility and tempestuous energy. A Mississippi steamboat manned by negro deck-hands will wood up a third quicker than one manned by the same number of whites, but white laborers of equal intelligence and under equal stimulus will cut twice as much wood, split twice as many rails, and hoe a third more corn in a day than negroes. On many plantations, religious exercises are almost the only habitual recreation not purely sensual, from steady dull labor, in which the negroes are permitted to indulge, and generally all other forms of mental enjoyment are discouraged. Religious exercises are rarely forbidden, and a greater freedom to individual impulses and talent is allowed while engaged in them than is ever tolerated in conducting mere amusements or educational exercises.

Naturally and necessarily all that part of the negro's nature which is otherwise suppressed, bursts out with an intensity and vehemence almost terrible to witness, in forms of religious worship and communion, and a "profession" of piety which it is necessary to make before one can take a very noticeable part in the customary social exercises, is almost universal, except on plantations where the ordinary tumultous religious meetings are discouraged, or in towns where other recreations are open to the slaves.[1]

RELIGIOUS INSTRUCTION OF SLAVES

With regard to the religious instruction of slaves, widely different practices of course prevail. There are some slaveholders, like Bishop Polk of Louisana, who oblige, and many others who encourage, their slaves to engage in religious exercises, furnishing them certain conveniences for the purpose, as described in the *Seaboard Slave States*.[2] Among the wealthier slave-owners, however, and in all those parts of the country where the enslaved portion of the population outnumbers the whites, there is generally a visible, and

[1] The following newspaper paragraph indicates the wholesale way in which slaves may be nominally Christianized :

"REVIVAL AMONG THE SLAVES.—Rev. J. M. C. Breaker, of Beaufort, S. C., writes to the *Southern Baptist* that within the last three months he has baptized by immersion three hundred and fifty persons, *all of them, with a few exceptions, negroes.* These conversions were the result of a revival which has been in progress during the last six months. On the 12th inst., he baptized two hundred and twenty-three converts—all blacks but three—and the ceremony, although performed with due deliberation, occupied only one hour and five minutes. This is nearly four a minute, and Mr. Breaker considers it a demonstration that the three thousand converted on the day of Pentecost could easily have been baptized by the twelve apostles—each taking two hundred and fifty—in an hour and thirteen minutes."

[2] Vol. II , p. 80 ff.

often an avowed distrust of the effect of religious exercises upon slaves, and even the preaching of white clergymen to them is permitted by many with reluctance.[1]   The prevailing impression among us, with regard to the important influence of slavery in promoting the spread of religion among the blacks, is an erroneous one in my opinion.   I have heard Northern clergymen speak as if they supposed a regular daily instruction of slaves in the truths of Christianity to be general.   So far is this from being the case, that although family prayers were held in several of the

[1] "Bishop Polk, of Louisiana, was one of the guests.   He assured me that he had been all over the country on Red River, the scene of the fictitious sufferings of 'Uncle Tom,' and that he had found the temporal and spiritual welfare of the negroes well cared for.   He had confirmed thirty black persons near the situation assigned to Legree's estate.   He is himself the owner of four hundred slaves, whom he endeavors to bring up in a religious manner.   He tolerates no religion on his estate but that of the Church, he baptizes all the children, and teaches them the catechism.   All, without exception, attend the Church service, and the chanting is creditably performed by them, in the opinion of their owner.   Ninety of them are communicants, marriages are celebrated according to the Church ritual, and the state of morals is satisfactory.   Twenty infants had been baptized by the bishop just before his departure from home, and he had left his whole estate, his keys, etc., in the sole charge of one of his slaves, without the slightest apprehension of loss or damage.   In judging of the position of this Christian prelate as a slave owner, the English reader must bear in mind that, by the laws of Louisiana, emancipation has been rendered all but impracticable, and that, if practicable, it would not necessarily be, in all cases, an act of mercy or justice."— *The Western World Revisited.* By the Rev Henry Caswall, M. A., author of *America and the American Church*, etc. Oxford, John Henry Parker, 1854.

fifty planters' houses in Mississippi and Alabama, in which I passed a night, I never in a single instance saw a field-hand attend or join in the devotion of the family.

In South Carolina a formal remonstrance, signed by over three hundred and fifty of the leading planters and citizens, was presented to a Methodist clergyman who had been chosen by the Conference of that State, as being a cautious and discreet person, to preach especially to slaves. It was his purpose, expressly declared beforehand, to confine himself to verbal instruction in religious truth. "Verbal instruction," replied the remonstrants, "will increase the desire of the black population to learn. * * * Open the missionary sluice, and the current will swell in its gradual onward advance. We thus expect *a progressive system of improvement* will be introduced, or will follow from the nature and force of circumstances, which, if not checked (though it may be shrouded in sophistry and disguise), *will ultimately revolutionize our civil institutions.*"

The missionary, the Rev. T. Tupper, accordingly retired from the field. The local newspaper, the *Greenville Mountaineer*, in announcing his withdrawal, stated that the great body of the people were manifestly opposed to the religious instruction of their slaves, even if it were only given orally.

Though I do not suppose this view is often avowed, or consciously held by intelligent citizens, such a formal, distinct, and effective manifestation of sentiment made by so important an integral portion of the slaveholding body, cannot be supposed to represent a merely local or occasional state of mind, and I have not been able to resist the impression, that even where the economy, safety, and duty of some sort of religious education of the slaves is conceded, so much caution, reservation, and restriction is felt to be necessary in their instruction, that the result in the majority of cases has been merely to furnish a delusive clothing of Christian forms and phrases, to the original vague superstition of the African savage.

THE CHURCH RECUMBENT

Upon the value of the statistics of "colored church membership," which are often used as evidence that the evils of slavery are fully compensated by its influence in Christianizing the slaves, some light is thrown by the following letter from the white pastor of a town church in that part of the South in which the whites are most numerous, and in which the negroes enjoy the most privileges.

" *To the Editor of the Richmond (Va.) Religious Herald.*

* * * "The truth is, the teachings of the pulpit (at least among Baptists) have nothing to do with the matter. Let me furnish a case in proof Of two churches which the writer serves, his immediate predecessor was pastor for about twenty-five years. It would be only necessary to give his name, to furnish the strongest and most satisfactory assurance that nothing which ever fell from his lips could be construed into the support of ignorance, superstition, or fanaticism. During the five or six years I have served these churches, whatever may have been my errors and failings, (and I am ready to admit that they have been numerous and grievous enough, in all conscience,) I know I have never uttered a sentiment which could be tortured into the support of the superstitions prevailing among the colored people   And yet, in both these churches, the colored members are as superstitious and fanatical as they are elsewhere.   Indeed, this was to be expected, for I certainly claim no superiority over my brethren in the ministry, and I am satisfied that many of them are far better qualified than I am to expose error and to root out superstition.   This state of things, then, is not due to the teachings of the pulpit.   Nor is it the result of private instructions by masters   Indeed, these last have been afforded so sparingly, till within a few years since, that they could produce but little effect of any sort. And, besides, those who own servants, and are willing to teach them, are far too intelligent to countenance superstition in any way.   I repeat the inquiry, then, why is it that so many of our colored members are ignorant, superstitious, and fanatical?   It is the effect of instructions received from leading men among themselves, and the churches are responsible for this effect, in so far as they receive into fellowship those who have listened to these instructions, ground their hopes upon them, and guide their lives by them.   Whatever we may say against superstition, so long as we receive into our churches those who are its slaves, they will believe that we think them Christians; and, naturally relying on our judgment as expressed by their reception, they will live deluded, and die but to be lost.

"But some one will say, 'We never receive colored persons when they manifest these superstitions—when they talk of visions, dreams, sounds,' etc.   This is right, as far as it goes. In every such case they should be rejected.   But superstition of a fatal character often exists where nothing is said about dreams and visions.   It is just as fatally superstitious to trust the sort of superstition which now prevails among the colored people.   They have found that sights and sounds will not answer before the whites, and now (reserving these, perhaps, for some chosen auditory of their own color), they substitute prayers and feelings.   In illustration permit me to record, in no spirit of levity, the stereotyped experience which generally passes current, and, in ninety-nine cases out of a hundred, introduces the colored candidate into the church.   The pastor is informed, by one of the 'colored deacons,' that a man wishes to offer to the church with a view to baptism.   The fact is announced, a meeting of the church called, and the candidate comes forward.

"*Pastor.* 'Well, John, tell me in a few words, in your own way, your religious experience. What have been your feelings, and what are your present hopes and purposes?'

"*John.* 'I see other people trying, and so I thought I would try too, as I had a soul to save. So I went to pray, and the more I pray the wus I felt, so I kept on praying, and the more I pray, the wus I felt. I felt heavy—I felt a weight—and I kept on praying till at last I felt light—I felt easy—I felt like I loved all Christian people—I felt like I loved everybody.'

"Now, this is positively the whole of the experience which is generally related by colored candidates for baptism. There may be a slight variation of expression now and then, but the sense is almost invariably the same. On this experience hundreds have been received into the churches—I have received many upon it myself. I am somewhat curious to know how many of the seventy, baptized by my good brother Bagby, told this tale. I'll warant not less than fifty. Have any of us been right in receiving persons on such a relation as this? In the whole of it, there is not one word of gospel, not one word about sorrow for sin, not one word about faith, not one word about Christ. I know that all these things are subsequently brought out by questions; and were this not the case, I have no idea that the candidate would be in any instance received. *But that these questions may be understood, they are made necessarily 'leading questions,' such as suggest their answers; and consequently, these answers are of comparatively little value.* * * * I am aware that, as brother Bagby suggests, private instructions by masters have been too much neglected. *But these can accomplish but little good, so long as they are counteracted by the teachings of leading colored members, in whose veiws, after all our efforts, the colored people will have most confidence.*"

Not the smallest suggestion, I observe, in all the long article from which the above is derived, is ventured, that the negroes are capable of education, or that their religious condition would improve if their general enlightenment of mind were not studiously prevented.

"I have often heard the remark made," says the Rev C. C. Jones, in a treatise on the *Religious Instruction of Slaves*, printed at Savannah, Georgia, 1842, "by men whose standing and office in the churches afforded them abundant opportunity for observation, that the more they have had to do with colored members, the less confidence they have been compelled to place in their Christian professions."

A portion of a letter written for publication by the wife of the pastor of a church in the capital of Alabama, given below, naïvely reveals the degree of enlightenment prevailing among the Christianized Africans at a point where their means of instruction are a thousand times better than they are on an average throughout the country.

"Having talked to him seriously, and in the strongest light held up to him the enormity of the crime in forsaking his lawful wife and taking another, Colly replied, most earnestly, and not taking in at all the idea of guilt, but deeply distressed at having offended his master :

"'Lor, Massa Harry, what was I to do, sir? She tuk all I could git, and more too, sir, to put on her back ; and tellin' de truf, sir, dress herself as no poor man's wife hav' any right to. I 'monstrated wid her, Massa, but to no purpose ; and den, sir, w'y I jis did all a decent man could do—lef' her, sir, for some oder nigger better off 'an I is.'

"'T was no use. Colly could not be aroused to conscientiousness on the subject.

"Not one in a thousand, I suppose, of these poor creatures, have any conception whatever of the sanctity of marriage ; nor can they be made to have ; yet, strange to say, they are perfect models of conjugal fidelity and devotion, while the temporary bondage lasts. I have known them to walk miles after a hard day's work, not only occasionally, but every night, to see the old woman, and cut her wood for her, etc. But to see the coolness with which they throw off the yoke is diverting in the extreme.

"I was accosted one morning in my husband's study by a respectable-looking negro woman, who meekly inquired if Mr. B was at home.

"'No, he is not. Is it any thing particular you want?—perhaps I can help you.'

"'Yes, ma'am; it's partickler business wid hisself.'

"Having good reason to believe it was the old story of 'a mountain in labor and brought forth a mouse,' I pressed the question, partly to save my better half some of the petty annoyances to which he was almost daily subjected by his sable flock, and partly, I own, to gratify a becoming and laudable curiosity, after all this show of mystery. Behold the answer in plain English, or rather nigger English.

"'I came to ask, please ma'am, if I might have another husband.'

"Just at this crisis, the Oracle entered, who, having authority, by a few spoken words, to join together those whom no man may put asunder, these poor people simply imagine him gifted with equal power to annul the contract with a breath of his mouth.

"I was heartily amused to find that this woman was really no widow, as I had supposed, but merely from caprice, or some reason satisfactory to herself, no doubt, took it into her head to drop her present spouse and look out for another. The matter was referred to the 'Quarterly Conference,' where an amusing scene occurred, which resulted in the discomfiture of the disconsolate petitioner, who returned to her home rather crest-fallen.

"These quarterly conference debates, for flights of oratory, and superlativeness of diction, beggar all description. Be it understood, that negroes, as a class, have more 'business' to attend to than any other people—that is, provided they can thereby get a chance to 'speak 'fore white folks.' To make a speech is glory enough for Sambo, if he happen to have 'the gift of gab'; and to speak before the preacher is an honor unparalleled. And, by the way, if the preacher have will and wit enough to manage and control the discordant elements of a negro Quarterly Conference, he will be abundantly rewarded with such respect and gratitude as man seldom may lay claim to. They account him but a very little 'lower than the angels'; and their lives, their fortunes, and their sacred honor, are equally his at command. But wo be to the unfortunate pastor who treats them with undue indulgence , they will besiege him daily and hourly with their petty affairs, and their business meetings will be such a monopoly of his time and patience, that but for the farcical character of the same, making them more like dramatic entertainments than sober realities, he would be in despair. Far into the short hours of morning will they speechify and magnify, until nothing but the voice of stern authority, in a tone of command not to be mistaken, can stop the torrent."

An Alabama gentleman whom I questioned with regard to the chastity of the so-called pious slaves confessed that four negro women had borne children in his own house, all of them at the time of delivery members in good standing of the Baptist church, and none of them calling any man husband. The only negro man in the house was also a church member, and he believed that he was the father of the four children. He said that he did not know of more than one negro woman whom he could suppose to be chaste, yet he knew hosts who were members of churches.[1]

[1] "A small farmer," who "has had control of negroes for thirty years and has been pursuing his present system with them for twenty years," and who, "owning but few slaves, is able," as he observes, "to do better by them" than large planters, writing to Mr. DeBow, says, "I have tried faithfully to break up immorality. I have not known an oath to be sworn for a long time. I know of no quarreling, no calling harsh names, and but little stealing. *Habits of amalgamation*

A Northern clergyman who had been some years in another town in Alabama, where also the means of instruction offered the slaves were unusually good, answered my inquiry, What proportion of the colored members of the churches in the town had any clear comprehension of the meaning of the articles of faith which they professed? "Certainly not more than one in seven."

The acknowledgment that "the colored people will, in spite of all our efforts, have more confidence in the views of leading colored members," made by the writer of the letter taken from the *Religious Herald*, has been generally made by all clergymen at the South with whom I have conversed. A clergyman of the Episcopal church, of very frank and engaging manners, said in my presence that he had been striving for seven years to gain the confidence of the small number of Africans belonging to his congregation, and with extreme humility he had been lately forced to acknowledge that all his apparent success hitherto had been most delusive. When asked how he accounted for it, he at once ascribed it to the negro's habitual distrust of the white race, and in discussing the causes of this distrust he asked how, if he pretended to believe that the Bible was the Word of God, addressed equally to all

---

I can not stop. I can only check it in name. I am willing to be taught, for I have tried everything I know." He has his field negroes attend his own family prayers on Sunday, prayer-meetings at four o'clock Sunday mornings, etc.— DeBow's *Resources*, vol. ii., p. 337.

the human race, he could explain to a negro's satisfaction why he should fear to put it directly into his hands and instruct him to read it and judge for himself of his duty? A planter present, a member of his church, immediately observed that these were dangerous views, and advised him to be cautious in the expression of them. The laws of the country forbade the education of negroes, and the church was, and he trusted always would remain, the bulwark of the laws. The clergyman replied that he had no design to break the laws, but he must say that he considered that the law which withheld the Bible from the negro was unnecessary and papistical in character.[1]

THE RESTRAINT UPON THE WHITE CLERGY

The *Methodist Protestant*, a religious newspaper edited by a clergyman in Maryland, where the slave population is to the free only in the ratio of one to twenty-five, lately printed an account of a slave auction in Java (translated from a Dutch paper), at which the father of a slave family was permitted to purchase his wife and children at a nominal price, owing to the

---

[1] The *Southern Presbyterian* in reviewing some observations made before a South Carolina Bible Society, in which it had been urged that if slaves were permitted to read the Bible, they would learn from it to be more submissive to the authority which the State gives the master over them, says that the speaker "seems to be uninformed of the fact that the Scriptures are read in our churches every Sabbath day, and those very passages which inculcate the relative duties of masters and servants in consequence of their textual, *i. e.* legally prescribed connections, are *more frequently read* than any other portions of the Bible."

humanity of the spectators   The account concluded as follows :

"It would be difficult to describe the joy experienced by these slaves on hearing the fall of the hammer which thus gave them their liberty , and this joy was further augmented by the presents given them by numbers of the spectators, in order that they might be able to obtain a subsistence till such a time as they could procure employment.

"These are the acts of a noble generosity that deserve to be remembered, and which, at the same time, testify that the inhabitants of Java begin to abhor the crying injustice of slavery, and are willing to entertain measures for its abolition."

To give currency to such ideas, even in Maryland, would be fatal to what clergymen call their "influence, " and which they everywhere value at a rather dangerous estimate ; accordingly, in the editorial columns prominence is given to the following salvo to the outraged sensibilities of the subscribers :

"SLAVE AUCTION IN JAVA

"A brief article, with this head, appears on the fourth page of our paper this week. It is of a class of articles we *never select*, because they are very often manufactured by paragraphists for a purpose, and are not reliable. It was put in by our printer in place of something we had *marked out*. We did not see this objectionable substitute until the outside form was worked off, and are therefore not responsible for it." [1]

THE EDUCATION OF THE WHITE RACE, UNDER THE NECESSITIES OF THE PRESENT SYSTEM

The habitual caution imposed on clergymen and public teachers must, and obviously does have an im-

[1] Organized action for the abolition of slavery in the island of Java, has since been authentically reported.

portant secondary effect, similar to that usually attributed by Protestants to papacy, upon the minds of all the people, discountenancing and retarding the free and fearless exercise of the mind upon subjects of a religious or ethical nature, and the necessity of accepting and apologizing for the exceedingly low morality of the normally religious slaves, together with the familiarity with this immorality which all classes acquire, renders the existence of a very elevated standard of morals among the whites almost an impossibility.[1]

In spite of the constant denunciations by the Southern newspapers, of those who continued to patronize

[1] Twice it happened to come to my knowledge that sons of a planter, by whom I was lodged while on this journey—lads of fourteen or sixteen—who were supposed to have slept in the same room with me, really spent the night, till after daybreak, in the negro cabins. A Southern merchant, visiting New York to whom I expressed the view I had been led to form of the evil of slavery in this way, replied that he thought I over-estimated the evil to boys on the plantations, but that it was impossible to over-estimate it in towns. "I have personal knowledge," he continued, "that there are but two lads, sixteen years old, in our town, [a small market town of Alabama,] who have not already had occasion to resort to remedies for the penalty of licentiousness." "When on my brother's plantation, just before I came North," said another Southern merchant, on his annual visit to New York, "I was informed that each of his family-servants were suffering from——, and I ascertained that each of my brother's children, girls and boys, had been informed of it and knew how and from whom it had been acquired. The negroes being their familiar companions, I tried to get my brother to send them North with me to school. I told him he might as well have them educated in a brothel at once, as in the way they were growing up."

Northern educational institutions, I never conversed
with a cultivated Southerner on the effects of slavery,
that he did not express a wish or intention to have his
own children educated where they should be free from
demoralizing associations with slaves. That this association is almost inevitably corrupting and dangerous,
is very generally (I may say, excepting by the extrem-
est fanatics of South Carolina, universally) admitted.
Now, although the children of a few wealthy men
may, for a limited period, be preserved from this danger, the children of the million can not be.   Indeed, it
requires a man of some culture, and knowledge of the
rest of the world, to appreciate the danger sufficiently
to guard at all diligently against it.   If habitual intercourse with a hopelessly low and immoral class is at
all bad in its effects on young minds, the people of the
South are, as a people, educated subject to this bad
influence, and must bear the consequences.   In other
words, if the slaves must not be elevated, it would
seem to be a necessity that the citizens should steadily
degenerate.

Change and grow more marked in their peculiarities
with every generation, they certainly do, very obviously.
"The South" has a traditional reputation for qualities
and habits in which, I think, the Southern people, as
a whole, are to-day more deficient than any other
nation in the world.   The Southern gentleman, as we
ordinarily conceive him to be, is as rare a phenomenon
in the South at the present day as is the old squire of
Geoffrey Crayon in modern England.   But it is unneces-

sary to argue how great must be the influence upon people of a higher origin, of habitual association with a race systematically kept at the lowest ebb of intellect and morals. It has been elaborately and convincingly described by Mr. Jefferson from his personal experience and observation of his neighbors. What he testified to be the effect upon the Virginians, in his day, of owning and associating with slaves, is now to be witnessed to a far greater and more deplorable extent throughout the whole South, but most deplorably in districts where the slave population predominates, and where, consequently, the action of slavery has been most unimpeded.[1]

[1] Jefferson fails to enumerate, among the evils of slavery, one of its influences which I am inclined to think as distinct and as baneful to us nationally as any other. How can men retain the most essential quality of true manhood who daily, without remonstrance or interference, see men beaten, whose position renders effective resistance totally impracticable—and not only men, but women, too! Is it not partially the result of this that self-respect seldom seems to suggest to an angry man at the South that he should use anything like magnanimity? that he should be careful to secure fair play for his opponent in a quarrel? A gentleman of veracity, now living in the South, told me that among his friends he had once numbered two young men, who were themselves intimate friends, till one of them, taking offence at some foolish words uttered by the other, challenged him. A large crowd assembled to see the duel, which took place on a piece of prairie ground. The combatants came armed with rifles, and at the first interchange of shots the challenged man fell disabled by a ball in the thigh. The other, throwing down his rifle, walked toward him, and, kneeling by his side, drew a bowie knife and deliberately butchered him. The crowd of bystanders not only permitted this, but the execrable assassin still lives in the community,

ABSENTEEISM.

What proportion of the larger cotton plantations are resided upon by their owners, I am unable to estimate with confidence Of those having cabin accommodations for fifty slaves each, which came under my observation from the road, while I was travelling through the cotton districts bordering the Mississippi River, I think more than half were unprovided with a habitation which I could suppose to be the ordinary residence of a man of moderate wealth.   In the more fertile and less healthy districts I should judge that the majority of slaves are left by their owners to the nearly unlimited government of hireling overseers the greater part of the time. Some of these plantations are owned by capitalists, who reside permanently and constantly in the North or in Europe.   Many are owned by wealthy Virginians and Carolinians who reside on what are called the "show plantations" of those States; plantations having all the character, though never the name, of mere country-seats, the exhausted soil of which will scarcely produce sufficient to feed and clothe the resident slaves, whose increase is constantly removed to colonize these richer fields of the West.

Still a large number are merely occasionally sojourning places of their owners, who naturally enough prefer

has since married, and, as far as my informant could judge, his social position has been rather advanced than otherwise, from thus dealing with his enemy. In what other English—in what other civilized or half-civilized community would such cowardly atrocity have been endured?

to live as soon as they can afford to do so, where the conveniences and luxuries belonging to a highly civilized state of society are more easily obtained than they can ever be in a country of large plantations. It is rare that a plantation would have a dozen intelligent families residing within a day's ride of it. Any society that a planter enjoys on his estate must, therefore, consist in a great degree of permanent guests. Hence the name for hospitality of wealthy planters. A large plantation is necessarily a retreat from general society, and is used by its owner, I am inclined to think, in the majority of cases, in winter, as Berkshire villas and farms are in summer by rich people of New York and Boston. I feel assured that this is the case with the plantations upon the Mississippi, and the bayous of Louisiana, upon the Arkansas, the Yazoo, and the Red rivers, and in the lowlands of Carolina and Georgia. I have never been on a plantation numbering fifty-field hands, the owner of which was accustomed to reside steadily through the year upon it. Still I am aware there are many such, and possibly it is a minority of them who are regularly absent with their families from their plantations during any considerable part of the year.

The summer visitors from the South to our Northern watering-places are, I judge, chiefly of the migratory, wealthy class. Such persons, it is evident are much less influenced in their character and habits, by association with slaves, than any other at the South. Their household arrangements, and the customs of

9

their house-servants must, of course, assimilate to
those of cultivated families in other parts of the world.
The Irish gentleman and the Irish peasant are not
more unlike, in their habits and manners, than some
of these large planters and the great multitude of slave
owners.

The number of the very wealthy is, of course, small,
yet as the chief part of the wealth of these consists in
slaves, no inconsiderable proportion of all the slaves
belong to men who deputize their government in
a great measure to overseers.   It may be computed,
(not, however, with confidence), from the census of
1850, that about one half the slaves of Louisiana and
one third those of Mississippi and Arkansas, belong to
estates of not less than fifty slaves each, and of these,
I believe, nine tenths live on plantations which their
owners reside upon, if at all, but transiently.

The number of plantations of this class, and the
proportion of those employed upon them to the whole
body of negroes in the country, is, as I have said,
rapidly increasing.   At the present prices of cotton
the large grower has such advantages over the small,
that the owner of a plantation of fifty slaves, favorably
situated, unless he lives very recklessly, will increase
in wealth so rapidly and possess such a credit that he
may soon establish or purchase other plantations, so
that at his death his children may be provided for
without reducing the effective force of negroes on any
division of his landed estate.   The excessive credit
given to such planters by negro dealers and tradesmen

renders this the more practicable. The higher the
price of cotton the higher is that of negroes, and
the higher the price of negroes the less is it in the
power of men of small capital to buy them. Large
plantations, of course, pay a much larger percentage on
the capital invested in them than smaller ones ; indeed
the only plausible economical defence of slavery is
simply an explanation of the advantages of associated
labor; advantages which are possessed equally by large
manufacturing establishments in which free laborers are
brought together and employed in the most effective
manner, and which I can see no sufficient reason for
supposing could not be made available for agriculture
did not the good results flowing from small holdings,
on the whole, counterbalance them. If the present
high price of cotton and the present scarcity of labor
at the South continues, the cultivation of cotton on
small plantations will by and by become unusual, for
the same reason that hand-loom weaving has become
unusual in the farm houses of Massachusetts.

But whatever advantages large plantations have,
they accrue only to their owners and to the buyers of
cotton ; the mass of the white inhabitants are dispersed over a greater surface, discouraged and driven
toward barbarism by them, and the blacks upon them,
while rapidly degenerating from all that is redeem-
ing in savage-life, are gaining nothing valuable of
civilization.

In the Report of the Grand Jury of Richland District,
South Carolina, in *eighteen hundred and fifty-four,*

calling for a re-establishment of the African slave trade,[1] it is observed, "as to the morality of this question, it is scarcely necessary for us to allude to it; when the fact is remarked that the plantations of Alabama, Mississippi, Louisiana, and Texas have been and are daily settled by the removal of slaves from the more northern of the Slave States, and that in consequence of their having been raised in a more healthy climate, and in most cases trained to pursuits totally different, the mortality even on the best-ordered farms is so great that in many instances the entire income is expended in the purchase of more slaves from the same source in order to replenish and keep up those plantations, while in *every case* the condition of the slave, if his life is spared, is made worse both physically and morally. * * * And if you look at the subject in a religious point of view, the contrast is equally striking, for when you remove a slave from the more northern to the more southern parts of the slaveholding States, you thereby diminish his religious opportunities."

I believe that this statement gives an exaggerated and calumnious report of the general condition of the slaves upon the plantations of the States referred to, containing, as they did in 1849, one third of the whole slave population of the South—but I have not been able to resist the conviction that in the districts where cotton is now grown most profitably to the planters,

---

[1] Richland District contains seven thousand white, and thirteen thousand slave population. The Report is published in the *Charleston Standard*, October 12, 1854.

the oppression and deterioration of the negro race is much more lamentable than is generally supposed by those who like myself have been constrained, by other considerations, to accept it as a duty to oppose temperately but determinately the modern policy of the South, of which this is an immediate result. Its effect on the white race, I still consider to be infinitely more deplorable.

In the important work of Dr. Davy on the *West Indies*, I find the following description of the poor whites of Barbadoes, who, by a comparison with Sir Charles Lyell's observations, and my own descriptions in the *Seaboard Slave States* (Vol. II., pages 41, 144), it may be seen correspond not only morally and intellectually, but remarkably also, in their physical appearance, with those of the old cotton plantation districts of the South.

"Relative to the whites, they may be divided into two classes—the poor laboring portion of them constituting the majority, and the smaller portion of them consisting of those in easy or affluent circumstances.

"The former are in many respects remarkable, and not less so in appearance than in character. Their hue and complexion are not such as might be expected; their color resembles more that of the Albino than of an Englishman. When exposed a good deal to the sun in a tropical climate, it is commonly of a sickly white, or light red, not often of a healthy brown; and they have generally light eyes and light-colored, sparse hair. In make they bear marks of feebleness, rather tall, loosely jointed, with little muscular development. In brief, their general appearance denotes degeneracy of corporeal frame, and reminds one of exotic plants vegetating in an uncongenial soil and climate.

"In character, morally and intellectually, they show marks

also of degeneracy, not less than physically. They are generally indolent and idle, ignorant and improvident, and often intemperate. Is it surprising, then, that they are poor, and objects of contempt? * * * What they are they have been made undoubtedly by circumstances, and this in the course of a few generations." [1]

Similar phenomena are found in the free race, I believe, wherever large slave-plantations are common Whether a gradual elevation of the slaves, would prove the entire destruction of the poor whites, as is held at the South, is certainly very doubtful. The effect of emancipation in Barbadoes, upon the whites, after some half dozen years only, is thus described by Dr. Davy:

"Previous to emancipation, the planters, for every sixty acres of land, had to provide a man for the militia (the chief purpose of which was to guard against the insurrection of their slaves). * * * He was supplied by his principal with a gun and ammunition, and had a house and two acres of land free of rent, on which he raised some vegetables and kept a cow, or two or three goats. Very idle himself, his wife worked with the needle, and got money for making clothes for the negroes" (p. 66). "Now that they are obliged to support themselves as they can, they are variously employed Those who possess a little land, or who rent a few acres, cultivate chiefly those crops which require least labor, and the smallest means, such as ground provisions, arrow-root, aloes, and perhaps a little cotton. I have seen one of them at work in a manner not a little characteristic: a hoe in one hand and umbrella in the other, which he held over his head, and a face-cloth over his face (a relief from reflected heat). Some who have been taught to read and write are employed as book-keepers by the proprietors of the larger estates, with a pay of about six dollars a month and board and lodging. Some are chiefly occupied in

---

[1] *The West Indies,* * * * *Founded on Notes and Observations Collected during a Three Years' Residence.* By John Davy, M. D., F.R.S., etc., Inspector General of Army Hospitals.

fishing. * * * Some gain a livelihood as carters and grooms, and some as field-laborers, a kind of labor which, when slaves were employed as laborers, they would have resisted *as insupportable degradation*. * * * All of them have the aristocratic feeling in its worst sense, the class pride acquired in time of slavery when they were an important portion of the privileged order; and it is marked in their manners and bearing. * * * They are not to be considered as altogether irreclaimable" (p. 71).

CHAPTER III

Vicksburg, March 18.—I arrived at this place last night, about sunset, and was told that there was no hotel in the town except on the wharf-boat, the only house used for that purpose having been closed a few days ago on account of a difference of opinion between its owner and his tenant.

There are no wharves on the Mississippi, or any of the Southern rivers. The wharf-boat is an old steamboat, with her paddle-boxes and machinery removed and otherwise dismantled, on which steamboats discharge passengers and freight. The main deck is used as a warehouse, and, in place of the furnace, has in this case a dramshop, a chandler's shop, a forwarding agency, and a telegraph office. Overhead, the saloon and staterooms remain and with the barroom and clerk's office, kitchen and barber's shop, constitute a stationary though floating hostelry.

Though there were fifty or more rooms, and not a dozen guests, I was obliged, about twelve o'clock, to admit a stranger who had been gambling all the evening in the saloon, to occupy the spare shelf of my closet. If a disposition to enjoy occasional privacy, or to exercise a choice in one's roommates were a sure symptom of a monomania for incendiarism, it could not be more carefully thwarted than it is at all public houses in this part of the world.

Memphis, March 20.—I reached here this morning in forty-eight hours by steamboat from Vickburg; distance four hundred miles; many stoppages and against the current; fare $10.

Here, at the "Commercial Hotel," I am favored with an unusually good-natured roommate. He is smoking on the bed—our bed—now, and wants to know what my business is here, and whether I carry a pistol about me; also whether I believe that it is n't lucky to play cards on Sunday; which I do most strenuously, especially as this is a rainy Sunday, and his second cigar is nearly smoked out.

This is a first-class hotel and has, of course, printed bills of fare, which in a dearth of other literature, are not to be dropped at the first glance. A copy of to-day's is presented on the following page.

Being in a distant quarter of the establishment when a crash of the gong announced dinner, I did not get to the table as early as some others. The meal was served in a large, dreary room exactly like a hospital ward; and it is a striking illustration of the celerity with which everything is accomplished in our young country, that beginning with the soup, and going on by the fish to the roasts, the first five dishes I inquired for, when at last I succeeded in arresting one of the negro boys, were "all gone," and as the waiter had to go to the head of the dining-room, or to the kitchen to

COMMERCIAL HOTEL.

BY D. COCKRELL.

BILL OF FARE.

MARCH 20

SOUP.

Oyster.

FISH.

Red.

BOILED

Jole and green.
Ham.
Corned beef,
Bacon and turnips.
Codfish egg sauce.
Beef heart egg sauce
Leg of mutton caper sauce,
Barbecued rabits,
Boiled tongue.

ROAST.

Veal.
Roast pig.
Moscovie Ducks.
Kentucky beef.
Mutton.
Barbecued shoat
Roast bear meat
Roast pork.

ENTREES

Fricasee pork
Calf-feet mushroom sauce.
Bear sausages.
Harricane tripe.
Stewed mutton.
Browned Rice.
Calf feet madeira sauce
Stewed turkey wine sauce
Giblets volivon.
Mutton omelett.
Beef's heart fricaseed.
Cheese macaroni
Chicken chops robert sauce.
Breast chicken madeira sauce.
Beef kidney pickle sauce.
Cod fish baked
Calf head wine sauce.

FRUIT.

Almonds.
Raisins.
Pecans

VEGETABLES.

Boiled Cabbage.
Turnips.
Cold Slaugh.
Hot slaugh.
Pickled beets.
Creole hominy.
Crout cabbage.
Oyster plant fried.
Parsneps gravied.
Stewed parsneps.
Fried cabbage.
Sweet potatoes spiced.
Carrot
Sweat potatoes baked.
Cabbage stuffed
Onions boiled.
Irish potatoes creamed and mashed.
Irish potatoes browned.
Boiled Shellots.
Scolloped carrots
Boiled turnips drawn butter
White beans.

PASTRY.

Currant pies
Lemon custard,
Rice pudding.
Cocoanut pie.
Cranberry pies
Sliced potato pie.
Chess cake,
Irish pudding.
Orange custard.
Cranberry shapes
Green peach tarts.
Green peach puff paste.
Grape tarts,
Huckle berry pies.
Pound Cake
Rheubarb tarts.
Plum tarts,
Calves feet jelly.
Blamonge
Oranga jelly.

ascertain this fact upon each demand, the majority of the company had left the table before I was served at all. At length I said I would take anything that was still to be had, and thereupon was provided immediately with some grimy bacon, and greasy cabbage. This I commenced eating, but I no sooner paused for a moment, than it was suddenly and surreptitiously removed, and its place supplied, without the expression of any desire on my part, with some other Memphitic chef d'œuvre, a close investigation of which left me in doubt whether it was that denominated "sliced potato pie," or "Irish pudding."

I congratulate myself that I have lived to see the day in which an agitation for reform in our GREAT HOTEL SYSTEM has been commenced, and I trust that a Society for the Revival of Village Inns will ere long form one of the features of the May anniversaries.

A stage-coach conveyed the railroad passengers from the hotel to the station, which was a mile or two out of town. As we were entering the coach the driver observed with a Mephistophelean smile that we "need n't calculate we were gwine to ride very fur" and accordingly, as soon as we had got into the country he stopped and asked all the men passengers to get out and walk, for, he added, "it was as much as his hoses could do to draw the ladies and the baggage" It was quite true; the road was so bad that the horses were obliged to stop frequently with the diminished load, and as there was a contract between myself and the proprietors by which, for a stipulated sum of money by me to them in hand

duly paid, they promised to convey me, as well as my
little baggage, I thought it would have been no more
than honest if they had looked out beforehand to have
either a stronger team, or a better road, provided. As
is the custom of our country, however, we allowed
ourselves to be thus robbed and forced to tiresome labor
with great good nature, and waded along through mud
ankle-deep, joking with the driver, and ready to put
our shoulders to the wheels if it should be necessary.
Two pieces of our baggage were jerked off in heavy
lurches of the coach; the owners picked them up and
carried them on their shoulders till the horses stopped
to breathe again. The train of course had waited
for us, and it continued to wait until another coach
arrived, when it started twenty minutes behind time.

After some forty miles of rail, nine of us were stowed
away in another stage-coach. The road was bad, the
weather foul. We proceeded slowly, were often in im-
minent danger of being upset, and once were all obliged
to get out and help the horses draw the coach out of a
slough; but with smoking, and the occasional circula-
tion of a small black bottle, and a general disposition
to be as comfortable as circumstances would allow, four
hours of stage-coaching proved less fatiguing than one
of the smoky rail-cars.

Among the passengers was a "Judge," resident in
the vicinity, portly, dignified, and well informed; and
a young man, who was a personal friend of the member
of Congress from the district, and who, as he informed
me, had, through the influence of this friend, a promise

from the President of honorable and lucrative employment under government. He was known to all the
other passengers, and hailed by every one on the roadside, by the title of Colonel. The Judge was ready to
converse about the country through which we were
passing, and while perfectly aware, as no one else
seemed to be, that it bore anything but an appearance
of prosperity or attractiveness to a stranger, he assured
me that it was really improving in all respects quite
rapidly. There were few large plantations, but many
small planters or rather farmers, for cotton, though the
principal source of cash income, was much less exclusively an object of attention than in the more southern
parts of the State. A larger space was occupied by the
maize and grain crops. There were not a few small
fields of wheat. In the afternoon, when only the Colonel and myself were with him, the Judge talked about
slavery in a candid and liberal spirit. At present
prices, he said, nobody could afford to own slaves,
unless he could engage them almost exclusively in
cotton-growing. It was undoubtedly a great injury to a
region like this, which was not altogether well adapted
to cotton, to be in the midst of a slaveholding country,
for it prevented efficient free labor. A good deal of
cotton was nevertheless grown hereabouts by white
labor—by poor men who planted an acre or two, and
worked it themselves, getting the planters to gin and
press it for them. It was not at all uncommon for men
to begin in this way and soon purchase negroes on
credit, and eventually become rich men. Most of the

plantations in this vicinity, indeed, belonged to men who had come into the country with nothing within twenty years. Once a man got a good start with negroes, unless the luck was much against him, nothing but his own folly could prevent his becoming rich. The increase of his negro property by births, if he took good care of it, must, in a few years, make him independent. The worst thing, and the most difficult to remedy, was the deplorable ignorance which prevailed. Latterly, however, people were taking more pride in the education of their children. Some excellent schools had been established, the teachers generally from the North, and a great many children were sent to board in the villages—county seats—to attend them. This was especially true of girls, who liked to live in the villages rather than on the plantations. There was more difficulty in making boys attend school, until, at least, they were too old to get much good from it.

The "Colonel" was a rough, merry, good-hearted, simple-minded man, and kept all the would-be sobersides of our coach body, in irrepressible laughter with queer observations on passing occurrences, anecdotes, and comic songs. It must be confessed that there is no charge which the enemies of the theatre bring against the stage, that was not duly illustrated, and that with a broadness which the taste of a metropolitan audience would scarcely permit. Had Doctor —— and Doctor —— been with me they would thereafter for ever have denied themselves, and discountenanced in others, the use of such a means of travel. The Colonel, notwithstanding, was of a most obliging disposition, and having ascertained in what direction I was going, enumerated at least a dozen families on the road, within some hundred miles, whom he invited me to visit, assuring me that I should find pretty girls in all of them, and a warm welcome, if I mentioned his name.

He told the Judge that his bar-bill on the boat, coming up from New Orleans, was forty dollars—seventeen dollars the first night. But he had made money—had won forty dollars of one gentleman. He confessed, however, that he had lost fifteen by another, "but he saw how he did it. He did not want to accuse him publicly, but he saw it and he purposed to write to him and tell him of it. He did not mean to insult the gentleman, only he did not want to have him think that he was so green as not to know how he did it."

While stopping for dinner at a village inn, a young man came into the room where we all were, and asked the coachman what was to be paid for a trunk which had been brought for him. The coachman said the charge would be a dollar, which the young man thought excessive. The coachman denied that was so, said that it was what he had often been paid; he should not take less. The young man finally agreed to wait for the decision of the proprietor of the line. There was a woman in the room; I noticed no loud words or angry tones, and had not supposed that there was the slightest excitement. I observed, however, that there was a profound silence for a minute afterwards, which was interrupted by a jocose remark of the coachman about the delay of our dinner. Soon after we re-entered the coach, the Colonel referred to the trunk owner, in a contemptuous manner. The Judge replied in a similar tone. "If I had been in the driver's place, I should have killed him, sure," said the Colonel. With great surprise, I ventured to ask for what reason. "Did not you see the fellow put his hand to his breast when the driver denied that he had ever taken less than a dollar for bringing a trunk from Memphis?"

"No, I did not; but what of it?"

"Why, he meant to frighten the driver, of course."

"You think he had a knife in his breast?"

"Of course he had, sir"

"But you would n't kill him for that, I suppose?"

"When a man threatens to kill me, you would n't have me wait for him to do it, would you, sir?"

The roads continued very heavy; some one remarked, "There 's been a heap of rain lately," and rain still kept falling. We passed a number of cotton-wagons which had stopped in the road; the cattle had been turned out and had strayed off into the woods, and the drivers lay under the tilts asleep on straw.

The Colonel said this sight reminded him of his old camp-meeting days. He used to be very fond of going to camp-meetings. "I used to go first for fun, and oh! Lord, haint I had some fun at camp-meetings? But after a while I got a conviction—need n't laugh, gentlemen. I tell you it was sober business for me. I 'll never make fun of that. The truth just is, I am a melancholy

case ; I thought I was a pious man once, I did—I 'm
damned if I did n't.   Don't laugh at what I say, now ;
I don't want fun made of that ; I give you my word I
experienced religion, and I used to go to the meetings
with as much sincerity and soberness, as anybody
could.   That was the time I learned to sing—learned to
pray too, I did ; could pray right smart.   I did think I
was a converted man, but of course, I aint, and I 'spose
't warnt the right sort, and I don't reckon I shall have
another chance.   A gentleman has the right to make
the most of this life, when he can't calculate on anything better than roasting in the next.   Aint that so
Judge ?   I reckon so.   You must n't think hard of me,
if I do talk wicked some.   Can't help it.''

So common is this sort of effervescing mixture of im-
piety and theology at the South, I doubt if the Colonel
was not perfectly sincere, though probably not wholly
unconscious of drollery, in these remarks.   At a Sunday dinner-table, at a village inn, two or three men
took seats, who had, as they said, ''been to the
preachin'.''   A child had been baptized, and the
preaching had been a defence of infant baptism.

'' I 'm damned,'' said one, ''ef he teched on the primary significance of baptism, at all—buryin' with
Jesus.''

'' They wus the weakest arguments for sprinklin'
that ever I heerd,'' said another—a hot, red-faced, cor-
pulent man—''and his sermon was two hours long, for
when he stopped I looked at my watch.   I thought it
should be a lesson to me, for I could n't help going

10

to sleep. Says I to Uncle John, says I—he sot next to
me, and I whispered to him—says I, ' When he gits to
Bunker Hill, you wake me up,' for I see he was bound
to go clean back to the beginnin' of things."

" Uncle John is an Episcopalian, aint he?"

" Yes."

" Well, there aint no religion in that, no how."

" No there aint "

" Well now, you would n't think it, but I 've studied
into religion a heap in my life."

" Don't seem to have done you much good."

" No it haint, not yet, but I 've studied into it, and
I know what it is."

" There aint but one way, Benny."

" I know it."

" Repent of your sins, and believe in Christ, and be
immersed, that 's all."

" I know it."

" Well, I hope the Lord 'll bring you to it, 'fore you
die."

" Reckon he will—hope so, sure."

" You would n't hardly think that fat man was a
preacher himself, would you?" said the landlady to
me, after they left.

" Certainly not."

" He is, though, but I don't think much of that
sort," and the landlady immediately began to describe
to me the religious history of the neighborhood. It
was some different here, she said, she reckoned, in
reply to a remark of mine, from what it was at the

North. Most respectable people became pious here
before they got to be very old, especially ladies.
Young ladies were always gay and went to balls till
they were near twenty years old, but from eighteen
to twenty-five they generally got religion, and then
they stopped right short and never danced or carried
on any after that. Sometimes it was n't till after they
were married, but there were n't many ladies who had
children that warn't pious. She herself was an exception, for she had three children and had not got
religion yet; sometimes she was frightened to think
how old she was—her children growing up about her;
but she did so like dancing—she hoped her turn would
come—she knew it would—she had a pious and praying mother, and she reckoned her prayers must be
heard, and so on.

I was forced by the stage arrangements to travel
night and day. The Colonel told me that I should be
able to get a good supper at a house where the coach
was to stop about midnight—" good honest fried bacon
and hot Christian corn-bread—nothing like it to fill a
man up and make him feel righteous You get a heap
better living up in this country than you can at the
St. Charles, for all the fuss they make about it. It 's
lucky you 'll have something better to travel on to-
night than them French friterzeed Dutch flabbergasted
hell-fixins: for you 'll have the————" (another most
extraordinary series of imprecations on the road over
which I was to travel).

Before dark all my companions left me, and in their

place I had but one, a young gentleman with whom I soon became very intimately acquainted. He was seventeen years old, so he said; he looked older; and the son of a planter in the "Yazoo bottoms." The last year he had "follered overseein'" on his father's plantation, but he was bound for Tennessee, now, to go to an academy, where he could learn geography. There was a school near home at which he had studied reading and writing and ciphering, but he thought a gentleman ought to have some knowledge of geography. At ten o'clock the next morning, the stage-coach having progressed at the rate of exactly two miles and a half an hour for the previous sixteen hours, during which time we had been fasting, the supper-house, which we should have reached before midnight, was still ten miles ahead, the driver sulky and refusing to stop until we reached it. We had been pounded till we ached in every muscle. I had had no sleep since I left Memphis. We were passing over a hill country which sometimes appeared to be quite thickly inhabited, yet mainly still covered with a pine forest, through which the wind moaned lugubriously.

I had been induced to make this trip, in no slight degree by reading the following description in a statistical article of DeBow's *Review :*

"The settling of this region is one among the many remarkable events in the history of the rise of the western States Fifteen years ago it was an Indian wilderness, and now it has reached and passed in its population other portions of the State of ten times its age, and this population, too, one of the finest in all the West. Great attention has been given to schools and education, and here, [at Memphis,] has been located the University of Mississippi; so amply endowed by the State, and now just going into operation under the auspices of some of the ablest professors from the Eastern colleges.   There is no overgrown wealth among them, and yet no squalid poverty; the people being generally comfortable, substantial and independent farmers.   Considering its climate, soil, wealth, and general character of its inhabitants, I should think no more desirable and delightful residence could be found than among the hills and sunny valleys of the Chickasaw Cession "[1]

And here among the hills of this Paradise of the Southwest, we were, Yazoo and I—he, savagely hungry, as may be guessed from his observations upon "the finest people of the West," among whose cabins in the pine wood, toiled our stage-coach.

The whole art of driving was directed to the discovery of a passage for the coach among the trees and through the fields, where there were fields, adjoining the road—the road itself being impassable.   Occasionally, when the coachman, during the night, found it necessary, owing to the thickness of the forest on each side, to take to the road, he would first leave the coach and make a survey with his lantern, sounding the ruts of the cotton-wagons, and finally marking out a channel by guiding-stakes which he cut from the underwood with a hatchet, usually carried in the holster.   If after diligent sounding, he found no passage sufficiently shallow, he would sometimes spend half an hour in preparing one, bringing rails from the nearest fence, or cutting brushwood for the purpose.   We were but once or twice during the night called upon to leave the

[1] See *Resources*, article "Mississippi," etc.

coach, or to assist in road-making, and my companion
frequently expressed his gratitude for this—gratitude
not to the driver, but to Providence, who had made a
country, as he thought, so unusually well adapted for
stage-coaching. The night before, he had been on a
much worse road, and was half the time, with numerous other passengers, engaged in bringing rails, and
prying the coach out of sloughs. They had been
obliged to keep on the track, because the water was
up over the adjoining country. Where the wooden
causeway had floated off, they had passed through
water so deep that it entered the coach body. With
our road of to-day, then, he could only express satisfaction ; not so with the residents upon it. " Look at
'em," he would say, " Just look at 'em ! What 's the
use of such people's living ? 'pears to me I 'd die if I
could n't live better 'n that. When I get to be Repre-
sentative, I am going to have a law made that all such
kind of men shall be took up by the State and sent to
the penitentiary, to make 'em work and earn something to support their families. I pity the women ; I
haint nuthin' agin them ; they work hard enough, I
know ; but the men—I know how 't is. They just
hang around groceries and spend all the money they
can get—just go round and live on other people, and
play keerds, and only go home to nights ; and the poor
women, they hev to live how they ken."

" Do you think it 's so ? It is strange we see no
men—only women and children."

" Tell you they 're off, gettin' a dinner out o' some-

body. Tell you, I know it's so. It's the way all
these people do. Why, there's one poor man I know,
that lives in a neighborhood of poor men, down our
way, and he's right industrious, but he can't get rich
and he never ken, cause all these other poor men live
on him.''

''What do you mean? Do they all drop in about
dinner time?''

'' No, not all on 'em, but some on 'em every day.
And they keep borrowin' things of him. He haint
spunk enough to insult 'em. If he'd just move into a
rich neighborhood and jest be a little sassy and not
keer so much what folks said of him, he'd get rich;
never knew a man that was industrious and sassy in
this country that did n't get rich, quick, and get niggers
to do his work for him. Anybody ken that's smart.
Thar's whar they tried to raise some corn. Warn't
no corn grow thar; that's sartin. Wonder what they
live on? See the stalks. They never made no corn.
Plowed right down the hill ! Did you ever see anything like it? As if this sile warn't poor enough
already. There now. Just the same. Only look at
'em ! 'Pears like they never see a stage afore. This
aint the right road, the way they look at us. No,
sartin, they never see a stage. Lord God ! see the
babies. They never see a stage afore. No, the stage
never went by here afore, I know. This damned
driver's just taken us round this way to show off what
he can do, and pass away the time before breakfast.
Could n't get no breakfast here if he would stop—'less

we ate a baby. That's right! step out where you ken
see her good; perhaps you 'll never see a stage again;
better look now, right sharp. Yes, oh yes, sartin;
fetch out all the babies. Haint you got no more?
Well, I should hope not. Now, what is the use of so
many babies? That's the worst on 't. I 'd get married to-morrow if I was n't sure I 'd hev babies. I
hate babies, can't bear 'em round me and won't hev
'em. I would like to be married. I know several
gals I 'd marry if 't war n't for that. Well, it 's a fact.
Just so. I hate the squallin' things I know I was
born a baby, but I could n't help it, could I? I wish
I had 'nt been. I hate the squallin' things. If I had
to hev a baby round me I should kill it.

"If you had a baby of your own, you 'd feel differently about it.

"That 's what they tell me. I s'pose I should,
but I don 't want to feel differently. I hate 'em. I
hate 'em."

The coach stopped at length. We got out and found
ourselves on the bank of an overflowed brook. A
part of the bridge was broken up, the driver declared
it impossible to ford the stream, and said he should
return to the shanty, four miles back, at which we
had last changed horses. We persuaded him to
take one of his horses from the team, and let us
see if we could not get across. I succeeded in
doing this without difficulty, and turning the horse
loose he returned. The driver, however, was still
afraid to try to ford the stream with the coach and

mails, and after trying our best to persuade him, I told him if he returned he should do it without me, hoping he would be shamed out of his pusillanimity. Yazoo joined me, but the driver having again recovered the horse upon which he had forded the stream, turned about and drove back. We pushed on, and after walking a few miles, came to a neat, new house, with a cluster of old cabins about it. It was much the most comfortable establishment we had seen during the day. Truly a " sunny valley " home of northern Mississippi. We entered quietly, and were received by two women who were spinning in a room with three outside doors all open, though a fine fire was burning, merely to warm the room, in a large fire-place, within. Upon our asking if we could have breakfast prepared for us, one of the women went to the door and gave orders to a negro, and in a moment after, we saw six or seven black boys and girls chasing and clubbing a hen round the yard for our benefit. I regret to add that they did not succeed in making her tender. At twelve o'clock we breakfasted, and were then accommodated with a bed, upon which we slept together for several hours. When I awoke, I walked out to look at the premises.

The house was half a dozen rods from the highroad, with a square yard all about it, in one corner of which was a small enclosure for stock, and a log stable and corn-crib. There were also three negro cabins; one before the house, and two behind it. The house was a neat building of logs, boarded over and painted on the outside. On the inside, the logs were neatly hewn to a plane face, and exposed. One of the lower rooms contained a bed, and but little other furniture; the other was the common family apartment, but also was furnished with a bed. A door opened into another smaller log house in the rear, in which were two rooms—one of them the family dining-room; the other the kitchen. Behind this was still another log erection, fifteen feet square, which was the smoke-house, and in which a great store of bacon was kept   The negro cabins were small, dilapidated and dingy; the walls were not chinked, and there were no windows—which, indeed, would have been a superfluous luxury, for there were spaces of several inches between the logs, through which there was unobstructed vision   The furniture in the cabins was of the simplest and rudest imaginable kind, two or three beds with dirty clothing upon them, a chest, a wooden stool or two, made with an axe, and some earthenware and cooking apparatus. Everything within the cabins was colored black by smoke. The chimneys of both the house and the cabins were built of splinters and clay, and on the outer side of the walls. At the door of each cabin were literally "heaps" of babies and puppies, and behind or beside it a pig-stye and poultry-coop, a ley-tub and quantities of home-carded cotton placed upon boards to bleach. Within each of them was a woman or two, spinning with the old-fashioned great wheel, and in the kitchen another woman was weaving coarse cotton shirtings with the ancient rude hand-loom. The mistress herself was spinning in the living-room, and asked, when we had grown acquainted, what women at the North could find to do, and how they could ever pass the time, when they gave up spinning and weaving. She made the common every-day clothing for all her family and her servants. They only bought a few "store-goods" for their "dress-up" clothes. She kept the negro girls spinning all through the winter, and at all times when they were not needed in the field She supposed they would begin to plant corn now in a few days, and then the girls would go to work out-of-doors. I noticed that all the bed-clothing, the towels, curtains, etc., in the house, were of homespun.

The proprietor, who had been absent on a fishing excursion, during the day, returned at dusk. He was a man of the fat, slow-and-easy style, and proved to be good-natured, talkative, and communicative. He had bought the tract of land he now occupied, and moved upon it about ten years before. He had made a large clearing and could now sell it for a good deal more than he gave for it. He intended to sell whenever he could get a good offer, and move on West. It was the best land in this part of the country, and he had got it well fenced, and put up a nice house: there were a great many people that like to have these things done for them in advance—and he thought he should not have to wait long for a purchaser. He liked himself to be clearing land, and it was getting too close settled about here to suit him. He did not have much to do but to hunt and fish, and the game was getting so scarce it was too much trouble to go after it. He did not think there were so many cat in the creek as there used to be either, but there were more gar-fish. When he first bought this land he was not worth much—had to run in debt—had n't but three negroes. Now, he was pretty much out of debt and owned twenty negroes, seven of them prime field-hands, and he reckoned I had not seen a better lot anywhere.

During the evening, all the cabins were illuminated by great fires, and, looking into one of them, I saw a very picturesque family group; a man sat on the ground making a basket, a woman lounged on a chest in the chimney-corner smoking a pipe, and a boy and two girls sat in a bed which had been drawn up opposite to her, completing the fireside circle. They were talking and laughing cheerfully.

The next morning when I turned out I found Yazoo looking with the eye of a connoisseur at the seven prime field-hands, who at half-past seven were just starting off with hoes and axes for their day's work. As I approached him, he exclaimed with enthusiasm:

"Aren't them a right keen lookin' lot of niggers?"

And our host soon after coming out, he immediately walked up to him, saying:

"Why, friend, them yer niggers o' yourn would be good for seventy bales of cotton, if you'd move down into our country."

Their owner was perfectly aware of their value, and said everything good of them.

"There's something ruther singlar, too, about my niggers ; I don't know as I ever see anything like it anywhere else."

"How so, sir?"

"Well, I reckon it's my way o' treatin' 'em, much as anything. I never hev no difficulty with 'em. Hen't licked a nigger in five year, 'cept maybe sprouting some of the young ones sometimes. Fact, my niggers never want no lookin' arter ; they jus tek ker o' themselves. Fact, they do tek a greater interest in the crops than I do myself. There's another thing— I 'spose 't will surprise you—there ent one of my niggers but what can read ; read good, too—better 'n I can, at any rate."

"How did they learn ?"

"Taught themselves. I b'lieve there was one on 'em that I bought, that could read, and he taught all the rest. But niggers is mighty apt at larnin,' a heap more'n white folks is."

I said that this was contrary to the generally received opinion.

"Well, now, let me tell you," he continued ; "I had a boy to work, when I was buildin', and my boys jus teachin' him night times and such, he warn't here more 'n three months, and he larned to read as well as any man I ever heerd, and I know he did n't know his letters when he come here. It did n't seem to me any white man could have done that ; does it to you, now ?"

"How old was he?"

"Warn't more 'n seventeen, I reckon."

"How do they get books—do you get them for them?"

"Oh, no ; get 'em for themselves."

"How?"

"Buy 'em."

"How do they get the money?"

"Earn it."

"How?"

"By their own work. I tell you my niggers have got more money 'n I hev."

"What kind of books do they get?"

"Religious kind a books ginerally—these stories ; and some of them will buy novels, I believe. They won't let on to that, but I expect they do it."

They bought them of peddlers. I inquired about the law to prevent negroes reading, and asked if it allowed books to be sold to negroes. He had never heard of any such law—did n't believe there was any. The Yazoo man said there was such a law—in his country　Negroes never had anything to read there. I asked our host if his negroes were religious, as their choice of works would have indicated.

"Yes ; all on 'em, I reckon. Don't s'pose you 'll believe it, but I tell you it 's a fact ; I haint heerd a swear on this place for a twelvemonth. They keep the Lord's day, too, right tight, in gineral "

"Our niggers is mighty wicked down in Yallerbush county," said my companion ; "they dance."

"Dance on Sunday?" I asked.

"Oh, no, we don't allow that."

"What do they do, then—go to meeting?"

"Why, Sundays they sleep mostly; they 've been at work hard all the week, you know, and Sundays they stay in their cabins and sleep and talk to each other. There 's so many of 'em together they don't want to go visiting off the place."

"Are your negroes Baptists or Methodists?" I inquired of our host.

"All Baptists; niggers allers want to be ducked, you know. They aint content to be just titch'd with water; they must be ducked in all over. There was two niggers jined the Methodists up here last summer, and they made the minister put 'em into the branch; they would n't jine 'less he 'd duck 'em."

"The Bible says baptize, too," observed Yazoo.

"Well, they think they must be ducked all under, or 't aint no good."

"Do they go o meeting?"

"Yes, they hev a meeting among themselves."

"And a preacher?"

"Yes; a nigger preacher."

"Our niggers is mighty wicked; they dance!" repeated Yazoo.

"Do you consider dancing so very wicked, then?" I asked.

"Well, I don't account so myself, as I know on, but they do, you know—the pious people, all kinds, except the 'Piscopers; some o' them, they do dance themselves, I believe. Do you dance in your country?"

"Yes."

"What sort of dances—cotillions and reels?"

"Yes, what do you?"

"Well, we dance cotillions and reels, too, and we dance on a plank; that's the kind of dancin' I like best."

"How is it done?"

"Why, don't you know that? You stand face to face with your partner on a plank and keep a dancin'. Put the plank up on two barrel heads, so it'll kind o' spring. At some of our parties—that's among common kind o' people, you know—it's great fun. They dance as fast as they can, and the folks all stand round and holler, '*Keep it up, John!*' '*Go it, Nance!*' '*Don't give it up so!*' '*Old Virginny never tire!*' '*Heel and toe, ketch a-fire!*' and such kind of observations, and clap and stamp 'em."

"Do your negroes dance much?"

"Yes, they are mighty fond on 't. Saturday night they dance all night, and Sunday nights, too. Day-time they sleep and rest themselves, and Sunday nights we let 'em dance and sing if they want. It does 'em good, you know, to enjoy theirselves."

"They dance to the banjo, I suppose?"

"Banjos and violins; some of 'em has got violins."

"I like to hear negroes sing," said I.

"Niggers is allers good singers nat'rally," said our host. "I reckon they got better lungs than white folks, they hev such powerful voices."

We were sitting at this time on the rail fence at the

corner of a hog-pen and a large, half-cleared field. In that part of this field nearest the house, among the old stumps, twenty or thirty small fruit trees had been planted. I asked what sorts they were.

"I don't know—good kinds tho', I expect; I bought 'em for that, at any rate."

"Where did you buy them?"

"I bought 'em of a feller that came peddlin' round here last fall; he said I 'd find 'em good."

"What did you pay for them?"

"A bit apiece."

"That 's very cheap, if they 're good for anything; you are sure they 're grafted, arn't you?"

"Only by what he said—he said they were grafted kinds. I 've got a paper in the housen he gin me, tells about 'em; leastways he said it did. They 's the curosest kinds of trees printed into it you ever heerd on. But I did not buy none, only the fruit kinds."

Getting off the fence I began to pick about the roots of one of them with my pocket-knife. After exposing the trunk for five or six inches below the surface, I said, "You 've planted these too deep, if they 're all like this. You should have the ground dished about it or it won't grow." I tried another, and after picking some minutes without finding any signs of the "collar," I asked if they had all been planted so deeply.

"I don't know—I told the boys to put 'em in about two feet, and I expect they did, for they fancied to have apple-trees growin'."

The catalogue of the tree-peddler, which afterwards

came into my possession, quite justified the opinion my host expressed of the kinds of trees described in it. The reader shall judge for himself, and I assure him that the following is a literal transcript of it, omitting the sections headed "Ancebus new," "Camelias," "Rhododendrums," "Bubbs Pæony," "Rosiers," "Wind's flowers of the greatest scarcity," "Bulbous Roots, and of various kinds of graines."

SPECIAL CATALOGUE
OF THE PLANTS, FLOWERS, SHRUBS IMPORTED BY
ROUSSET
MEMBER OF SEVERAL SOCIETIES.
At PARIS (France), boulevard of Hopital, and at CHAMBERY, faubourg de Mache.

Mr Rousset beg to inform they are arrived in this town, with a large assortment of the most rare vegetable plants, either flowerd on fruit bearer, onion bulbous, seeds, &c., &c. Price very moderate.

Their store is situated

CHOIX D'ARBRES A FRUIT.

CHOICE OF FRUIT TREES

PEAR TREES.

1 Good Louisa from Avranche.
2 Winter's Perfume.
3 Saint-John-in-Iron.
4 Leon-the-Clerc
5 Bergamot from England.
6 Duchess of Angoulême.
7 Goulu-Morceau
8 Tarquin Pear.
9 Summer's Good (large) Christian.
10 Good Turkisk Christian
11 Grey (large) Beurré.
12 Royal Beurré from England.

1 Bon-Chrétien d'été
2 — d'hiver.
3 — de Pâque.
4 Doyenné blanc.
5 Duchesse d'Angora-New
6 Belle Angevine foodante.
7 Crassane d'hiver
8 Louise d'Orleans, sucré.
9 Double fleur hâtif.
10 Angélique de Tour.

1 Borgamotte de Milan, gros
2 — d'Aiençon, très-gros.
3 Beurré gris d'hiver.
4 — Amanlis
5 — d'Hardenpoint précoce.
6 Fortunè, fondant
7 Josephine, chair fine.
8 Martin-sec, sucré
9 Messire, gris
10 Muscat d'etè
11 Doyenné d'automne
12 — d'hiver, sucré.
13 Virgouleuse fondonte
14 Bezy-Lamotte
15 Gros-Blanquet

APPLES.

1 Renetto of Spain.
2 — Green
3 Apple Coin
4 — Friette
5 Calville, white, winter's fruit.
6 — red, autuma's fruit.
7 — red, winter's fruit
8 Violet or of the Four-Taste.
9 Renette from England, or Gold Apple.

10 Golden Renette, yellow, backwards plant.
11 White Renette, of a great perfume
12 Renette, red, winter's fruit.

1 Renette, yellow, hearly fruit
2 — grey, very delicate
3 — Princess noble.
4 Apple d'Api
5 — d'Eve
6 Winter's Postophe
7 Plein gney fenouillet
8 Renette franc
9 — of St Laurent.
10 Sammers Numbourg
11 Belle du Harve
12 Belle Hollandaise

1 Violet Apple or of the 4 taste; the fruit may by preserved 2 years
2 Princess Renette, of a gold yellow, spotted with red of a delicious taste
3 White Renette from Canada, of which the skin is lite scales strange by its size
4 The Cythère Apple.
5 The Caynoite Apple
6 Apple Trees with double flowers Blooms twice a year, Camélia's flowers like
106 others kinds of Apples of the newest choice.

APRICOTS.

1 The Ladie's Apricots.
2 The Peach Apricots.
3 The Royal Apricots
4 The Gros Musog Apricots.
5 The Pourret Apricots
6 Portugal Apricots
7 Apricats monstruous from America, of a gold yellow, of an enormous size, and of the pine's apple taste

PEACH TREES.

1 Peach Grosse Mignonne
2 — Bello Beauty.
3 — Godess
4 — Beauty of Paris.
5 — from Naples! said without stone.
6 Brugnon, musc taste.
7 Admirable; Belle of Vitry.
8 The Large Royal.
9 Monstruous Pavie.
10 The Cardinal, very forward.
11 Good Workman.
12 Lêtitia Bonaparte
13 The Prince's Peach, melting in the mouth
14 The Prince's Peach from Africa, with large white fruit weighing pound and half each, hearly, new kind
50 others new kinds of Peach Trees

PLUM TREES.

1 Plum Lamorte.
2 Surpasse Monsieur
3 Damas with musc taste
4 Royale of Tours.
5 Green Gage, of a violet colour.
6 Large Mirabelle
7 Green Gage, golded.
8 Imperial, of a violet colour.
9 Empress, of a white colour.
10 Ste-Catherine, zellow, sugar taste like

CHERRY TREES.

1 Cherry from the North
2 — Royal, gives from 18 to 20 cherries weihing one pound, 4 diferentes kinds.
3 Cherry Reina Hortense
4 — Montmorency
5 — with thort stalk (Gros-Gobet)
6 — Le Mercier
7 — Four for a pound.
8 Cherry Beauty of Choicy.
9 — The English.
10 Cherry-Duck
11 — Créole with bunches.
12 — Bigarrot or monster of new Mézel

CURRANT TREES.

1 Currant Three with red bunches (grapes)
2 Currant Three with white bunches.
3 Gooseberries of 1st choice. (Raspberries) six kinds of alégery.
4 New kind of currants, of which the grapes are as big as the wine grapes

GRAPES WINES.

1 Chasselas of Fontainebleau, with large gold grains.
2 Chasselas, black very good.
3 — red, of musc teste.
4 Verdal, the swetest and finest fruit for desert
5 White Muscadine grape, or of Frontignan.
6 Muscat of Alexandrie, musc taste
7 Cornichon, white, sweet sugar like, very good
8 Tokay, red and white.
9 Verju from Bordeaux large yellow fruit.
10 St Peter large and fine fruit.
11 Red Muscadine Graper
12 Raisin of Malaga.
13 The Celestial Wine Mree, or the amphibious grain, weighing 2 ounces, the grain of a red and violet colour.

NEW STRAWBERRY PLANTS.

1 The Strawberry Cremont.
2 — — the Queen.
3 — — monster, new kind
4 — — from Cllih.
5 Caperon of a raspberry taste.
6 Scarlat from Venose, very forward plant.
7 Prince Albert, fruit of very greatz beauty
8 Grinston colalant, very large.
9 Rose-Berrv, big fruit and of a long form.
10 Bath cherry, very good.
11 The Big Chinese Strawberry. weihing 16 to a pound, produce fruit all year round, of the pine apple's taste
12 Vilmoth full.

NEW FIG TREES OF A MONSTRUOUS SIZE

1 Diodena white, of a large size.
2 Duchess of Maroc, green fruit.
3 Doone-à-Dieu, blue fruit.
4 La Sanspareille, yellow fruit.

The Perpetual Raspberry Tree, imported from Indies producing a fruit large as an egg, taste delicious 3 kinds, red, violet and white.

The Raspberry Tree from Fastolff, red fruit, very good of an extraordinary size, very hearly forward plant.

Cherry Currant Tree, with large bunchés, it has a great production. Its numerous and long bunches cover entirely the old wood and looks like grapes; the fruit of a cherry pink colour is very large and of the best quality

Asparagus from Africa, new kinds, good to eat the same year of their planting (seeds of two years). 1000 varieties of annual and perpetual flower's grains also of kitchen garden grains

PAULNOVIA INPERIALIS. Magnificent hardy plant from 12 to 15 yards of higth ; its leave come to the size of 75 to 80 centimeter and its fine and larg flowers of a fine blue, gives when the spring comes, a soft and agréable perfume
Besides these plants the amateur will fine at M. ROUSSET, stores, a great number of other Plants and Fruit Trees of which would be to long to describe.

NOTICE

The admirable and strange plant called *Trompette du Jugement* (The Judgment Trompette), of that name having not yet found its classification.
This marvellous plant was send to us from China by the clever and courageous botanist collector, M. Fortune, from l'Himalaya, near summet of the Chamalari Macon
This splendid plant deserves the first rank among all kinds of plant wich the botanical science has produce till now in spite of all the new discoveries
This bulbous plant gives several stems on the same subject It grows to the height of 6 feet. It is furnished with flowers from bottom to top. The bud looks by his from like a big cannon ball of a heavenly blue The center is of an aurora yellowish colour. The vegetation of that plant is to fouitfull that when it is near to blossom it gives a great heat when tassing it in hand, and when the bud opens it produces a naite Similar to a pislole shot. Immediately the vegetation takes fire and burns like alcohol about an hour and half The flowers succeeding one to the other gives the satisfaction of having flowers during 7 or 8 months
The most intense cold can not hurt this plant and can be culvivated in pots, in appartments or gpeen houses.
We call the public attention to this plant as a great curiosity.

Havre—Printed by F. HUE, rue de Paris, 89.

" But come," said the farmer, "go in ; take a drink. Breakfast 'll be ready right smart."

"I don't want to drink before breakfast, thank you."

" Why not ? "

" I 'm not accustomed to it, and I don't think it 's wholesome."

Not wholesome to drink before breakfast! That was "a new kink" to our jolly host, and troubled him as much as a new "ism" would an old fogy. Not wholesome? He had always reckoned it warn't very wholesome not to drink before breakfast. He did not expect I had seen a great many healthier men than he was, had I? and he always took a drink before breakfast If a man just kept himself well strung up, without ever stretching himself right tight, he did n't reckon damps or heat would ever do him much harm. He had never had a sick day since he came to this place, and he reckoned that this was owin' considerable to the good rye whiskey he took. It was a healthy trac' of land, though, he believed, a mighty healthy trac'; everything seemed to thrive here. We must see a nigger-gal that he was raisin'; she was just coming five, and would pull up nigh upon a hundred weight.

" 'Two year ago," he continued, after taking his dram, as we sat by the fire in the north room, "when I had a carpenter here to finish off this house, I told one of my boys he must come in and help him. I reckoned he would larn quick, if he was a mind to. So he came in, and a week arterwards he fitted the plank and laid this floor, and now you just look at it; I don't believe any man could do it better. That was two year ago, and now he's as good a carpenter as you ever see. I bought him some tools after the carpenter left, and he can do anything with 'em—make a table or a chest of drawers or anything. I think niggers is somehow nat'rally ingenious; more so 'n white folks. They is wonderful apt to any kind of slight."

I took out my pocket-map, and while studying it, asked Yazoo some questions about the route East. Not having yet studied geography, as he observed, he could not answer. Our host inquired where I was going, that way. I said I should go on to Carolina.

"Expect you're going to buy a rice-farm, in the Carolinies, aint you? and I reckon you're up here speckylating arter nigger stock, aint you now?"

"Well," said I, "I wouldn't mind getting that fat girl of yours, if we can make a trade. How much a pound will you sell her at?"

"We don't sell niggers by the pound in this country."

"Well, how much by the lump?"

"Well, I don't know; reckon I don't keer about sellin' her just yet."

After breakfast, I inquired about the management of the farm. He said that he purchased negroes, as he was able, from time to time. He grew rich by the improved salable value of his land, arising in part from their labor, and from their natural increase and improvement, for he bought only such as would be likely to increase in value on his hands.   He had been obliged to spend but little money, being able to live and provide most of the food and clothing for his family and his people by the production of his farm.   He made a little cotton, which he had to send some distance to be ginned and baled, and then wagoned it seventy miles to a market; also raised some wheat, which he turned into flour at a neighboring mill, and sent to the same market.   This transfer engaged much of the winter labor of his man-slaves.

I said that I supposed the Memphis and Charleston railroad, as it progressed east, would shorten the distance to which it would be necessary to draw his cotton, and so be of much service to him   He did not know that.   He did not know as he should ever use it.   He expected they would charge pretty high for carrying cotton, and his niggers had n't anything else to do.   It did not really cost him anything now to send it to Memphis, because he had to board the niggers and the cattle anyhow, and they did not want much more on the road than they did at home.

He made a large crop of corn, which, however, was mainly consumed by his own force, and he killed annually about one hundred and fifty hogs, the bacon of which was all consumed in his own family and by his people, or sold to passing travellers.   In the fall, a great many drovers and slave-dealers passed over the road with their stock, and they frequently camped against his house, so as to buy corn and bacon of him. This they cooked themselves.

There were sometimes two hundred negroes brought along together, going South. He did n't always have bacon to spare for them, though he killed one hundred and fifty swine. They were generally bad characters, and had been sold for fault by their owners. Some of the slave-dealers were high-minded honorable men, he thought; " high-toned gentlemen, as ever he saw, some of 'em was."

Niggers were great eaters, and wanted more meat than white folks ; and he always gave his as much as they wanted, and more, too. The negro cook always got dinner for them, and took what she liked for it ; his wife did n't know much about it. She got as much as she liked, and he guessed she did n't spare it. When the field-hands were anywhere within a reasonable distance, they always came up to the house to get their dinner. If they were going to work a great way off, they would carry their dinner with them. They did as they liked about it. When they had n't taken their dinner, the cook called them at twelve o'clock with a conch. They ate in the kitchen, and he had the same dinner that they did, right out of the same frying-pan —it was all the same, only they ate in the kitchen, and he ate in the room we were in, with the door open between them.

I brought up the subject of the cost of labor, North and South He had no apprehension that there would ever be any want of laborers at the South, and could not understand that the ruling price indicated the state of the demand for them. He thought negroes would increase more rapidly than the need for their labor. "Niggers," said he, "breed faster than white folks, a 'mazin' sight, you know; they begin younger."

"How young do they begin?"

"Sometimes at fourteen; sometimes at sixteen, and sometimes at eighteen."

"Do you let them marry so young as that?" I inquired. He laughed, and said, "They don't very often wait to be married."

"When they marry, do they have a minister to marry them?"

"Yes, generally one of their own preachers."

"Do they with you?" I inquired of Yazoo.

"Yes, sometimes they hev a white minister, and sometimes a black one, and if there ar'n't neither handy, they get some of the pious ones to marry 'em. But then very often they only just come and ask our consent, and then go ahead, without any more ceremony. They just call themselves married. But most niggers likes a ceremony, you know, and they generally make out to hev one somehow, They don't very often get married for good, though, without trying each other, as they say, for two or three weeks, to see how they are going to like each other."

I afterwards asked how far it was to the post-office. It was six miles. "One of my boys," said our host, "always gets the paper every week. He goes to visit his wife, and passes by the post-office every Sunday. Our paper haint come, though, now, for three weeks. The mail don't come very regular." All of his

negroes, who had wives off the place, left an hour
before sunset on Saturday evening. One of them,
who had a wife twenty miles away, left at twelve
o'clock Saturday, and got back at twelve o'clock
Monday.

"We had a nigger once," said Yazoo, "that had
a wife fifteen miles away, and he used to do so; but he
did some rascality once, and he was afraid to go again.
He told us his wife was so far off, 't was too much
trouble to go there, and he believed he 'd give her up.
We was glad of it. He was a darned rascally nigger
—allers getting into scrapes. One time we sent him
to mill, and he went round into town and sold some of
the meal. The storekeeper would n't pay him for 't,
'cause he had n't got an order   The next time we
were in town, the storekeeper just showed us the bag
of meal;—said he reckoned 't was stole; so when we
got home we just tied him up to the tree and licked
him. He 's a right smart nigger; rascally niggers
allers is smart. I 'd rather have a rascally nigger than
any other—they 's so smart allers. He is about the
best nigger we 've got.

"I have heard," said I, "that religious niggers
were generally the most valuable. I have been told
that a third more would be given for a man if he were
religious."

"Well, I never heerd of it before," said he. Our
host thought there was no difference in the market
value of sinners and saints.

"Only," observed Yazoo, " the rascalier a nigger is,

the better he'll work.   Now that yer nigger I was
tellin' you on, he's worth more'n any other nigger
we've got.   He's a yaller nigger."

I asked their opinion as to the comparative value of
black and yellow negroes.   Our host had two bright
mulatto boys among his—did n't think there was
much difference, "but allers reckoned yellow fellows
was the best a little ; they worked smarter.   He would
rather have them."   Yazoo would not; he " did n't
think but what they'd work as well; but he did n't
fancy yellow negroes 'round him ; would rather have
real black ones."

I asked our host if he had no foreman or driver for
his negroes, or if he gave his directions to one of them
in particular for all the rest.   He did not.   They all
did just as they pleased, and arranged the work among
themselves.   They never needed driving.

" If I ever notice one of 'em getting a little slack, I
just talk to him ; tell him we must get out of the grass,
and I want to hev him stir himself a little more, and
then, maybe, I slip a dollar into his hand, and when he
gits into the field he'll go ahead, and the rest seeing
him, won't let themselves be distanced by him.   My
niggers never want no lookin' arter.   They tek more interest in the crop than I do myself, every one of 'em."

Religious, instructed, and seeking further enlightenment ; industrious, energetic, and self-directing ; well
fed, respected, and trusted by their master, and this
master an illiterate, indolent, and careless man !   A
very different state of things, this, from what I saw on

the great cotton planter's estate, where a profit of one hundred thousand dollars was made in a single year, but where five hundred negroes were constantly kept under the whip, where religion was only a pow-wow or cloak for immorality, and where the negro was considered to be of an inferior race, especially designed by Providence to be kept in the position he there occupied! A very different thing; and strongly suggesting what a very different thing this negro servitude might be made in general, were the ruling disposition of the South more just, democratic, and sensible.

About half past eleven, a stage-coach, which had come earlier in the morning from the East, and had gone on as far as the brook, returned, having had our baggage transferred to it from the one we had left on the other side. In the transfer a portion of my baggage was omitted and never recovered. Up to this time our host had not paid the smallest attention to any work his men were doing, or even looked to see if they had fed the cattle, but had lounged about, sitting upon a fence, chewing tobacco, and talking with us, evidently very glad to have somebody to converse with. He went in once again, after a drink; showed us the bacon he had in his smoke-house, and told a good many stories of his experience in life, about a white man's "dying hard" in the neighborhood, and of a tree falling on a team with which one of his negroes was plowing cotton, "which was lucky"—that is, that it did not kill the negro—and a good deal about "hunting" when he was younger and lighter.

Still embarrassed by an old idea which I had brought
to the South with me, I waited, after the coach came
in sight, for Yazoo to put the question, which he
presently did, boldly enough.

"Well ;   reckon we're goin' now.   What's the
damage ? "

"Well ; reckon seventy-five cents 'll be right."

CHAPTER IV

THE INTERIOR COTTON DISTRICTS

I HAVE considered the condition and prospects of the white race in the South a much more important subject, and one, at this time, much more in want of exposition than that of the African. But the great difference in the mode of life of the slaves when living on large plantations, and when living on farms or in town establishments, or on such small plantations that they are intimately associated with white families, has seemed to me to have been so much overlooked by writers, that I have departed widely from the narrative with which this volume commenced, and drawn from my travelling notes of a previous year, to more fully display it.

Continuing the horseback journey commenced in the rich cotton-bearing soils which border the Mississippi River, I turned eastward, not far above Natchez, and pursued an indirect route towards Tuscaloosa in Alabama. The country grew less fertile, and the plantations smaller. The number of whites (not of negroes), living upon plantations of the class chiefly described thus far in this volume (and, in two instances, at length in my first volume), is, of course, small. The more common sort of plantations and the common middle-class planter, can hardly be seen by a tourist in any other way than that I now pursued, travelling in the interior, away from the rivers and the ordinary lines of communication, and independently of public conveyances; there is consequently less general knowledge of them, I apprehend, than of any other portion of the population of the South, yet of the class properly termed "the planters" they constitute probably nine tenths.

The prices of "improved" plantation land varies from five to ten dollars per acre, according to its fertility and the vicinity to a market; near large towns only does it command more.[1] As the richest soils are in the lowest situations—frequently on the borders of marshes and streams—the most productive plantations are seldom healthy, and their proprietors very generally live for a part of the summer, I am informed, in the neighboring towns, where they constitute congenial society for each other. Comparatively few of the towns, however, are thus favored; all that I saw in central Mississippi, with the exception of Jackson,[2] the capital,

[1] "The value of the best cotton plantations on the uplands of Natchez is about £4 an acre, which is little more than half that which soils of similar quality are worth in Canada West."— *North America: Its Agriculture, etc.*, page 271.

[2] The capital is a rather fine town externally. At the principal hotel, in some departments of which there is the usual "first-class" regal magnificence, napkins, silver-plated forks and candelabra, there was, at the time of my visit, and, as I learn from a recent traveller, there is still, no *cabinet d'aisance*. On inquiring for it, I was advised by the landlord himself to go to a cypress swamp, perhaps a quarter of a mile distant, and

were forlorn, poverty-stricken collections of shops, groggeries, and lawyers' offices, mingled with unsightly and usually dilapidated dwelling-houses. Moreover, I found that many a high-sounding name (figuring on the same maps in which towns of five thousand inhabitants in New England, New York, and Pennsylvania are omitted), indicated the locality of merely a grocery or two, a blacksmith shop, and two or three log cabins. I passed through two of these map towns without knowing that I had reached them, and afterwards ascertained that one of them consisted of a deserted blacksmith shop and a cabin in which the postmaster lived, and the other, of a single grocery.

The majority of the interior plantations which came under my observation belong to resident planters, and are from four hundred to one thousand acres in extent, the average being perhaps six hundred acres [1] The number of negroes on each varies from ten to forty, more frequently being between twenty and thirty. Where there are fewer than ten negroes, the owners are frequently seen holding a plow among them;

---

there was evidence enough that this was daily resorted to for the purpose, not only by the other guests of the hotel, but by a large portion of the inhabitants of the town. The reader need be under no fear of drawing a false inference from this fact, with regard to the degree in which the South generally is possessed of all modern civilized convenience.

[1] When the largest share of the labor is not intended to be applied to the cotton crop, but is divided among various crops, as is usually the case where less than four hundred acres are held in possession by the proprietor, I term the enterprise a farm in distinction from a plantation.

where there are over twenty, a white overseer is usually employed, the owner perhaps directing, but seldom personally superintending, the field labor.

The characteristics of this latter class of cotton-planters vary much. I shall, I think, be generally rightly understood if I say that the majority of them possess more dignity of bearing and manner, that they give a stranger an impression of greater "respectability" than the middle class of farmers at the North and in England, while they have less general information and less active and inquiring minds. The class of farmers in New England and New York, with whom I compare them, have rarely received any education beyond that of the public schools, which, in the last generation, afforded a very meagre modicum of instruction. The planters of whom I speak, I judge to have usually spent a short time at boarding-schools or institutions of a somewhat superior order to the common, or "primary" schools of the country—but their acquisition of knowledge subsequently to their school-days by newspapers and books, and by conversation, has been very small.

It is frequently the case, however, that the planter has started as a poor, and entirely self-dependent young man, the basis of whose present fortune consisted of his savings from the wages earned by him as overseer—these are commonly as illiterate as the very poorest of our Northern agricultural laborers. Yet again there are those who, beginning in the same way, have acquired, while so employed, not only a capital with which to purchase land and slaves, but a valuable stock of experience and practical information, and somewhat of gentlemanly bearing from intercourse with their employers. In respect to the enjoyment of material comforts, and the exercise of taste in the arrangment of their houses and grounds, the condition of these planters, while it is superior to that of the Texans, is far below that of Northern farmers of one quarter their wealth. But an acquaintance with their style of living can only be obtained from details, and these I shall again give by extracts from my journal, showing how I chanced to be entertained night after night, premising that I took no little pains to select the most comfortable quarters in the neighborhood, which I reached at the close of the day. To avoid repetition, I will merely say with regard to diet, that bacon, corn-bread, and coffee invariably appeared at every meal ; but, besides this, either at breakfast or supper, a fried fowl, "biscuit" of wheat flour, with butter were added—the biscuit invariably made heavy, doughy, and indigestible with shortening (fat), and brought to table in relays, to be eaten as hot as possible with melting butter. Molasses usually, honey frequently, and, as a rare exception, potatoes and green peas were added to the board. Whiskey was seldom offered me, and only once any other beverage except the abominable preparation which passes for coffee.

Until I reached the softly rounded hills, with occasional small prairies, through which flows the Tombigbee, in the eastern part of the State, the scenery

was monotonous and sombre The predominating
foliage is that of the black-oak, black-jack, and pine,
except in the interval lands, where the profuse and
bright-colored vegetation common to the latitude is
generally met with in great variety.

Last of May.   Yesterday was a raw, cold day, wind
northeast, like a dry northeast storm at home.   Fortunately I came to the pleasantest house and household
I had seen for some time.   The proprietor was a native
of Maryland, and had travelled in the North ; a devout
Methodist, and somewhat educated.   He first came
South, as I understood, for the benefit of his health, his
lungs being weak.   The climate here is very mild ; lung
complaints, though not infrequent, not nearly as common as in Maryland.   Of a number of Northern people
whom he had known to come here with consumption,
only one or two had recovered.   There are several
in the country now, he said, young women teaching
school.   This immediate locality, he considered very
healthy ; he had a family (including about fifteen negroes) of twenty, and had never been visited by any
sickness more serious than chills and fever ; but on
lower and richer ground, they suffered much from typhus fever, pneumonia, and malignant typhus.

His first dwelling, a rude log cabin, was still standing,
and was occupied by some of his slaves.   The new
house, a cottage, consisting of four rooms and a hall,
stood in a small grove of oaks ; the family were quiet,
kind, and sensible.

When I arrived, the oldest boy was at work, holding a plow in the cotton-field, but he left it and came at once, with confident and affable courtesy, to entertain me

My host had been in Texas, and after exploring it quite thoroughly, concluded that he much preferred to remain where he was. He found no part of that country where good land, timber, and a healthy climate were combined : in the west he did not like the vicinage of the Germans and Mexicans ; moreover, he did n't "fancy" a prairie country. Here, in favorable years, he got a bale of cotton to the acre. Not so much now as formerly. Still, he said, the soil would be good enough for him here, for many years to come.

I said that he was a Methodist ; he was also an extreme pro-slavery man. He had seen in his religious newspaper an account of Mr. Fillmore's being shown a large Alabama plantation on a Sunday ; Mr. Fillmore had expressed himself highly delighted and surprised with the manner in which the slaves were taken care of, being obliged to attend church, etc. He hoped it would do Mr. Fillmore good. He had been opposed to him in politics, and he doubted now if he could be trusted. They would try to make him President again, he supposed, for they were working hard to make the South think him her friend. There was no knowing about anything of that kind now. There was New York, my State, who could tell anything about her now-a-days ? It seemed to him she was controlled by fanatics, demagogues, and foreigners, who were purchased by the highest bidder ; she was no more to be depended upon than a weathercock.   One year she pointed one way, the next, directly opposite.   The South could no more depend on the Democrats than on the Whigs in New York, that was his opinion.

I went five times to the stable without being able to find the servant there.   I was always told that "the boy" would feed my horse, and take good care of him, when he came ; and so at length, I had to go to bed, trusting to this assurance.   I went out just before breakfast and found the horse with only ten *dry* cobs in the manger.   I searched for the boy ; could not find him, but was told that my horse had been fed.   I said, "I wish to have him fed more—as much as he will eat." Very well, the boy should give him more.   When I went out after breakfast, the boy was leading out the horse.   I asked him if he had given him corn this morning.

"Oh yes, sir."

"How many ears did you give him ? "

"Ten or fifteen—or sixteen, sir ; he eats very hearty."

I went into the stable and saw that he had had no more, *i. e.*, after the feed of the evening ; there were the same ten cobs (dry) in the manger.   I doubted, indeed, from their appearance, if the boy had fed him at all the night before.   I fed him with leaves myself, but could not get into the corn crib.   The proprietor was, I do not doubt, perfectly honest, but very likely the negro stole the corn for his own hogs and fowls.

The next day I rode more than thirty miles, having

secured a good feed of corn for the horse at mid-day.
At nightfall I was much fatigued, but had as yet failed
to get lodging. It began to rain and grow dark, and
I kept the road with difficulty. Finally, about nine
o'clock, I came to a large, comfortable house.

An old lady sat in the veranda, of whom I asked if
I could be accommodated for the night: "Reckon so,"
she replied ; then after a few moments' reflection, without rising from her chair she shouted, "Gal !—gal!"
Presently a girl came.

"Missis?"

"Call Tom !"

The girl went off, while I remained, waiting for a
more definite answer. At length she returned: "Tom
aint there, missis."

"Who is there?"

"Old Pete."

"Well, tell him to come and take this gentleman's
horse."

Pete came, and I went with him to the gate where
I had fastened my horse. Here he called for some
younger slave to come and take him down to the pen,
while he took off the saddle.

All this time it was raining, but any rapidity of
movement was out of the question. Pete continued
shouting. "Why not lead the horse to the pen yourself?" I asked. "I must take care of de saddle and
tings, massa ; tote 'em to de house whar dey 'll be safe.
Dese niggers is so treacherous can't leave nothin' roun'
but dey 'll hook suthing off of it."

Next morning, at dawn of day, I saw honest Pete come into the room where I was in bed and go stealthily to his young master's clothes, probably mistaking them for mine. I moved, and he dropped them, and slunk out to the next room, where he went loudly to making a fire. I managed to see Belshazzar well fed night and morning.

There were three pretty young women in this house, of good manners and well dressed, except for the abundance of rings and jewelry which they displayed at breakfast. I've no doubt they had enjoyed the advantages of some "Institute," where they had been put clean through from "the elementary studies" to "Waxwork and *Watts on the Mind.*" One of them surprised me, therefore, not a little at the table. I had been offered, in succession, fried ham and eggs, sweet potatoes, apple-pie, corn-bread, boiled eggs, and molasses ; this last article I declined, and passed it to the young lady opposite, looking to see how it was to be used. She had, on a breakfast plate, fried ham and eggs and apple-pie, and poured molasses between them.

June — I stopped last evening at the house of a man who was called " Doctor " by his family, but who was, to judge from his language, very illiterate. His son, by whom I was first received, followed me to the stable. He had ordered a negro child to lead my horse, but as I saw the little fellow could n't hold him I went myself He had no fodder (corn-leaves), and proposed to give the horse some shucks (corn-husks) dipped in salt water, and, as it was now too late to go farther, I assented. Belshazzar licked them greedily, but would not eat them, and they seemed to destroy his appetite for corn, for late in the evening, having groped my way into the stable, I found seven small ears of corn, almost untasted, in the manger. I got the young man to come out and give him more.

The "Doctor" returned from "a hunt," as he said, with no game but a turtle, which he had taken from a "trot line"—a line, with hooks at intervals, stretched across the river.

The house was large, and in a good-sized parlor or common room stood a handsome centre table, on which were a few books and papers, mostly Baptist publications. I sat here alone in the evening, straining my eyes to read a wretchedly-printed newspaper, till I was offered a bed. I was very tired and sleepy, having been ill two nights before. A physician, whom I had been obliged to consult, informed me that severe illness was frequently occasioned here by an exposure of the abdomen to the cool night air, an accident to which the irritation of insects must often subject sleepers. The bed was apparently clean, and I embraced it with pleasure.

My host, holding a candle for me to undress by (there was no candlestick in the house), called to a boy on the outside to fasten the doors, which he did by setting articles of furniture against them. When I had got into bed he went himself into an inner room, the door of which he closed and fastened in the same manner. No sooner was the light withdrawn than I was attacked by bugs   I was determined, if possible, not to be kept awake by them, but they soon conquered me.   I never suffered such incessant and merciless persecution from them before.   In half an hour I was nearly frantic, and leaped out of bed.   But what to do?   There was no use in making a disturbance about it; doubtless every other bed and resting-place in the house was full of them.   I shook out my day clothes carefully and put them on, and then pushing away the barricade, opened the door and went into the parlor.   At first I thought that I would arrange the chairs in a row and sleep on them; but this I found impracticable, for the seats of the chairs were too narrow, and moreover of deerskin, which was sure to be full of fleas if not of bugs. Stiff and sore and weak, I groaningly lay down where the light of the moon came through a broken window, for bugs feed but little except in darkness, and with my saddle-bags for a pillow, again essayed to sleep. Fleas! instantly.   I rolled and scratched for hours There was nothing else to be done; I was too tired to sit up, even if that would have effectually removed the annoyance.   Finally I dozed—not long, I think, for I was suddenly awakened by a large insect dropping upon my eye.   I struck it off, and at the moment it stung me.   My eyelid swelled immediately and grew painful, but at length I slept in spite of it.   I was once more awakened by a large beetle which fell on me from the window; once more I got to sleep, till finally at four o'clock I awoke with that dryness of the eyes which indicates a determination of the system to sleep no more. It was daylight, and I was stiff and shivering, the inflammation and pain of the sting in my eyelid had in a great degree subsided. I put on my boots and hat, pushed back the bolt of the outside door-lock with my thumb, and went to the stable. The negroes were already at work in the field. Belshazzar had had nearly as bad a place to sleep in as I, the floor of the stall, being of earth, had been trodden into two hollows at each end, leaving a small rough hillock in the centre. Bad as it was, however, it was the best in the stable; only one in four of the stalls having a manger that was not broken down. A little black girl and boy were cleaning their master's horses—mine they were afraid of. They had put some fresh corn in his manger, however, and as he refused to eat I took a curry-comb and brush, and for the next two hours gave him the first thorough grooming he had enjoyed since I owned him. I could not detect the reason of his loss of appetite. I had been advised by an old Southern traveller to examine the corn when my horse refused to eat—if corn were high I might find that it had been greased. From the actions of the horse, then and subsequently, I suspect some trick of this kind was here practiced upon me. When I returned to the house and asked to wash, water was given me in a vessel which, though I doubted the right of my host to a medical diploma, certainly smelt strongly of the shop—it was such as is used by apothecaries in mixing drugs. The title of doctor is often popularly given in the South to drug-

gists and venders of popular medicines; very probably
he had been one, and had now retired to enjoy the
respectability of a planter.

June ——.—I saddled and rode on immediately after
breakfast; but as soon as the dew had dried off the
grass, and I could find an abandoned plantation, I
turned aside from the road and wandered through the
old fields till I came upon a thicket of broad-leafed
black-jacks, with glades of grass only a little broken
by bushes. I then unsaddled, and fastening Belshazzar with a lariat where he could either graze or lie in
the shade of a pine-tree, I laid my blanket on the
ground among the black-jacks, and in two minutes was
rapidly overtaking my lost night's rest.

Awakening suddenly, I find that Belshazzar, his
rope stretched to its utmost tension, has got close to
me, and stands strongly braced, with nostrils dilated,
eyes and ears bent on the swamp below us, where a
pack of hounds are rushing past in full frantic cry.
Gradually the music dies away in the distance ; we see
nothing of deer, or fox, or nigger, hounds, or hunts-
men. Belshazzar returns to feed, and Jude coils down
to sleep again upon her form. But I have slept enough;
so I wash myself from canteen and get dinner, write up
my journal, and am off again.

A PIOUS SLAVE

Soon I met a very ragged old negro, of whom I
asked the way, and at what house within twelve miles

I had better stop. He advised me to go to one more than twelve miles distant.

"I suppose," said I, "I can stop at any house along the road here, can't I? They 'll all take in travellers?"

"Yes, sir, if you 'll take rough fare, such as travellers has to, sometimes. They 're all dam'd rascals along dis road, for ten or twelve miles, and you 'll git nothin' but rough fare. But I say, massa, rough fare 's good enough for dis world; aint it, massa? Dis world aint nothin'; dis is hell, dis is, I calls it; hell to what 's a comin' arter, ha! ha! Ef you 's prepared? you says I don't look much 's if I was prepared, does I? nor talk like it, nuther. De Lord he cum to me in my cabin in de night time, in de year '45."

"What?"

"De Lord! massa, de bressed Lord! He cum to me in de night time, in de year '45, and he says to me, says he, 'I 'll spare you yet five year longer, old boy!' So when '50 cum round I thought my time had cum, sure, but as I did n't die, I reckon de Lord has 'cepted of me, and I 'specs I shall be saved, dough I don't look much like it, ha! ha! ho! ho! de Lord am my rock, and he shall not perwail over me. I will lie down in green pastures and take up my bed in hell, yet will not his mercy circumwent me Got some tobaccy, master?"

A little after sunset I came to an unusually promising plantation, the dwelling being within a large inclosure, in which there was a well-kept Southern sward shaded by fine trees. The house, of the usual form, was

painted white, and the large number of neat out-
buildings seemed to indicate opulence, and, I thought,
unusual good taste in its owner. A lad of sixteen received me, and said I could stay; I might fasten my
horse, and when the negroes came up he would have
him taken care of. When I had done so, and had
brought the saddle to the veranda, he offered me a
chair, and at once commenced a conversation in the
character of entertainer. Nothing in his tone or manner would have indicated that he was not the father of
the family and proprietor of the establishment. No
prince royal could have had more assured and non-
chalant dignity. Yet a Northern stable-boy or ap-
prentice, of his age, would seldom be found as
ignorant.

" Where do you live, sir, when you are at home?"
he asked.

" At New York."

" New York is a big place, I expect?"

" Yes, very big."

" Big as New Orleans, is it?"

" Yes, much bigger."

" Bigger 'n New Orleans? It must be a bully city."

" Yes; the largest in America."

" Sickly there now, sir?"

" No, not now; it is sometimes."

" Like New Orleans, I suppose, sir?"

" No, never so bad as New Orleans sometimes is."

" Right healthy place, I expect?"

" Yes, I believe so, for a place of its size."

" What diseases do you have there, sir ? "

" All sorts of diseases—not so much fever, however, as you have here."

"Measles and hooping cough, sometimes, I reckon ? "

" Yes, 'most all the time, I dare say."

" All the time !   People must die there right smart. Some is dyin' 'most every day, I expect ? "

" More than a hundred every day, I suppose."

" Gosh ! a hundred every day ! Almighty sickly place 't must be ? "

" I don't think it is any more sickly than it is here. It is such a large place, you see—seven hundred thousand people."

" Seven hundred thousand—expect that 's a heap of people, aint it ? "

His father, a portly, well-dressed man, soon came in, and learning that I had been in Mexico, said, " I suppose there 's a heap of Americans flocking in and settling up that country along on the line, aint there, sir ? "

" No, sir, very few. I saw none, in fact—only a few Irishmen and Frenchmen, who call themselves Americans. Those were the only foreigners I saw except negroes."

" Niggers ! Where were they from ? "

" They were runaways from Texas."

" But their masters go there and get them again, don't they ? "

" No, sir, they can't."

" Why not ? "

"The Mexicans are friendly to the niggers, and protect them."

"But why not go to the Government?"

"The Government considers them as free, and will not let them be taken back."

"But that's stealing, that is; just the same as stealing, sir. Why don't our Government make them deliver them up? What good is the Government to us if it don't preserve the rights of property, sir? Niggers are property, aint they? and if a man steals my property, aint the Government bound to get it for me? Niggers are property, the same as horses and cattle, and nobody's any more right to help a nigger that's run away than he has to steal a horse."

He spoke very angrily, and was excited. Perhaps he was indirectly addressing me, as a Northern man, on the general subject of fugitive slaves. I said that it was necessary to have special treaty stipulations about such matters. The Mexicans lost their *peons*—bounden servants; they ran away to our side, but the United States Government never took any measures to restore them, nor did the Mexicans ask it. "But," he answered, in a tone of indignation, "those are not niggers, are they? They are white people, just as white as the Mexicans themselves, and just as much right to be free."

My horse stood in the yard till quite dark, the negroes not coming in from the cotton-field. I proposed twice to take him to the stable, but was told not to—the niggers would come up soon and attend to him. Just as we were called to supper, the negroes began to make their appearance, getting over a fence with their hoes, and the master called to one to put the horse in the stable, and to "take good care of him." "I want him to have all the corn he'll eat," said I. "Yes, sir—feed him well; do you hear, there?"

The house was meagrely furnished within, not nearly as well as the most common New England farm-house. I saw no books and no decorations. The interior wood-work was unpainted

At supper there were three negro girls in attendance—two children of twelve or fourteen years of age, and an older one, but in a few moments they all disappeared. The mistress called aloud several times, and at length the oldest came, bringing in hot biscuit.

"Where's Suke and Bet?"

"In the kitchen, missus."

"Tell them both to come to me, right off."

A few minutes afterwards, one of the girls slunk in and stood behind me, at the farthest point from her mistress. Presently she was discovered.

"You, Bet, are you there? Come here! come here to me! close to me! (*Slap, slap, slap.*) Now, why don't you stay in here? (*Slap, slap, slap*, on the side of the head) I know! you want to be out in the kitchen with them Indians! (*Slap, slap, slap.*) Now see if you can stay here." (*Slap !*) The other girl didn't come in at all, and was forgotten

As soon as supper was over my hostess exclaimed, "Now, you Bet, stop crying there, and do you go

right straight home ; mind you run every step of the
way, and if you stop one minute in the kitchen you 'd
better look out   Begone ! '' During the time I was in
the house she was incessantly scolding the servants, in
a manner very disagreeable for me to hear, though
they seemed to regard it very little.

The Indians, I learned, lived some miles away, and
were hired to hoe cotton. I inquired their wages.
"Well, it costs me about four bits (fifty cents) a day,"
(including food, probably). They worked well for a
few days at a time ; were better at picking than at
hoeing. "They don't pick so much in a day as niggers, but do it better" The woman said they were
good for nothing, and her husband had no business to
plant so much cotton that he could n't 'tend it with his
own slave hands.

While at table a young man, very dirty and sweaty,
with a ragged shirt and no coat on, came in to supper.
He was surly and rude in his actions, and did not
speak a word ; he left the table before I had finished,
and lighting a pipe, laid himself at full length on the
floor of the room to smoke. This was the overseer.

Immediately after supper the master told me he was
in the habit of going to bed early, and he would now
show me to my room. He did so, and left me alone
without a candle. It was dark, and I did not know
the way to the stables, so I soon went to bed. On a
feather bed I did not enjoy much rest, and when I
at last awoke and dressed, breakfast was just ready.
I said I would go first to look after my horse, and did

so, the master following me. I found him standing
in a miserable stall, in a sorry state ; he had not been
cleaned, and there were no cobs or other indications
of his having been fed at all since he had been there.
I said to my host ·

" He has not been fed, sir ! "

"I wonder ! haint he? Well, I 'll have him fed.
I s'pose the overseer forgot him."

But, instead of going to the crib and feeding him at
once himself, he returned to the house and blew a
horn for a negro ; when one came in sight from the
cotton-fields, he called to him to go to the overseer for
the key of the corn-crib and feed the gentleman's
horse, and asked me to now come to breakfast. The
overseer soon joined us as at supper ; nothing was said
to him about my horse, and he was perfectly silent,
and conducted himself like an angry or sulky man in
all his actions. As before, when he had finished
his meal, without waiting for others to leave the
table, he lighted a pipe and lay down to rest on the
floor. I went to the stable and found my horse had
been supplied with seven ears of corn only I came
back to ask for more, but could find neither master nor
overseer. While I was packing my saddle-bags pre-
paratory to leaving, I heard my host call a negro to
"clean that gentleman's horse and bring him here."
As it was late, I did not interpose. While I was
putting on the bridle, he took off the mosquito tent
attached to the saddle and examined it I told him
why I carried it.

"You won't want it any more," said he; "no mosquitoes of any account where you are going; you'd better give it to me, sir, I should like to use it when I go a-fishing; mosquitoes are powerful bad in the swamp." After some further solicitations, as I seldom used it, I gave it to him. Almost immediately afterwards he charged me a dollar for my entertainment, which I paid, notwithstanding the value of the tent was several times that amount. Hospitality to travellers is so entirely a matter of business with the common planters.

I passed the hoe-gang at work in the cotton-field, the overseer lounging among them carrying a whip; there were ten or twelve of them; none looked up at me. Within ten minutes I passed five who were plowing, with no overseer or driver in sight, and every one stopped their plows to gaze at me.

I reached a village before noon, and as I was confident the negro had neglected to feed my horse the evening previous, I stopped and bought some oats for him, which he ate with great avidity. Oats is a fodder crop here only; no grain is ever threshed out except for seed. A negro in the stable asked if I were "gwine on Tuscaloosy way?"

"Yes"

"Oh, I wish I could go wid you."

"Why, have you friends there?"

"I has dat, both black and white. Does you live in Tuscaloosy, massa?"

"No, I live at the North, in New York."

"At the North! Oh, dat's de country for to live in. Wish I could go dar wid you, right now. Dat's de country : a man can live dar, and a nigger too, and no devilishness dar 'cept what a man does to hisself."

He was born in Virginia, owned in Tuscaloosa, and was hired out to a man here. He did not like this place at all, but would rather live here than go any "further down." He seemed to have great dread of going "further down" (South).

"Why?"

"Niggers doesn't have no Sunday dar, massa. Niggers has to work and white folks has muster ; dey drums and fifes de whole bressed day ; dat yer'll sound strange on a Sunday to a Northern man, eh?"

I told him I didn't think it was so. He didn't know, but so the niggers here had told him. A report of steamboat negroes from New Orleans and the sugar districts, probably.

A MISSISSIPPI SLAVEHOLDING ABOLITIONIST

Yesterday I met a well-dressed man upon the road, and inquired of him if he could recommend me to a comfortable place to pass the night.

"Yes, I can," said he ; "you stop at John Watson's. He is a real good fellow, and his wife is a nice, tidy woman ; he's got a good house, and you'll be as well taken care of there as in any place I know."

"What I am most concerned about is a clean bed," said I.

"Well, you are safe for that, there."

So distinct a recommendation was unusal, and when I reached the house he had described to me, though it was not yet dark, I stopped to solicit entertainment.

In the gallery sat a fine, stalwart man, and a woman who in size and figure matched him well. Some ruddy, fat children were playing on the steps. The man wore a full beard, which is very uncommon in these parts. I rode to a horse-block near the gallery, and asked if I could be accommodated for the night. "Oh, yes, you can stay here if you can get along without anything to eat; we don't have anything to eat but once a week." "You look as if it agreed with you; I reckon I'll try it for one night." "Alight, sir, alight. Why, you came from Texas, did n't you? Your rig looks like it," he said, as I dismounted. "Yes, I've just crossed Texas, all the way from the Rio Grande." "Have you, though? Well, I'll be right glad to hear something of that country." He threw my saddle and bags across the rail of the gallery, and we walked together to the stable.

"I hear that there are a great many Germans in the western part of Texas," he said presently.

"There are a great many; west of the Guadalupe, more Germans than Americans born."

"Have they got many slaves?"

"No."

"Well, won't they break off and make a free State down there, by and by?"

"I should think it not impossible that they might."

"I wish to God they would; I would like right well

to go and settle there if it was free from slavery. You
see Kansas and all the Free States are too far north for
me ; I was raised in Alabama, and I don't want to
move into a colder climate , but I would like to go
into a country where they had not got this curse of
slavery."

He said this not knowing that I was a Northern
man . greatly surprised, I asked, " What are your objections to slavery, sir ! "

" Objections ! The first 's here" (striking his
breast) ; " I never could bring myself to like it. Well,
sir, I know slavery is wrong, and God 'll put an end to
it. It 's bound to come to an end, and when the end
does come, there 'll be woe in the land. And, instead
of preparing for it, and trying to make it as light as
possible, we are doing nothing but make it worse and
worse. That 's the way it appears to me, and I 'd
rather get out of these parts before it comes. Then
I 've another objection to it. I don't like to have
slaves about me. Now, I tell a nigger to go and feed
your horse ; I never know if he 's done it unless I go
and see ; and if he did n't know I would go and see,
and would whip him if I found he had n't fed him,
would he feed him ? He 'd let him starve. I 've got
as good niggers as anybody, but I never can depend on
them ; they will lie, and they will steal, and take advantage of me in every way they dare. Of course
they will if they are slaves. But lying and stealing
are not the worst of it. I 've got a family of children,
and I don't like to have such degraded beings round

my house while they are growing up. I know what the consequences are to children, of growing up among slaves.''

I here told him that I was a Northern man, and asked if he could safely utter such sentiments among the people of this district, who bore the reputation of being among the most extreme and fanatical devotees of slavery. '' I 've been told a hundred times I should be killed if I were not more prudent in expressing my opinions, but, when it comes to killing, I 'm as good as the next man, and they know it. I never came the worst out of a fight yet since I was a boy. I never am afraid to speak what I think to anybody. I don't think I ever shall be.''

'' Are there many persons here who have as bad an opinion of slavery as you have ?''

'' I reckon you never saw a conscientious man who had been brought up among slaves who did not think of it pretty much as I do—did you?''

'' Yes, I think I have, a good many.''

'' Ah, self-interest warps men's minds wonderfully, but I don't believe there are many who don't think so, sometimes — it 's impossible, I know, that they don't.''

Were there any others in this neighborhood, I asked, who avowedly hated slavery ? He replied that there were a good many mechanics, all the mechanics he knew, who felt slavery to be a great curse to them, and who wanted to see it brought to an end in some way. The competition in which they were constantly made to feel themselves engaged with slave-labor was degrading to them, and they felt it to be so. He knew a poor, hard-working man who was lately offered the services of three negroes for six years each if he would let them learn his trade, but he refused the proposal with indignation, saying he would starve before he helped a slave to become a mechanic.[1] There was a good deal of talk now among them about getting laws passed to prevent the owners of slaves from having them taught trades, and to prohibit slave-mechanics from being hired out. He could go out to-morrow, he supposed, and in the course of a day get two hundred signatures to a paper alleging that slavery was a curse to the people of Mississippi, and praying the Legislature to take measures to relieve them of it as soon as

[1] At Wilmington, North Carolina, on the night of the 27th of July, (1857,) the frame-work of a new building was destroyed by a number of persons and a placard attached to the disjointed lumber, stating that a similar course would be pursued in all cases, against edifices that should be erected by negro contractors or carpenters, by one of which class of men the house had been constructed. There was a public meeting called a few days afterwards, to take this outrage into consideration, which was numerously attended. Resolutions were adopted, denouncing the act, and the authorities were instructed to offer a suitable reward for the detection and conviction of the rioters. "The impression was conveyed at the meeting," says the *Wilmington Herald*, "that the act had been committed by members of an organized association, said to exist here, and to number some two hundred and fifty persons, and possibly more, who, as was alleged, to right what they considered a grievance in the matter of negro competition with white labor, had adopted the illegal course of which the act in question was an illustration." Proceedings of a similar significance have occurred at various points, especially in Virginia.

practicable. (The county contains three times as many slaves as whites.)

He considered a coercive government of the negroes by the whites, forcing them to labor systematically, and restraining them from a reckless destruction of life and property, at present to be necessary. Of course, he did not think it wrong to hold slaves, and the profits of their labor were not more than enough to pay a man for looking after them—not if he did his duty to them. What was wrong, was making slavery so much worse than was necessary. Negroes would improve very rapidly, if they were allowed, in any considerable measure, the ordinary incitements to improvement. He knew hosts of negroes who showed extraordinary talents, considering their opportunities : there were a great many in this part of the country who could read and write, and calculate mentally as well as the general run of white men who had been to schools. There were Colonel ——'s negroes, some fifty of them ; he did not suppose there were any fifty more contented people in the world ; they were not driven hard, and work was stopped three times a day for meals ; they had plenty to eat, and good clothes ; and through the whole year they had from Friday night to Monday morning to do what they liked with themselves. Saturdays, the men generally worked in their patches (private gardens,) and the women washed and mended clothes. Sundays, they nearly all went to a Sabbath School which the mistress taught, and to meeting, but they were not obliged to go ; they could come and go as they pleased all

Saturday and Sunday; they were not looked after at all. Only on Monday morning, if there should any one be missing, or any one should come to the field with ragged or dirty clothes, he would be whipped. He had often noticed how much more intelligent and sprightly these negroes all were than the common run; a great many of them had books and could read and write; and on Sundays they were smartly dressed, some of them better than he or his wife ever thought of dressing. These things were purchased with the money they made out of their patches, working Saturdays.

There were two other large plantations near him, in which the negroes were turned out to work at half-past three every week-day morning—I might hear the bell ring for them—and frequently they were not stopped till nine at night, Saturday nights the same as any other. One of them belonged to a very religious lady, and on Sunday mornings at half-past nine she had her bell rung for Sunday School, and after Sunday School they had a meeting, and after dinner another religious service. Every negro on the plantation was obliged to attend all these exercises, and if they were not dressed clean they were whipped. They were never allowed to go off the plantation, and if they were caught speaking to a negro from any other place they were whipped. They could all of them repeat the Catechism, he believed, but they were the dullest, and laziest, and most sorrowful-looking negroes he ever saw.

As a general rule, the condition of the slaves, as

regards their material comfort, had greatly improved within twenty years. He did not know that it had in other respects. It would not be a bit safer to turn them free, to shift for themselves, than it would have been twenty years ago. Of this he was quite confident. Perhaps they were a little more intelligent, knew more, but they were not as capable of self-guidance, not as much accustomed to work and contrive for themselves, as they used to be, when they were not fed and clothed nearly as well as now.

Beyond the excessive labor required of them on some plantations, he did not think slaves were often treated with unnecessary cruelty. It was necessary to use the lash occasionally. Slaves never really felt under any moral obligation to obey their masters. Faithful service was preached to them as a Christian duty, and they pretended to acknowledge it, but the fact was that they were obedient just so far as they saw that they must be to avoid punishment; and punishment was necessary, now and then, to maintain their faith in their master's power. He had seventeen slaves, and he did not suppose that there had been a hundred strokes of the whip on his place for a year past.

He asked if there were many Americans in Texas who were opposed to slavery, and if they were free to express themselves. I said that the wealthy Americans there, were all slaveholders themselves; that their influ- ence all went to encourage the use of slave-labor, and render labor by whites disreputable. " But are there not a good many Northern men there?" he asked.

The Northern men, I replied, were chiefly merchants or speculators, who had but one idea, which was to make money as fast as they could; and nearly all the little money there was in that country was in the hands of the largest slaveholders.

If that was the way of things there, he said, there could not be much chance of its becoming a Free State. I thought the chances were against it, but if the Germans continued to flock into the country, it would rapidly acquire all the characteristics of a free-labor community, including an abundance and variety of skilled labor, a home market for a variety of crops, denser settlements, and more numerous social, educational, and commercial conveniences. There would soon be a large body of small proprietors, not so wealthy that the stimulus to personal and active industry would have been lost, but yet able to indulge in a good many luxuries, to found churches, schools, and railroads, and to attract thither tradesmen, mechanics, professional men, and artists. Moreover, the laborers who are not landholders would be intimately blended with them in all their interests; the two classes not living dissociated from each other, as was the case generally at the South, but engaged in a constant fulfilment of reciprocal obligations. I told him that if such a character of society could once be firmly and extensively established before the country was partitioned out into these little independent negro kingdoms, which had existed from the beginning in every other part of the South, I did not think any laws would be necessary to prevent slavery. It might be a Slave State, but it would be a free people.

On coming from my room in the morning, my host met me with a hearty grasp of the hand. "I have slept very little with thinking of what you told me about western Texas. I think I shall have to go there. If we could get rid of slavery in this region, I believe we would soon be the most prosperous people in the world. What a disadvantage it must be to have your ground all frozen up and to be obliged to fodder your cattle five months in the year, as you do at the North. I don't see how you live. I should like to buy a small farm near some town where I could send my children to school—a farm that I could take care of with one or two hired men. One thing I wanted to ask you, are the Germans learning English at all?" "Oh, yes ; they teach the children English in their schools." "And have they good schools ?" "Wherever they have settled at all closely, they have. At New Braunfels, they employ American as well as German teachers, and instructions can be had in the classics, natural history, and the higher mathematics." "Upon my word, I think I must go there," he replied. (Since then, as I hear, an educational institution of a high character, has been established, by German influence, in San Antonio, teachers in which are from Harvard.)

When I left, he mounted a horse and rode on with me some miles, saying he did not often find an intelligent man who liked to converse with him on the question of slavery. It seemed to him there was an epidemic

insanity on the subject.   It is unnecessary to state
his views at length.   They were precisely those
which used to be common among all respectable men at
the South.   I have recently received a letter from him,
in which, after alluding to the excitement which the
Kansas question has produced, he says he thinks a considerable change of sentiment has occurred, in consequence of reading and talking about Kansas difficulties,
among his neighbors.   He is fully determined to go to
western Texas, and reckons as many as ten families and
thirty single men would go with him, if there were a
prospect that free servants and laborers could be hired
there and negroes be kept away.

As we rode, an old negro met and greeted us warmly.
My companion hereupon observed that he had never
uttered his sentiments in the presence of a slave, but in
some way all the slaves in the country had, he thought,
been informed what they were, for they all looked to
him as their special friend.   When they got into trouble,
they would often come to him for advice or assistance.
This morning, before I was up, a negro came to him
from some miles distant, who had been working for a
white man on Sundays till he owed him three dollars,
which, now that the negro wanted it, he said he could
not pay.   He had given the negro the three dollars, for
he thought he could manage to get it from the white
man.

He confirmed the impression I had formed of the
purely dramatic and deceptive character of what passed
for religion with most of the slaves.   One of his slaves

was a preacher, and a favorite among them. He sometimes went to plantations twenty miles away—even further—on a Sunday, to preach a funeral sermon, making journeys of fifty miles a day, on foot. After the sermon a hat would be passed around, and he sometimes brought home as much as ten dollars. He was a notable pedestrian; and once when he had committed some abominable crime for which he knew he would have to be punished, and had run away, he (Mr. Watson) rode after him almost immediately, often got in sight of him, but did not overtake him until the second day, when starting early in the morning he overhauled him crossing a broad, smooth field. When the runaway parson saw that he could not escape, he jumped up into a tree and called out to him, with an aggravatingly cheerful voice, "I gin ye a good run dis time, did n't I, massa?" He was the most rascally negro, the worst liar, thief, and adulterer on his place. Indeed, when he was preaching, he always made a strong point of his own sinfulness, and would weep and bellow about it like a bull of Bashan, till he got a whole camp meeting into convulsions.

This phrase reminds me of a scene which I witnessed in New Orleans, and as I have not yet described any of the religious services of the negroes, except that observed at a funeral, I will here give an account of it, which was written the same day.

A SLAVE RELIGIOUS SERVICE IN NEW ORLEANS

Walking this morning through a rather mean neigh-

borhood I was attracted, by a loud chorus singing, to
the open door of a chapel or small church. I found
a large congregation of negroes assembled within, and
the singing being just then concluded, and a negro
preacher commencing a sermon, I entered an empty
pew near the entrance. I had no sooner taken a seat
than a negro usher came to me and, in the most polite
manner, whispered, " Won't you please to let me give
you a seat, higher up, master, 'long o' tudder white
folks ? "

I followed him to the uppermost seat, facing the
pulpit, where there were three other white persons.
One of them was a woman—old, very plain, and not
as well dressed as many of the negroes ; another looked
like a ship's officer, and was probably a member of the
police force in undress—what we call a spy when we
detect it in Europe ; both of these remained diligently
and gravely attentive during the service , the third was
a foreign-looking person, very flashily dressed, and
sporting a yellow-headed walking-stick, and much
cheap jewelry.

The remainder of the congregation consisted entirely
of colored persons, many of them, however, with light
hair and hardly any perceptible indications of having
African blood. On the step of the chancel were a
number of children, and among these one of the love-
liest young girls that I ever saw. She was a light
mulatto, and had an expression of unusual intelligence and vivacity. During the service she frequently
smiled, I thought derisively, at the emotions and

excitement betrayed by the older people about her. She was elegantly dressed, and was accompanied by a younger sister, who was also dressed expensively and in good taste, but who was a shade darker, though much removed from the blackness of the true negro, and of very good features and pleasant expression.

The preacher was nearly black, with close woolly-hair. His figure was slight, he seemed to be about thirty years of age, and the expression of his face indicated a refined and delicately sensitive nature. His eye was very fine, bright, deep and clear; his voice and manner generally quiet and impressive.

The text was, "I have fought the good fight, I have kept the faith; henceforth there is laid up for me a crown of glory;" and the sermon was an appropriate and generally correct explanation of the customs of the Olympic games, and a proper and often eloquent application of the figure to the Christian course of life Much of the language was highly metaphorical; the figures long, strange, and complicated, yet sometimes, however, beautiful. Words were frequently misplaced, and their meaning evidently misapprehended, while the grammar and pronunciation were sometimes such as to make the idea intended to be conveyed by the speaker incomprehensible to me. Vulgarisms and slang phrases occasionally occurred, but evidently without any consciousness of impropriety on the part of the speaker or his congregation.

As soon as I had taken my seat, my attention was attracted by an old negro near me, whom I supposed

14

for some time to be suffering under some nervous complaint : he trembled, his teeth chattered, and his face, at intervals, was convulsed. He soon began to respond aloud to the sentiments of the preacher, in such words as these : " Oh, yes ! " " That 's it, that 's it ! " " Yes, yes—glory—yes ! " and similar expressions could be heard from all parts of the house whenever the speaker's voice was unusually solemn, or his language and manner eloquent or excited.

Sometimes the outcries and responses were not confined to ejaculations of this kind, but shouts, and groans, terrific shrieks, and indescribable expressions of ecstasy—of pleasure or agony—and even stamping, jumping, and clapping of hands, were added. The tumult often resembled that of an excited political meeting ; and I was once surprised to find my own muscles all stretched, as if ready for a struggle— my face glowing, and my feet stamping—having been infected unconsciously, as men often are, with instinctive bodily sympathy with the excitement of the crowd. So wholly unintellectual was the basis of this excitement, however, that I could not, when my mind retroverted to itself, find any connection or meaning in the phrases of the speaker that remained in my memory; and I have no doubt it was his " action " rather than his sentiments, that had given rise to the excitement of the congregation.

I took notes as well as I could of a single passage of the sermon. The preacher having said that among the games of the arena, were "raaslin" (wrestling) and

boxing, and described how a combatant determined to
win the prize, would come boldly up to his adversary
and stand square before him, looking him straight in
the eyes, and while he guarded himself with one hand,
would give him "a lick" with the other, continued in
these words . "Then would he stop, and turn away his
face, and let the adversary hit back? No, my brethren,
no, no ! he 'd follow up his advantage, and give him
another lick ; and if he fell back, he 'd keep after him,
and not stop !—and not faint !—not be content with
merely driving him back !—but he 'd *persevere!* (yes,
glory!) and hit him again! (that 's it, hit him again!
hit him again! oh, glory! hi! hi' glory !) drive him
into the corner! and never, never stop till he had him
down ! (glory, glory, glory!) and he had got his foot
on his neck, and the crown of wild olive leaves was
placed upon his head by the lord of games. (Ha ! ha !
glory to the Lord! etc) It was the custom of the
Olympian games, my brethren, for the victor to be
crowned with a crown of wild olive leaves; but sometimes, after all, it would n't be awarded right, because
the lord of the games was a poor, frail, erroneous man,
and maybe he couldn't see right, or maybe he was n't
an honest man, and would have his favorite among
the combatants, and if his favorite was beaten, he
would not *allow* it, but would declare that he was the
victor, and the crown would descend on *his* head
(*glory !*) But there ain't no danger of that in our
fight with the world, for our Lord is throned in justice.
(Glory !—oh, yes! yes'—sweet Lord! sweet Lord!)

He seeth in secret, and he knoweth all things, and there's no chance for a mistake, and if we only will just persevere and conquer, and conquer and persevere (yes, sir! oh, Lord, yes!), and persevere—not for a year, or for two year, or ten year ; nor for seventy year, perhaps ; but if we persevere—(yes! yes!) if we persevere —(oh! Lord! help us!)—if we persevere unto the end —(oh! oh! glory! glory! glory!)—until he calls us home! (Frantic shouting.) Henceforth there is laid up for us a crown of immortal glory—(ha! ha! HA!) —not a crown of wild olive leaves that begin to droop as soon as they touch our brow, (oh! oh! oh!) but a crown of immortal glory! That fadeth not away! Never begins to droop! But is immortal in the heavens!" Tremendous uproar, many of the congregation on their feet, and uttering cries and shrieks impossible to be expressed in letters. The shabby gentleman by my side, who had been asleep, suddenly awakened, dropped his stick, and shouted with all his might, "Glory to the Lord!"

The body of the house was filled by the audience ; there were galleries, but few persons were in them, on one side, two or three boys, and on the other, on the seat nearest the pulpit, about a dozen women.

The preacher was drawing his sermon to a close, and offering some sensible and pertinent advice, soberly and calmly, and the congregation was attentive and comparatively quiet, when a small old woman, perfectly black, among those in the gallery, suddenly rose, and began dancing and clapping her hands ; at first, with a

slow and measured movement, and then with increasing rapidity, at the same time beginning to shout
"*ha! ha!*" The women about her arose also, and
tried to hold her, as there appeared great danger that
she would fall out of the gallery, and those below, left
their pews that she might not fall upon them.

The preacher continued his remarks—much the best
part of his sermon—but it was plain that they were
wasted ; every one was looking at the dancing woman
in the gallery, and many were shouting and laughing
aloud (in joyful sympathy, I suppose). His eye flashed
as he glanced anxiously from the woman to the people,
and then stopping in the middle of a sentence, a sad
smile came over his face; he closed the book, and
bowed his head upon his hands to the desk. A voice
in the congregation struck into a tune, and the whole
congregation rose and joined in a roaring song. The
woman was still shouting and dancing, her head thrown
back and rolling from one side to the other. Gradually her shout became indistinct, she threw her arms
wildly about instead of clapping her hands, fell back
into the arms of her companions, then threw herself
forward and embraced those before her, then tossed
herself from side to side, gasping, and finally sunk to
the floor, where she remained at the end of the song,
kicking, as if acting a death struggle.

Another man now rose in the pulpit, and gave out a
hymn, naming number and page, and holding a book
before him, though I thought he did not read from it,
and I did not see another book in the house. Having

recited seven verses, and repeated the number and page
of the hymn, he closed the book and commenced to ad-
dress the congregation. He was a tall, full-blooded
negro, very black, and with a disgusting expression of
sensuality, cunning, and vanity in his countenance, and
a pompous, patronizing manner—a striking contrast,
in all respects, to the prepossessing quiet and modest
young preacher who had preceded him. He was
dressed in the loosest form of the fashionable sack over-
coat, which he threw off presently, showing a white
vest, gaudy cravat, and a tight cut-away coat, linked
together at the breast with jet buttons. He commenced
by proposing to further elucidate the meaning of the
apostle's words ; they had an important bearing, he said
which his brother had not had time to bring out adequately before the congregation. At first he leaned
carelessly on the pulpit cushion, laughing cunningly,
and spoke in a low, deep, hoarse, indistinct, and confidential tone, but soon he struck a higher key, drawling
his sentences like a street salesman, occasionally breaking out into a yell with all the strength of extraordinarily powerful lungs, at the same time taking a striking
attitude and gesturing in an extraordinary manner.
This would create a frightful excitement in the people,
and be responded to with the loudest and most terrific
shouts. I can compare them to nothing else human I
ever heard. Sometimes he would turn from the audience and assume a personal opponent to be standing
by his side in the pulpit. Then, after battling for a
few minutes in an awful and majestic manner with this

man of Belial, whom he addressed constantly as "sir!" he would turn again to the admiring congregation, and in a familiar, gratulatory, and conversational tone explain the difficulty into which he had got him, and then again suddenly turn back upon him, and in a boxing attitude give another knock-down reply to his heretical propositions.

His language was in a great part unintelligible to me, but the congregation seemed to enjoy it highly, and encouraged and assisted him in his combat with "Sir" Knight of his imagination most tumultuously, and I soon found that this poor gentleman, over whom he rode his high horse so fiercely, was one of those "who take unto themselves the name of BAPTIST," and that the name of his own charger was "*Persever-ance-of-the-Saints*

The only intelligible argument that I could discover, was presented under the following circumstances. Having made his supposed adversary assert that "if a man would only just believe and let him bury him under de water, he would be saved,"—he caught up the big pulpit Bible, and using it as a catapult, pretended to hurl from it the reply,—"Except ye persevere and fight de good fight unto de end, ye shall be damned!" "That's it, that's it!" shouted the delighted audience. "Yes! you shall be damned! Ah! you've got it now, have ye! Pooh!—Wha's de use o' his tellin' us dat ar?" he continued, turning to the congregation with a laugh; "wha's de use on't, when we know dat a month arter he's buried 'em under the water—whar do

we find 'em? Ha! ah ha! Whah? In de grog shop!
(Ha! ha! ha! ha!) Yes we do, don't we? (Yes! yes!)
In de rum-hole! (Ha! ha! ha! Yes! yes! oh Lord)
and we know de spirit of rum and de Spirit of God
has n't got no 'finities. (Yah! ha! ha! yes! yes! dat's
it! oh, my Jesus! Oh! oh! glory! glory!) Sut' nly,
sah! You may launch out upon de ocean a drop of oil
way up to Virginny, and we'll launch annudder one
heah to Lusiana, and when dey meets—no matter how
far dey been gone—dey'll unite! Why, sah? Because
dey's got de 'finities, sah! But de spirit of rum haint
got nary sort o' 'finity with de Spirit—" etc.

Three of the congregation threw themselves into
hysterics during this harangue, though none were so
violent as that of the woman in the gallery. The man
I had noticed first from his strange convulsive motions,
was shaking as if in a violent ague, and frequently
snatched the sleeve of his coat in his teeth as if he
would rend it. The speaker at length returned to the
hymn, repeated the number and page and the first two
lines. These were sung, and he repeated the next, and
so on, as in the Scotch Presbyterian service. The congregation sang; I think every one joined, even the children,
and the collective sound was wonderful. The voices of
one or two women rose above the rest, and one of these
soon began to introduce variations, which consisted
mainly of shouts of oh! oh! at a piercing height.
Many of the singers kept time with their feet, balancing themselves on each alternately, and swinging their
bodies accordingly. The reading of the lines would

be accompanied also by shouts, as during the previous discourse.

When the preacher had concluded reading the last two lines, as the singing again proceeded, he raised his own voice above all, turned around, clapped his hands, and commenced to dance, and laughed aloud, first with his back, and then his face to the audience.

The singing ceased, but he continued his movements, leaping, with increasing agility, from one side of the pulpit to the other.   The people below laughed and shouted, and the two other preachers who were shut into the pulpit with the dancer, tried hard to keep out of his way, and threw forward their arms and shoulders, to fend off his powerful buffets as he surged about between them.   Swinging out his arms at random, with a blow of his fist he knocked the great Bible spinning off the desk, to the great danger of the children below ; then threw himself back, jamming the old man, who was trying to restrain him, against the wall.

At the next heave, he pitched headforemost into the young preacher, driving him through the door and falling with him half down the stairs, and after bouncing about a few moments, jerking his arms and legs violently, like a supple-jack, in every direction, and all the time driving his breath with all the noise possible between his set teeth, and trying to foam at the mouth and act an epileptic fit, there he lay as if dead, the young preacher, with the same sad smile, and something of shame on his face, sitting on the stair holding his head on his shoulder, and grasping one of his hands, while his feet were extended up into the pulpit.

The third man in the pulpit, a short, aged negro, with a smiling face, and a pleasing manner, took the Bible, which was handed up to him by one of the congregation, laid it upon the desk, and, leaning over it, told the people, in a gentle conversational tone, that the "love feast" would be held at four o'clock; gave some instructions about the tickets of admission, and severely reproved those who were in the habit of coming late, and insisting upon being let in after the doors were locked. He then announced that the doxology would be sung, which accordingly followed, another woman going into hysterics at the close. The prostrate man rose, and released the young preacher, who pronounced the Apostles' blessing, and the congregation slowly passed out, chatting and saluting one another politely as they went, and bearing not the slightest mark of the previous excitement.

The night after leaving Mr. Watson's I was kindly received by a tradesman, who took me, after closing his shop, to his mother's house, a log cabin, but more comfortable than many more pretentious residences at which I passed a night on this journey. For the first time in many months tea was offered me. It was the coarse Bohea, sweetened with honey, which was stirred into the tea as it boiled in a kettle over the fire, by the old lady herself, whose especial luxury it seemed to be. She asked me if folks ever drank tea at the North, and when I spoke of green tea, said she had never heard of that kind of tea before   They owned a number of slaves, but the young man looked after my horse himself.   There was a good assortment of books and newspapers at his house, and the people were quite intelligent and very amiable.

A NIGHT WITH A "POOR WHITE"

The next day I passed a number of small Indian farms, very badly cultivated—the corn nearly concealed by weeds.   The soil became poorer than before, and the cabins of poor people more frequent. I counted about ten plantations, or negro-cultivated farms, in twenty miles.   A planter, at whose house I called after sunset, said it was not convenient for him to accommodate me, and I was obliged to ride until it was quite dark.   The next house, at which I arrived, was one of the commonest sort of cabins.   I had passed twenty like it during the day, and I thought I would take the opportunity to get an interior knowledge of them.   The fact that a horse and wagon were kept, and that a considerable area of land in the rear of the cabin was planted with cotton, showed that the family were by no means of the lowest class, yet, as they were not even able to hire a slave, they may be considered to represent very favorably, I believe, the condition of the poor whites of the plantation districts.   The whites of the county, I observe, by the census, are three to one of the slaves ; in the nearest adjoining county, the proportion is reversed ; and within a few miles the soil was richer, and large plantations occurred.

It was raining and nearly nine o'clock.   The door of the cabin was open, and I rode up and conversed with the occupant as he stood within.   He said that he was not in the habit of taking in travellers, and his wife was about sick, but if I was a mind to put up with common fare he did n't care.   Grateful, I dismounted and took the seat he had vacated by the fire, while he led away my horse to an open shed in the rear—his own horse ranging at large, when not in use, during the summer.

The house was all comprised in a single room, twenty-eight by twenty-five feet in area, and open to the roof above.   There was a large fireplace at one end and a door on each side—no windows at all. Two bedsteads, a spinning-wheel, a packing-case, which served as a bureau, a cupboard, made of rough hewn slabs, two or three deerskin-seated chairs, a Connecticut clock, and a large poster of Jayne's patent medicines, constituted all the visible furniture either useful or ornamental in purpose.   A little girl immediately, without having had any directions to do so, got a frying-pan and a chunk of bacon from the cupboard, and cutting slices from the latter, set it frying for my supper.   The woman of the house sat sulkily in a chair tilted back and leaning against the logs, spitting occasionally at the fire, but took no notice of me, barely nodding when I saluted her.   A baby lay crying on the floor.   I quieted it, and amused it with my watch till the little girl, having made "coffee" and put a piece of corn-bread on the table with the bacon, took charge of it.

I hoped the woman was not very ill.

"Got the headache right bad," she answered. "Have the headache a heap, I do. Knew I should have it to-night. Been cuttin' brush in the cotton this afternoon. Knew 't would bring on my headache. Told him so when I begun "

As soon as I had finished my supper and fed Jude, the little girl put the fragments and the dishes in the cupboard, shoved the table into a corner, and dragged a quantity of quilts from one of the bedsteads, which she spread upon the floor, and presently crawled among them out of sight for the night. The woman picked up the child—which, though still a suckling, she said was twenty-two months old—and nursed it, retaking her old position. The man sat with me by the fire, his back towards her The baby having fallen asleep was laid away somewhere, and the woman dragged off another lot of quilts from the beds, spreading them upon the floor. Then taking a deep tin pan, she filled it with alternate layers of corn-cobs and hot embers from the fire. This she placed upon a large block which was evidently used habitually for the purpose, in the centre of the cabin. A furious smoke arose from it, and we soon began to cough. "Most *too* much smoke," observed the man Hope 't will drive out all the gnats, then," replied the woman (There is a very minute flying insect here, the bite of which is excessively sharp.)

The woman suddenly dropped off her outer garment and stepped from the midst of its folds in her petticoat ;

then, taking the baby from the place where she had deposited it, lay down and covered herself with the quilts upon the floor. The man told me that I could take the bed which remained upon one of the bedsteads, and kicking off his shoes only, rolled himself into a blanket by the side of his wife. I ventured to take off my cravat and stockings, as well as my boots, but almost immediately put my stockings on again, drawing their tops over my pantaloons. The advantage of this arangement was that, although my face, eyes, ears, neck, and hands were immediately attacked, the vermin did not reach my legs for two or three hours Just after the clock struck two, I distinctly heard the man and the woman, and the girl and the dog scratching, and the horse out in the shed stamping and gnawing himself. Soon afterward the man exclaimed, "Good God Almighty—mighty ! mighty ! mighty !'" and jumping up, pulled off one of his stockings, shook it, scratched his foot vehemently, put on the stocking, and lay down again with a groan. The two doors were open, and through the logs and the openings in the roof I saw the clouds divide, and the moon and stars reveal themselves. The woman, after being nearly smothered by the smoke from the pan, which she had originally placed close to her own pillow, rose and placed it on the sill of the windward door, where it burned feebly and smoked lustily, like an altar to the Lares, all night. Fortunately the cabin was so open that it gave us little annoyance, while it seemed to answer the purpose of keeping all flying insects at a distance.

When, on rising in the morning, I said that I would like to wash my face, water was given me for the purpose in an earthen pie-dish. Just as breakfast, which was of exactly the same materials as my supper, was ready, rain began to fall, presently in such a smart shower as to put the fire out and compel us to move the table under the least leaky part of the roof.

At breakfast occurred the following conversation :

" Are there many niggers in New York ? "

" Very few."

" How do you get your work done ? "

" There are many Irish and German people constantly coming there who are glad to get work to do.".

" Oh, and you have them for slaves ? "

" They want money and are willing to work for it. A great many American-born work for wages, too "

" What do you have to pay ? "

" Ten or twelve dollars a month."

" There was a heap of Irishmen to work on the railroad ; they was paid a dollar a day ; there was a good many Americans, too, but mostly they had little carts and mules, and hauled dirt and sich like. They was paid twenty-five or thirty dollars a month and found."

" What did they find them ? "

" Oh, blanket and shoes, I expect ; they put up kind o' tents like for 'em to sleep in all together. "

" What food did they find them ? "

" Oh, common food ; bacon and meal "

" What do they generally give the niggers on the plantations here ? "

" A peck of meal and three pound of bacon is what they call 'lowance, in general, I believe. It takes a heap of meat on a big plantation. I was on one of William R. King's plantations over in Alabamy, where there was about fifty niggers, one Sunday last summer, and I see 'em weighin' outen the meat. Tell you, it took a powerful heap on it. They had an old nigger to weigh it out And he warn't no ways partickler about the weight. He just took it and chopped it off, middlins, in chunks, and he 'd throw 'em into the scales, and if a piece weighed a pound or two over he wouldn't mind it ; he never took none back. Aint niggers all-fired sassy at the North ? ''

" No, not particularly.''

" Aint they all free, there ? I hearn so.''

" Yes.''

" Well, how do they get along when they 's free ? ''

" I never have seen a great many, to know their circumstances very well. Right about where I live they seem to me to live quite comfortably ; more so than the niggers on these big plantations do, I should think.''

" Oh ! They have a mighty hard time on the big plantations. I 'd ruther be dead than to be a nigger on one of these big plantations.''

" Why, I thought they were pretty well taken care of on them.''

The man and his wife both looked at me as if surprised, and smiled.

" Why, they are well fed, are they not ? ''

" Oh, but they work 'em so hard. My God, sir, in

pickin' time on these big plantations they start 'em to work 'fore light, and they don't give 'em time to eat "

" I supposed they generally gave them an hour or two at noon "

" No, sir ; they just carry a piece of bread and meat in their pockets and they eat it when they can, standin' up. They have a hard life on 't, that 's a fact. I reckon you can get along about as well withouten slaves as with 'em, can't you, in New York ? "

" In New York there is not nearly so large a proportion of very rich men as here. There are very few people who farm over three hundred acres, and the greater number—nineteen out of twenty, I suppose—work themselves with the hands they employ. Yes, I think it 's better than it is here, for all concerned, a great deal. Folks that can't afford to buy niggers get along a great deal better in the Free States, I think ; and I guess that those who could afford to have niggers get along better without them."

" I no doubt that 's so. I wish there warn't no niggers here. They are a great cuss to this country, I expect. But 't would n't do to free 'em ; that would n't do no how ! "

GET RID OF THE NIGGERS

" Are there many people here who think slavery a curse to the country ? "

" Oh, yes, a great many. I reckon the majority would be right glad if we could get rid of the niggers. But it would n't never do to free 'em and leave 'em

15

here. I don't know anybody, hardly, in favor of that. Make 'em free and leave 'em here and they'd steal every thing we made. Nobody couldn't live here then.''

These views of slavery seem to be universal among people of this class. They were repeated to me at least a dozen times.

NIGGER PANICS

'' Where I used to live [Alabama], I remember when I was a boy—must ha' been about twenty years ago—folks was dreadful frightened about the niggers. I remember they built pens in the woods where they could hide, and Christmas time they went and got into the pens, 'fraid the niggers was risin.' ''

'' I remember the same time where we was in South Carolina,'' said his wife ; '' we had all our things put up in bags, so we could tote 'em, if we heerd they was comin' our way.''

They did not suppose the niggers ever thought of rising now, but could give no better reason for not supposing so than that ''everybody said there warn't no danger on't now.''

Hereabouts the plantations were generally small, ten to twenty negroes on each ; sometimes thirty or forty. Where he used to live they were big ones—forty or fifty, sometimes a hundred on each. He had lived here ten years. I could not make out why he had not accumulated wealth, so small a family and such an inexpensive style of living as he had. He generally planted twenty to thirty acres, he said; this year he had sixteen in cotton and about ten, he thought, in corn. Decently cultivated, this planting should have produced him five hundred dollars' worth of cotton, besides supplying him with bread and bacon—his chief expense, apparently. I suggested that this was a very large planting for his little family; he would need some help in picking time. He ought to have some now, he said; grass and bushes were all overgrowing him; he had to work just like a nigger; this durnation rain would just make the weeds jump, and he did n't expect he should have any cotton at all There war n't much use in a man's trying to get along by himself; everything seemed to set in agin him. He'd been trying to hire somebody, but he could n't, and his wife was a sickly kind of a woman.

His wife reckoned he might hire some help if he'd look round sharp

My horse and dog were as well cared for as possible, and a "snack" of bacon and corn-bread was offered me for noon, which has been unusual in Mississippi. When I asked what I should pay, the man hesitated and said he reckoned what I had had was n't worth much of anything; he was sorry he could not have accommodated me better. I offered him a dollar, for which he thanked me warmly. It was the first instance of hesitation in charging for a lodging which I have met with from a stranger at the South.

CHAPTER V

THE PIEDMONT COTTON DISTRICT

NORTHERN ALABAMA

OMITTING a portion of my journey, in which the general characteristics of the country through which I passed differed not materially from those of the district described in the last chapter, I resume my narrative at the point where, in my progress northward, it was first evident that cotton was no longer the all-important object of agricultural interest, other crops receiving, at least, equal attention.

June —. I have to-day reached a more distinctly hilly country—somewhat rocky and rugged, but with inviting dells. The soil is sandy and less frequently fertile ; cotton-fields are seen only at long intervals, the crops on the small proportion of cultivated land being chiefly corn and oats. I notice also that white men are more commonly at work in the fields than negroes, and this as well in the cultivation of cotton as of corn.

The larger number of the dwellings are rude log huts, of only one room, and that unwholesomely crowded. I saw in and about one of them, not more than fifteen feet square, five grown persons and as

many children. Occasionally, however, the monotony
of these huts is agreeably varied by neat, white, frame
houses. At one such I dined to-day, and was comfortably entertained. The owner held a number of
slaves, but made no cotton. He owned a saw-mill,
was the postmaster of the neighborhood, and had been
in the Legislature.

I asked him why the capital had been changed from
Tuscaloosa to Montgomery. He did not know. "Because Montgomery is more central and easy of access,
probably," I suggested. "No, I don't think that had
anything to do with it." "Is Tuscaloosa an unhealthy place?" "No, sir; healthier than Montgomery, I reckon." "Was it then simply because the
people of the southern districts were stronger, and
used their power to make the capital more convenient
of access to themselves?" "Well, no, I don't think
that was it, exactly. The fact is, sir, the people here
are not like you Northern people; they don't reason
out everything so. They are fond of change, and
they got tired of Tuscaloosa; the Montgomery folks
wanted it there and offered to pay for moving it, so
they let 'em have it; 't was just for a change " "If
there really was no better reason, was it not rather
wasteful to give up all the public buildings at Tuscaloosa?" "Oh, the Montgomery people wanted it so
bad they promised to pay for building a new State
House; so it did not cost anything. "

Quite on a par with the economics of Southern
commercial conventions.

COTTON-GROWING FARMERS

I passed the night at the second frame house that I saw during the day, stopping early in order to avail myself of its promise of comfort. It was attractively situated on a hill-top, with a peach orchard near it. The proprietor owned a dozen slaves, and "made cotton," he said, "with other crops" He had some of his neighbors at tea and at breakfast; sociable, kindly people, satisfied with themselves and their circumstances, which I judged from their conversation had been recently improving. One coming in, remarked that he had discharged a white laborer whom he had employed for some time past, the others congratulated him on being "shet" of him; all seemed to have noticed him as a bad, lazy man; he had often been seen lounging in the field, rapping the negroes with his hoe if they did n't work to suit him. "He was about the meanest white man I ever see," said a woman; "he was a heap meaner 'n niggers. I reckon niggers would come somewhere between white folks and such as he." "The first thing I tell a man," said another, "when I hire him, is, 'If there's any whippin' to be done on this place I want to do it myself.' If I saw a man rappin' my niggers with a hoe-handle, as I see him, durned if I would n't rap him—the lazy whelp."

One of the negroes complimented my horse. "Dar's a heap of genius in dat yar hoss's head!" The proprietor looked after the feeding himself.

These people were extremely kind; inquiring with the simplest good feeling about my domestic relations, and the purpose of my journey. When I left, one of them walked a quarter of a mile to make sure that I went upon the right road. The charge for entertainment, though it was unusually good, was a quarter of a dollar less than I have paid before, which I mention, not as Mr. De Bow would suppose,[1] out of gratitude for the moderation, but as an indication of the habits of the people, showing, as it may, either closer calculation, or that the district grows its own supplies, and can furnish food cheaper than those in which attention is more exclusively given to cotton.

June —. The country continues hilly, and is well populated by farmers, living in log huts, while every mile or two, on the more level and fertile land, there is a larger farm, with ten or twenty negroes at work. A few whites are usually working near them, in the same field, generally plowing while the negroes hoe.

WARM WORK FOR WOMAN-KIND

About noon, my attention was attracted towards a person upon a ledge, a little above the road, who was throwing up earth and stone with a shovel. I stopped to see what the purpose of this work might be, and perceived that the shoveller was a woman, who, presently discovering me, stopped and called to others behind her, and immediately a stout girl and two younger children, with a man, came to the edge

[1] See De Bow's *Review*, for August, 1857, p. 117.

and looked at me. The woman was bare-headed, and otherwise half-naked, as perhaps needed to be, for her work would have been thought hard by our stoutest laborers, and it was the hottest weather of the summer, in the latitude of Charleston, and on a hill-side in the full face of the noon sun. I pushed my horse up the hill until I reached them, when another man appeared, and in answer to my inquiries, told me that they were getting out iron ore. One was picking in a vein, having excavated a short adit; the other man picked looser ore exterior to the vein. The woman and children shovelled out the ore and piled it on kilns of timber, where they roasted it to make it crumble. It was then carted to a forge, and they were paid for it by the load. They were all clothed very meanly and scantily. The woman worked, so far as I could see, as hard as the men. The children, too, even to the youngest —a boy of eight or ten—were carrying large lumps of ore and heaving them into the kiln, and shovelling the finer into a screen to separate the earth from it.

Immediately after leaving them I found a good spot for nooning. I roped my horse out to graze, and spread my blanket in a deep shade. I noticed that the noise of their work had ceased, and about fifteen minutes afterwards, Jude suddenly barking I saw one of the men peering at me through the trees, several rods distant. I called to him to come up. He approached rather slowly and timidly, examined the rope with which my horse was fastened, eyed me vigilantly, and at length asked if I was resting myself. I replied that I was; and he said that he did not know but I might be sick, and had come to see me. I thanked him, and offered him a seat on my blanket, which he declined. Presently he took up a newspaper that I had been reading, looked at it a moment, then told me he could n't read. "Folks don't care much for edication round here; it would be better for 'em, I expect, if they did." He then began to question me closely about my circumstances—where I came from, whither I was going, etc.

When his curiosity was partially appeased he suddenly laughed in a silly manner, and said that the people he had been working with had watched me after I left them; they saw me ride up the hill and stop, ride on again, and finally take off my saddle, turn my horse loose and tote my saddle away, and they were much frightened, thinking I must be crazy at least. When he started to come toward me they told him he would 'nt dare to go to me, but he saw how it was, well enough—I was just resting myself.

"If I should run down hill now," said he, "they 'd start right off and would n't stop for ten mile, reckoning you was arter me. That would be fun; oh, we have some good fun here sometimes with these green folks. There 's an amazin' ignorant set round here."

I asked if they were foreigners.

"Oh, no; they are common, no-account people;

they used to live over the hill, here; they come right nigh starvin' thar, I expect."

They had not been able to get any work to do, and had been "powerful poor," until he got them to come here They had taken an old cabin, worked with him, and were doing right well now. He did n't let them work in the vein—he kept that for himself—but they worked all around, and some days they made a dollar and a half—the man, woman, and children together. They had one other girl, but she had to stay at home to take care of the baby and keep cattle and hogs out of their "gardien." He had known the woman when she was a girl; "she was always a good one to work. She'd got a voice like a bull, and she was as smart as a wildcat; but the man war n't no account"

He had himself followed this business (mining) since he was a young man, and could earn three dollars a day by it if he tried; he had a large family and owned a small farm; never laid up anything, always kept himself a little in debt at the store.

He asked if I had not found the people "more friendly like" up in this country to what they were down below, and assured me that I would find them grow more friendly as I went further north, so at least he had heard, and he knew where he first came from (Tennessee) the people were more friendly than they were here. "The richer a man is," he continued, pursuing a natural association of ideas, "and the more niggers he's got, the poorer he seems to live. If you

want to fare well in this country you stop to poor folks'
housen, they try to enjoy what they 've got, while
they ken, but these yer big planters they don't care
for nothin' but to save. Now, I never calculate to save
anything ; I tell my wife I work hard and I mean to
enjoy what I earn as fast as it comes.''

Sometimes he "took up bee-huntin' for a spell," and
made money by collecting wild honey. He described
his manner of finding the hives and securing the honey,
and, with a hushed voice, told me a "secret," which
was, that if you carried three leaves, each of a different
tree (?) in your hand, there was never a bee would dare
to sting you.

I asked about his children. He had one grown-up
son, who was doing very well ; he was hired by the
gentleman who owned the forge, to cart ore. He had
nothing to do but to drive a team ; he did n't have to
load, and had a nigger to take care of the horses when
his day's teaming was done.

ARTICLES OF FEMININE LUXURY

His wages were seven dollars a month, and board
for himself and wife. They ate at the same table with
the gentleman, and had good living, beside having
something out of the store, "tobacco and so on—tobacco for both on 'em, and two people uses a good deal
of tobacco, you know ; so that 's pretty good wages—
seven dollars a month, beside their keep and tobacco.''
Irishmen, he informed me, had been employed occasionally at the forge. "They do well at first, only
they is apt to get into fights all the time ; but after

they 've been here a year or two, they get to feel so independent and keerless-like, you can't get along with
'em.'' He remained about half an hour, and not
till he returned did I hear again the noise of picking
and shovelling, and cutting timber.

At the forges, I was told, slave labor is mainly
employed—the slaves being owned by the proprietors
of the forges.

"PLEASE TO REMEMBER," ETC.

I spent that night at a large inn in a village. In the
morning as I sat waiting in my room, a boy opened
the door. Without looking up I asked, "Well?"

"I did n't say nuthin', sar," with a great grin.

"What are you waiting there for?" "Please, massa,
I b'leve you 's owin' me suthin', sar." "Owing you
something? What do you mean?" "For drying
yer clothes for yer, sar, last night" I had ordered
him immediately after tea to go up stairs and get my
clothes, which had been drenched in a shower, and
hang them by the kitchen fire, that they might be
dry if I should wish to leave early in the morning.
When I went to my bedroom at nine o'clock I found
the clothes where I had left them. I went down and
reported it to the landlord, who directly sent the boy
for them. In the morning, when I got them again I
found they were not dry except where they were
burned   I told him to be gone ; but with the door half
open, he stood putting in his head bowing and grinning.
"Please, sar, massa sent me out of an errand, and I was

afeard you would be gone before I got back; dat's the reason why I mention it, sar; dat's all, sar; I hope you'll skuse me, sar."

A SPORTING FARMER AND NIGGER-HUNTING

During the afternoon I rode on through a valley, narrow and apparently fertile, but the crops indifferent. The general social characteristics were the same that I met with yesterday.

At night I stopped at a large house having an unusual number of negro cabins and stables about it. The proprietor, a hearty old farmer, boasted much of his pack of hounds, saying they had pulled down five deer before he had shot at them. He was much interested to hear about Texas, the Indians and the game. He reckoned there was "a heap of big varmint out thar."

His crop of cotton did not average two bales to the hand, and corn not twenty bushels to the acre.

He amused me much with a humorous account of an oyster supper to which he had been invited in town, and his attempts to eat the "nasty things" without appearing disconcerted before the ladies.

An old negro took my horse when I arrived, and half an hour afterward came to me and asked if I wanted to see him fed. As we walked toward the stables, he told me that he always took care not to forget gentlemen's hosses, and to treat them well; "then," he said, bowing and with emphasis, "they looks out and don't forget to treat me well."

The same negro was called to serve me as a candlestick at bedtime. He held the candle till I got into bed. As he retired I closed my eyes, but directly afterward, perceiving the light return, I opened them. Uncle Abram was bending over me, holding the candle, grinning with his toothless gums, winking and shaking his head in a most mysterious manner

"Hush! massa," he whispered. "You hain't got something to drink, in dem saddle-bags has you, sar?"

My host wanted much to buy or borrow Jude of me; offering to return her to me in New York, with the best pup, and without expense to me, if I would let him get a litter from her.

I have been asked for my dog at every house in which I have stopped on the road, and, on an average, twice a day beside, since I left Natchez. Gentlemen inquire respectfully: "Would not you like to give away that dog, sir?" Negroes: "Don't you want to gib me dat dog, sar?" Boys: "Please, sir, gin me that dog, sir?" and children, black and white, demand it peremptorily · "Gin me dat dog."

The farmer told me something about "nigger dogs;" they did n't use foxhounds, but bloodhounds—not pure, he thought, but a cross of the Spanish bloodhound with the common hounds or curs. There were many men, he said, in the country below here, who made a business of nigger-hunting, and they had their horses trained, as well as the dogs, to go over any common fence or if they could n't leap it, to break it down. Dogs were trained, when pups, to follow a negro—not allowed to catch one, however, unless they were quite young, so that they could n't hurt him much, and they were always taught to hate a negro, never being permitted to see one except to be put in chase of him. He believed that only two of a pack were kept kennelled all the time—these were old, keen ones, who led the rest when they were out; they were always kept coupled together with a chain, except when trailing. He had seen a pack of thirteen who would follow a trail two days and a half old, if rain had not fallen in the mean time. When it rained immediately after a negro got off, they had to scour the country where they supposed he might be, till they scented him.

When hard pushed, a negro always took to a tree; sometimes, however, they would catch him in an open field. When this was the case the hunter called off the dogs as soon as he could, unless the negro fought—"that generally makes 'em mad (the hunters), and they 'll let 'em tear him a spell. The owners don't mind having them kind o' niggers tore a good deal; runaways aint much account no how, and it makes the rest more afraid to run away when they see how they are sarved." If they caught the runaway within two or three days, they got from $10 to $20; if it took a longer time, they were paid more than that; sometimes $200. They asked their own price; if an owner should think it exorbitant, he supposed, he said, in reply to an inquiry, they 'd turn the nigger loose, order him to make off, and tell his master to catch his own niggers.

HILL-FOLKS ON SUNDAY

June —, Sunday.—I rode on, during the cool of the morning, about eight miles, and stopped for the day at a house pleasantly situated by a small stream, among wooded hills. During the forenoon, several men and three women, with their children, gathered at the house. All of them, I concluded, were non-slave-holders, as was our host himself; though, as one told me, "with his five boys he makes a heap more crop than Mrs. ——, who's got forty niggers." "How is that?" Well, she's a woman and she can't make the niggers work; she won't have an overseer, and niggers won't work, you know, unless there's somebody to drive 'em."

Our host, when I arrived, had just been pulling weeds out of his potato patch, which he mentioned as an apology for not being a little clean, like the rest.

Beside the company I have mentioned, and the large family of the house, there was another traveller and myself to dinner, and three bountiful tables were spread, one after another.

The traveller was said to be a Methodist preacher, but gave no indication of it, except that he said grace before meat, and used the Hebrew word for Sunday. He was, however, a man of superior intelligence to the others, who were ignorant and stupid, though friendly and communicative. One asked me "what a good nigger man could be bought for in New York"; he didn't seem surprised or make any further inquiry

when I told him we had no slaves there.   Some asked
me much about crops, and when I told them that my
crops of wheat for six years had averaged twenty-eight
bushels, and that I had once reaped forty from a single
acre, they were amazed beyond expression, and anxious
to know how I "put it in."   I described the process
minutely, which astonished them still more ; and one
man said he had often thought they might get more
wheat if they put it in differently ; he had thought that
perhaps more wheat would grow if more seed were
sown, but he never tried it.   The general practice,
they told me, was to sow wheat on ground from which
they had taken maize, without removing the maize
stumps, or plowing it at all ; they sowed three pecks
of wheat to the acre, and then plowed it in—that was
all.   They used the cradle, but had never heard of
reaping-machines ; the crop was from five to ten bushels an acre, ten bushels was extraordinary, six was not
thought bad.   Of cotton, the ordinary crop was five
hundred pounds to the acre, or from one to two bales
to a hand.   Of maize, usually from ten to twenty
bushels to the acre ; last year not over ten ; this
year they thought it would be twenty-five on the best
land.

HUNTING TALES

The general admiration of Jude brought up the topic
of negro dogs again, and the clergyman told the story
of a man who hunted niggers near where he lived.
He was out once with another man, when, after a long

16

search, they found the dogs barking up a big cotton-
wood tree. They examined the tree closely without
finding any negro, and concluded that the dogs must
have been foiled, and they were about to go away,
when Mr. ———, from some distance off, thought he
saw a negro's leg very high up in the tree, where the
leaves and moss were thick enough to hide a man lying
on the top of a limb with his feet against the trunk.
He called out, as if he really saw a man, telling him
to come down, but nothing stirred. He sent for an
axe, and called out again, saying he would cut the
tree to the ground if he did n't come down. There was
no reply. He then cut half through the tree on one side,
and was beginning on the other, when the negro hal-
loed out that if he would stop he would come down.
He stopped cutting, and the negro descended to the
lowest limb, which was still far from the ground, and
asked the hunter to take away his dogs, and promise
they should n't tear him. But the hunter swore he 'd
make no conditions with him after having been made
to cut the tree almost down.

The negro said no more, but retained his position until the tree was nearly cut in two. When it began to
totter, he slid down the trunk, the dogs springing upon
him as soon as he was within their reach He fought
them hard, and got hold of one by the ear ; that made
them fiercer, and they tore him till the hunter was
afraid they 'd kill him, and stopped them.

I asked if dogs were often allowed to tear the negroes when they caught them ?

" When the hunters come up they always call them off, unless the nigger fights. If the nigger fights 'em that makes 'em mad, and they let 'em tear him good," said the clergyman.

There were two or three women present, and the young men were sparking with them in the house, sitting on beds for want of sofas, the chairs being all in use outside ; the rest of the company sat on the gallery most of the time, but there was little conversation. It was twice remarked to me, "Sunday 's a dull day—nothing to do."

As the Methodist and I were reading after dinner, I noticed that two or three were persuading the others to go with them somewhere, and I asked where they proposed to go. They said they wanted to go over the mountain to hunt a bull.

" To shoot him ?"

"Oh, no, it 's a working bull ; they got his mate yesterday. There aint but one pair of cattle in this neighborhood, and they do all the hauling for nine families." They belonged, together with their wagon, to one man, and the rest borrowed of him. They wanted them this week to cart in their oats. The stray bull was driven in toward night, yoked with another to a wagon, and one of the women, with her family, got into the wagon and was carried home. The bulls were fractious and had to be led by one man, while another urged them forward with a cudgel.

Last night a neighbor came into the house of Uncle Abram's master, and in the course of conversation about crops, said that on Sunday he went over to John Brown's to get him to come out and help him at his harvesting. He found four others there for the same purpose, but John said he did n't feel well, and he reckoned he could n't work. He offered him a dollar and a half a day to cradle for him, but when he tried to persuade him, John spoke out plainly and said, "he 'd be d—d if he was going to work anyhow"; so he said to the others, "Come, boys, we may as well go; you can't make a lazy man work when he 's determined he won 't." He supposed that remark made him mad, for on Thursday John came running across his cotton patch, where he was plowing. He did n't speak a word to him, but cut along over to his neighbor's house, and told him that he had shot two deer, and wanted his hounds to catch 'em, promising to give him half the venison if he succeeded. He did catch one of them, and kept his promise.

This man Brown, they told me, had a large family and lived in a little cabin on the mountain. He pretended to plant a corn patch, but he never worked it, and did n't make any corn. They reckoned he lived pretty much on what corn and hogs he could steal, and on game. The children were described as pitiably "scrawny," half-starved little wretches. Last summer his wife had come to one of them, saying they had no corn, and she wanted to pick cotton to earn some. He had let her go in with the niggers and pick. She kept at it for two days, and took her pay in corn. Afterward he saw her little boy "toting" it to the mill to be ground—much too heavy a load for him.

I asked if there were many such vagabonds.

"Yes, a great many on the mountain, and they make a heap of trouble. There is a law by which they might be taken up [if it could be proved that they have no 'visible means of support'] and made to work to support their families; but the law is never used."

Speaking of another man, one said: "He'll be here to breakfast, at your house for dinner, and at Dr. ——'s to supper, leaving his family to live as they best can." They "reckoned" he got most of his living in that way, while his family had to get theirs by stealing. He never did any work except hunting, and they "reckoned" he killed about as many shoats and yearlings as deer and turkeys.

They said that this sort of people were not often intemperate; they had no money to buy liquor with; now and then, when they'd sold some game or done a little work to raise some money, they'd have a spree; but they were more apt to gamble it off or spend it for fine clothes and things to trick out their wives.

June —. To-day, I am passing through a valley of thin, sandy soil, thickly populated by poor farmers. Negroes are rare, but occasionally neat, new houses, with other improvements, show the increasing prosperity of the district   The majority of the dwellings are small log cabins of one room, with another separate cabin for a kitchen; each house has a well, and a garden enclosed with palings. Cows, goats, mules, and swine, fowls and doves are abundant. The people are more social than those of the lower country, falling readily into friendly conversation with a traveller. They are very ignorant ; the agriculture is wretched and the work hard   I have seen three white women hoeing field crops to-day.   A spinning-wheel is heard in every house, and frequently a loom is clanging in the gallery, always worked by women ; every one wears homespun. The negroes have much more individual freedom than in the planting country, and are not unfrequently heard singing or whistling at their work.

CHAPTER VI

THE HIGHLANDERS

THE northernmost cotton-fields, which I observed, were near the Tennessee line. This marks a climatic division of the country, which, however, is determined by change of elevation rather than of latitude. For a week or more afterwards, my course was easterly, through parts of Tennessee and Georgia into North Carolina, then northward, and by various courses back into Tennessee, when, having finally crossed the Appalachians for the fourth time, I came again to the tobacco plantations of the Atlantic slope in Virginia

AGRICULTURAL NOTES IN THE HIGHLANDS

The climate of this mountain region appears not to differ very greatly from that of Long Island, Southern New Jersey, and Pennsylvania. It is, perhaps, more variable, but the extremes both of heat and cold are less than are reached in those more northern and less elevated regions. The usual crops are the same, those of most consequence being corn, rye, oats, and grass. Fruit is a more precarious crop, from a greater liability to severe frosts after the swelling of buds in the spring. The apple-crop has been thus totally destroyed in the year of my journey, so that in considerable orchards I did not see a single apple. Snow had fallen several inches in depth in April, and a severe freezing night following, even young shoots, which had begun to grow, forest trees, and leaves which had expanded, were withered

The summer pasture continues about six months. The hills generally afford an excellent range, and the mast is usually good, much being provided by the chestnut, as well as the oak and smaller nut-bearing trees The soil of the hills is a rich dark vegetable deposit, and they are cultivated upon very steep slopes. It is said to wash and gully but little, being very absorptive. The valleys, and gaps across the mountain ranges, are closely settled, and all the feasible level ground that I saw in three weeks was fenced, and either under tillage or producing grass or hay. The agricultural management is nearly as bad as possible. Corn, planted without any manure, even by farmers who have large stocks of cattle, is cultivated for a long series of years on the same ground ; the usual crop being from twenty to thirty bushels to the acre. Where it fails very materially, it is thought to be a good plan to shift to rye Rye is sown in July, broadcast, among the growing corn, and incidentally covered with a plow and hoes at the "lay by" cultivation of the corn. It is reaped early in July the following year with cradles, an acre yielding from five to fifteen bushels. The following crop of corn is said to be much the better for the interpolation. Oats, and in the eastern parts, buckwheat, are sown in fallow land, and the crops appeared to be excellent, but I could learn of never a measurement. Herd's-grass (*Agrostis vulgaris*) is sown on the valley lands (rarely on the steep slopes of the mountains), with oats, and the crop, without any further labor, pays for mowing and making into hay for from four to eight years afterward. Where it becomes mossy, weedy, and thin, it is often improved by harrowing or scarifying with a small "bull-tongue," or coulter-plow, and meadows thus made and occasionally assisted, are considered "permanent." The hay from them soon becomes in large part, however, coarse, weedy, and bushy.

Natural meadows are formed on level land in the valleys, which is too wet for cultivation, by felling the timber and cutting up the bushes as close to the ground as practicable, in August. The grass is cut the following year in June, and again in August or September, at which time the new growth of bushes yield to the scythe. The sprouts cease to spring after the second or third year. Clover is a rare crop, but appears well, and is in some localities a spontaneous production. Hay is stored but little in barns, the larger part being stacked in fields. The hay-fields are pastured closely, and with evident bad effect, in the spring and autumn.

Horses, mules, cattle, and swine, are raised extensively, and sheep and goats in small numbers, throughout the mountains, and afford almost the only articles of agricultural export. Although the mountains are covered during three months of the winter with snow several inches in depth, and sometimes (though but rarely) to the depth of a foot or more, and the nights, at least, are nearly always freezing, I never saw any sort of shelter prepared for neat stock. In the severest weather they are only fed occasionally, hay or corn being served out upon the ground, but this is not done daily, or as a regular thing, even by the better class of farmers. One of these, who informed me that his neighbor had four hundred head that were never fed at all, and never came off the mountain, in consequence of which "heaps of them" were starved and frozen to death every year, said that he himself gave his stock a feed "every few days," sometimes not oftener than "once in a week or two." The cattle are of course small, coarse, and "raw-boned." They are usually sold to drovers from Tennessee when three years old, and are driven by them to better lowland pastures, and more provident farmers, by whom they are fattened for the New York market. During the past five or six years, in consequence of the increasing competition, the drovers have purchased also the two-year-olds.

No dairy products are sold. I saw no cheese ; but butter of better quality than I found elsewhere at the South is made by all farmers for their own tables. Mules are raised largely. The mares with foals are usually provided with a pen and shed, and fed with corn, cut oats (the grain and straw chopped together), and hay, daily during winter. This is done by no means universally, however In no single case did I find stabling and really comfortable shelter prepared for a stock of mules ; as a consequence, the mules are inferior in size and constitution to those of Kentucky, Tennessee, and Missouri, and command less prices when driven to the plantations of South Carolina and Georgia—the market for which they are raised.

The business of raising hogs for the same market, which has formerly been a chief source of revenue to the mountain region, has greatly decreased under the competition it has latterly met with from Tennessee and Kentucky. It is now a matter of inferior concern except in certain places where the chestnut mast is remarkably fine. The swine at large in the mountains look much better than I saw them anywhere else at the South. It is said that they will fatten on the mast alone, and the pork thus made is of superior taste to that made with corn, but lacks firmness. It is the custom to pen the swine and feed them with corn for from three to six weeks before it is intended to kill them. In some parts of the mountains the young swine are killed a great deal by bears. Twenty neigh-bors, residing within a distance of three miles, being met at a corn-shucking, last winter, at a house in which I spent the night in North Carolina, account had been taken of the number of swine each supposed himself to have lost by this enemy during the previous two months, and it amounted to three hundred.

Bears, wolves, panthers, and wild-cats are numerous, and all kill young stock of every description. Domestic dogs should also be mentioned among the beasts of prey, as it is the general opinion of the farmers that more sheep are killed by dogs than by all other animals. Sheep-raising and wool-growing should be, I think, the chief business of the mountains. If provided with food in deep snows, a hardy race of sheep could be wintered on the mountains with comfort. At present no sheep are kept with profit. I have no doubt they might be, were shepherds and dogs kept with them constantly, and were they always folded at night. Eagles are numerous, and prey upon very young lambs and pigs.

Many of the farmers keep small stocks of goats, for the manageable quantity of excellent fresh meat the kids afford them, when killed in summer. Their milk is seldom made use of. They require some feeding in winter, and the new-born kids, no adequate shelter ever being provided for them, are often frozen to death. Goats, in all parts of the South, are more generally kept by farmers than at the North.

The agricultural implements employed are rude and inconvenient. A low sled is used in drawing home the crops of small grain. As it is evident that large loads may be moved with a sled across declivities where it would be impracticable to use a cart or wagon, hillside farmers, elsewhere, might frequently find it advantageous to adopt the plan.

Slaves, I was often told, were "unprofitable property" in the mountains, except as they increase and improve in salable value. Two men, on different occasions, in mentioning the sources of revenue of the farmers in their respective districts, spoke of the sale of negroes in the same sentence with that of cattle and swine. "A nigger," said one of them, "that would n't bring over $300, seven years ago, will fetch $1000, cash, quick, this year; but now, hogs, they aint worth so much as they used to be; there's so many of 'em driven through here from Tennessee, they've brought the price down"

Of the people who get their living entirely by agriculture, few own negroes; the slaveholders being chiefly professional men, shop-keepers, and men in office, who are also land owners, and give a divided attention to farming.

The disadvantages attendant upon slave-labor are more obvious where slaves are employed in small numbers together, because the proportion of the labor of the agricultural establishment which requires discretion and trustness on the part of the laborer or vigilant superintendence, and "driving," at many different points, at the same moment, on that of the overseer, is much smaller on a farm than on a plantation. A man can compel the uninterrupted labor of a gang of fifty cotton-hoers almost as absolutely as he can that of a gang of five, and it takes scarcely more superintendence to make sure of the proper feeding of thirty mules, when they are collected in their stable, than of three. For this reason the bad economy of slavery is more obvious to the unthinking people, where it exists in the mild and segregated form in which it is found, when found at all, in those highland districts, than in the large properties of the cotton and sugar districts, The direct moral evils of slavery, however, are less— even less proportionately to the number of slaves, because the slaves being of necessity less closely superintended, and their labor being directed to a greater variety of employments, their habits more resemble those of ordinary free laborers, they exercise more responsibility, and both in soul and intellect they are more elevated ; and this may be said generally of the Northern or farming, as compared with those of the Southern or planting Slave States.

The condition of a slave, however, must always carry with it the strongest temptations to falsehood and eye-service, and slavery, in its mildest character, must be prejudicial to the morals and to the prosperity of the country in which it exists. How this appears in the highland region I can easily show.

In a valley of unusual breadth and fertility, where the farmers were wealthier and the slaves more numerous than usual, I came, one afternoon, upon a herd of uncommonly fine cattle, as they were being turned out of a field by a negro woman. She had given herself the trouble to let down but two of the seven bars of the fence, and they were obliged to leap over a barrier at least four feet high. Last of all came, very unwillingly, a handsome heifer, heavy with calf; the woman urged her with a cudgel and she jumped, but lodging on her belly, as I came up she lay bent, and, as it seemed, helplessly hung upon the top bar. I was about to dismount to help her, when the woman struck her severely, and with a painful effort she boggled over. I spent the night at the best farm, and with the best educated man I met in all the mountain region—this, indeed, was rather below the mountain district proper, in a valley of the eastern Piedmont region. He spoke with some pride of the improvement in the quality of the stock and agriculture of the neighborhood, and asked if I had not seen some fine cattle during the afternoon. I replied that I had, and at the same time mentioned the incident I have just related. "Ha! yes," said he, "that's just a piece of nigger-work. She ought to have had fifty given her right off. But a nigger always will be lazy and careless." "But," said his son, a young man of eighteen, "niggers can be made to do right." "No, they can not," returned the father, "they can never be trusted to do right. I never had a nigger that would even plow to suit me unless while I was standing right over him. And who wants to spend all his life in scolding?" Then to me, "If I could get such hired men as you can in New York, I'd never have another nigger on my place ; but the white men here who will labor, are not a bit better than negroes. You have got to stand right over them all the time, just the same ; and then, if I should ask, now, one of my white men to go and take care of your horse, he'd be very apt to tell me to do it myself, or, if he obeyed, he would take pains to do so in some way that would make me sorry I asked him ; then if I should scold him, he would ask me if I thought he was a nigger, and refuse to work for me any more.''

Wherever there are slaves, I have found that farmers universally testify that white laborers adopt their careless habits, and that they are even more indifferent than negröes to the interests of their employers. Southerners sometimes deny that "slavery degrades labor,'' or prevents industry among the free, and I have been shown individual instances of hard-working white men to prove this. Perhaps it would be more strictly correct to say that slavery breeds unfaithful, meretricious, inexact, and non-persistent habits of working. This influence of slavery extends to the mountains, although the people are much more industrious than those of the low lands. It continued to be my custom to bivouac in the woods during the hottest part of the day. One fine morning in July, I stopped about ten o'clock, at a fork in the road, to inquire my way of a couple of young men who were binding grain in an adjoining field. They both left their work and came to the fence before answering me, but as soon as I could with civility interrupt the conversation they desired, I rode on. Just beyond the fork, a brook, having a grassy bank, and a hill crowned by a forest upon one side, crossed the road. The view down the valley was fine, and thinking I was unlikely to find a pleasanter spot later, I rode on into the woods until I reached a shady opening, took off my saddle, and soon brought my horse back to the brook crossing to graze. I then turned down the brook till I found a deep, clear pool,

where I bathed; then coming back toward my horse
saw that the men had followed me all this time. I
went on to my saddle, and presently saw them ap-
proach and lie down near the horse. I walked towards
them, but before I came within speaking distance they
rose and returned to their work. Half an hour later I
was awakened by Jude, and found they had again left
the field and were coming toward me. I restrained the
dog and they approached, one whittling a stick, but
aimlessly and to no purpose or shape, unlike a Yankee.
Whittling away, he addressed me :

" ''Low yer minin'." (Searching for ore-beds.)

" No, sir."

" ''Low yer travellin'."

" Yes."

" ''Lowed yer was."

"''Low that hoss was raised in the mountings," said
the other.

" No; he was raised in Texas."

" What sort of dog do you call that?"

" A bull terrier."

"''Lowed 't was a sort of bully dog," and so on.
They were very ignorant. Reckoned if I was going
to New York I would not come back here—people that
went that way hardly ever did. I asked if many went
from here to New York. "There was a heap gone to
Texies," they said; "but they allowed New York was
beyond the Texies." (Texas.)

They remained standing fully an hour near me. At
length I went to the horse to give him a little corn;

17

they followed me down, and I left them watching him eat it. Before they again returned to their work, they had lost not less than three hours of the finest harvesting morning of the season; and this is a fair illustration of the way in which the poor white farmers of the Slave States are generally found to attend to their business

Extreme poverty is rare in the mountains, but a smaller proportion of the people live in a style corresponding to that customary among what are called in New England "fore-handed folks," than in any other part of the civilized world which I have visited. The number who can be classed as moderately well-informed, using the New England rural standard, is extremely small. I did not meet in a whole month more than two or three natives who seemed to have enjoyed equal advantages of education with the lowest class of New England (native) working people. Each of those above the average in this respect I shall speak of distinctly.

The great majority live in small and comfortless log huts, two detached cabins usually forming the habitation of a family. These are rarely provided with glass windows, many are even without a port; yet the winter is more severe even than in England. The interior of one frame house, in which I spent a night, forty by thirty feet in dimensions, and two stories in height, occupied by a family of much more than the usual wealth, received light in the lower story only by the door and the occasional interstices of the boarding, and in the upper, by two loopholes, unfurnished with shutters.

The table is usually abundantly provided, its only marked difference from that of the lower country being the occasional presence of unleavened rye bread, made with saleratus and fat, unlike any rye bread I have eaten elsewhere, but more palatable to me than the usual corn bread. Butter is always offered in the mountains, and is usually good.

The women, as well as the men, generally smoke, and tobacco is grown for home use. They are more industrious than the men, often being seen at work in the fields, and at spinning-wheels and hand-looms in almost every house. I was less troubled by vermin than in the low country, yet so much so that I adopted the habit of passing the night on the floor of the cabins, rather than in their beds. The furniture of the cabins is rather less meagre than that of a similar class of habitations in the lower region. In the northern parts, it is common to see a square frame in which are piled a dozen bed quilts. Notwithstanding the ignorance of the people, books are more common than even in the houses of the slave-owners on the planting districts. They seemed fond of reading aloud, those who were able —in a rather doleful and jolting manner. Their books are generally the cheapest and tawdriest of religious holiday books, as Mr. Sears' publications, Fox's *Martyrs*, the *Biography of Distinguished Divines*, with such others as *The Alarm to the Unconverted* and *The Cause and Cure of Infidelity*; not such as *Pil-*

grim's Progress, or *Robinson Crusoe,* neither of which did I ever meet with.

The generally open-hearted, frank, and kindly char-acter of the people, the always agreeable scenery, usually picturesque, and in some parts grandly beauti-ful, and the salubrious atmosphere, cool at night, and though very hot, rarely at all enervating at mid-day, made this part of my journey extraordinarily pleasant. I would have been willing to continue it for months. My horse and dog, now almost every day bountifully fed on suitable food, were in good condition and spirits, and resting on Sundays, I could calculate to make twenty-six miles a day. The dog, notwithstanding the roads were much more stony and hotter than in the low country, was now never foot-sore, which I attribute to the frequency of mountain streams in which she could cool herself. Nor did my horse, though climbing and descending mountains, get seri-ously saddle-galled. The only precaution I took against this danger, was to wash his back twice a day with cold water, and to be sure that the saddle-blanket was laid on smoothly, and was quite clean even from dust. My expenses were not over one dollar a day, the usual charge for a night being from fifty to seventy-five cents, or little more than half that charged me by Mississippi planters for much poorer entertainment.

I resume the narrative of my journey, chiefly in the form of extracts from my diary, as before.

June 29.—At nightfall I entered a broader and more populous valley than I had seen before during the day, but for some time there were only small single-room log cabins, at which I was loth to apply for lodging. At length I reached a large and substantial log house with negro cabins. The master sat on the stoop. I asked if he could accommodate me.

"What do you want?"

"Something to eat for myself and horse, and room to sleep under your roof."

"The wust on 't is," he said, getting up and coming toward me, "we have n't got much for your horse."

"You 've got corn, I suppose."

"No, haint got no corn but a little that we want for ourselves, only just enough to bread us till corn comes again."

"Well, you have oats?"

"Haint got an oat."

"Have n't you hay?"

"No."

"Then I must go further, for my horse can't travel on fodder.'

"Haint got nary fodder nuther."

A TENNESSEE SQUIRE

Fortunately I did not have to go much further before I came to the best house I had seen during the day, a large, neat, white house, with negro shanties, and an open log cabin in the front yard. A stout, elderly, fine-looking woman, in a cool white muslin dress sat upon the gallery, fanning herself. Two little negroes had just brought a pail of fresh water, and she was drinking of it with a gourd, as I came to the gate. I asked if it would be convenient for her to accommodate me for the night, doubtingly, for I had learned to distrust the accommodations of the wealthy slave-holders

"Oh yes, get down, fasten your horse there, and the niggers will take care of him when they come from their work. Come up here and take a seat."

I brought in my saddle-bags

"Bring them in here, into the parlor," she said, "where they 'll be safe."

The interior of the house was furnished with unusual comfort. "The parlor," however, had a bed in it. As we came out she locked the door.

We had not sat long, talking about the weather, (she was suffering much from the heat) when her husband came. He was very hot also, though dressed cooly enough in merely a pair of short-legged, unbleached cotton trousers, and a shirt with the bosom spread open—no shoes nor stockings. He took his seat before speaking to me, and after telling his wife it was the hottest day he ever saw, squared his chair toward me, threw it back so as to recline against a post, and said gruffly, "Good evening, sir; you going to stay here to-night?"

I replied, and he looked at me a few moments without speaking. He was in fact so hot that he spoke with difficulty. At length he got breath and asked abruptly: "You a mechanic, sir, or a dentist, eh—or what?"

I presently asked what railroad it was that I had crossed about six miles east of Chattanooga. I had not expected to find any railroad in this direction. He answered pompously that it was "the Atlantic and Pacific Railroad. It began at Charleston and ended at Chattanooga, but was to be carried across to a place called Francisco in California."

Valuable information, but hardly as interesting as that which the old lady gave me soon afterward. We had been talking of Texas and the emigration. She said "there was a new country they had got annexed to the United States now, and she reckoned people would all be for going to that, now it was annexed. They called it Nebrasky; she did n't know much about it, but she reckoned it must be a powerful fine country, they 'd taken so much trouble to get possession of it."

Supper was cooked by two young women, daughters of the master of the house, assisted by two little negro boys The cabin in front of the house was the kitchen, and when the bacon was dished up, one of the boys struck an iron triangle at the door. "Come to supper," said the host, and led the way to the kitchen, which was also the supper-room. One of the young ladies took the foot of the table, the other seated herself apart by the fire, and actually waited on the table, though the two negro boys stood at the head and foot, nominally waiters, but always anticipated by the Cinderella, when anything was wanted.

A big lout of a youth who came from the field with the negroes, looked in, but seeing me, retired. His father called, but his mother said "'t would n't do no good—he was so bashful."

Speaking of the climate of the country, I was informed that a majority of the folks went barefoot all winter, though they had snow much of the time four or five inches deep, and the man said he did n't think most of the men about here had more than one coat, and they never wore any in the winter except on holidays. "That was the healthiest way," he reckoned, "just to toughen yourself and not wear no coat; no matter how cold it was, he did n't wear no coat.

The master held a candle for me while I undressed, in a large room above stairs; and gave me my choice of the four beds in it. I found one straw bed (with, as usual, one sheet), on which I slept comfortably. At midnight I was awakened by some one coming in. I rustled my straw, and a voice said, "Who is there in this room?"

"A stranger passing the night; who are you?"

"All right; I belong here. I 've been away and just come home"

He did not take his clothes off to sleep. He turned out to be an older son who had been fifty miles away, looking after a stray horse. When I went down stairs in the morning, having been awakened early by flies, and the dawn of day through an open window, I saw the master lying on his bed in the "parlor," still asleep in the clothes he wore at supper. His wife was washing herself on the gallery, being already dressed for the day; after drying her face on the family towel, she went into the kitchen, but soon returned, smoking a pipe, to her chair in the doorway.

Yet everything betokened an opulent and prosperous farmer—rich land, extensive field crops, a number of negroes, and considerable herds of cattle and horses. He also had capital invested in mines and railroads, he told me. His elder son spoke of him as "the squire."

A negro woman assisted in preparing breakfast (she had been employed in the field labor the night before), and both the young ladies were at the table. The squire observed to me that he supposed we could buy hands very cheap in New York. I said we could hire them there at moderate wages. He asked if we could n't buy as many as we wanted, by sending to Ireland for them and paying their passage. He had supposed we could buy them and hold them as slaves for a term of years, by paying the freight on them. When I had corrected him, he said, a little hesitatingly, "You don't have no black slaves in New York?" "No, sir" "There's niggers there, aint there, only they're all free?" "Yes, sir." "Well, how do they get along so?" "So far as I know, the most of them live pretty comfortably." (I have changed my standard of comfort lately, and am inclined to believe that the majority of the negroes at the North live more comfortably than the majority of the whites at the South.) "I wouldn't like that," said the old lady. "I would n't like to live where niggers was free, they are bad enough when they are slaves: it's hard enough to get along with them here, they're so bad. I reckon that niggers are the meanest critters on earth ; they are so mean and nasty'' (she expressed disgust and indignation very strongly in her face). '' If they was to think themselves equal to we, I don't think white folks could abide it—they 're such vile saucy things.'' A negro woman and two boys were in the room as she said this.

At night I was again troubled to find a house at which my horse could be suitably fed, and was finally directed to a place at some distance off my direct road. To reach it, I followed a cart path up a pretty brook in a mountain glen, till I came to an irregular-shaped cattle yard, in the midst of which was a rather picturesque cabin, the roof being secured by logs laid across it and held in place by long upright pins. The interior consisted of one large ''living-room,'' and a '' lean-to,'' used as a kitchen, with a sleeping loft over half the living-room For furniture, there were two bedsteads, which occupied one third of the room ; a large and a small table, on the latter of which lay a big Bible, and other books ; several hide-bottomed chairs, two chests, shelves with crockery, and a framed lithographic portrait of Washington on the white horse. Women's dresses hung as a curtain along the foot of one bed ; hides, hams, and bunches of candles from the rafters. An old man and his wife, with one hired man, were the occupants ; they had come to this place from North Carolina two years before. They were very good, simple people ; social and talkative, but at frequent intervals the old man, often in the midst of conversation interrupting a reply to a question put by myself, would groan aloud and sigh out, "Glory to God!" "Oh, my blessed Lord!" "Lord, have mercy on us!" or something of the sort, and the old woman would respond with a groan, and then there would be silence for reflection for a few moments, as if a dead man were in the house, and it had been forgotten for a time. They talked with great geniality and kindness, however, and learning that I was from New York, said that I had reminded them, "by the way I talked," of some New York people who had moved near to where they had lived in North Carolina, and whom they seemed to have much liked. "They was well larned people," the old man said; "though they warn't rich, they was as well larned as any, but they was the most friendly people I ever see. Most of our country folks, when they is well larned, is too proud, they won't hardly speak civil to the common; but these Yorkers was n't so, the least bit; they was the civilest people I ever seed. When I seed the gals coming over to our housen, I nat'rally rejoiced; they always made it so pleasant. I never see no people who could talk so well."

He and his wife frequently referred to them afterwards, and complimented me by saying that "they should have known me for a Yorker by my speeching so much like them."

I said, in answer to their inquiry, that I had found the people of this part of the country remarkably friendly and sociable. The old man said he had "always heard this was so, and it was nat'ral it should be. There warn't no niggers here ; where there was niggers, people could n't help getting a cross habit of speaking " He asked if New York were not a Free State, and how I liked that. I answered, and he said he 'd always wished there had n't been any niggers here (the old woman called out from the other room, that she wished so, too), but he would n't like to have them free. As they had got them here, he did n't think there was any better way of getting along with them than that they had. There were very few in the district, but where they came from there were more niggers than whites. They had had three themselves ; when they decided to move up here into the mountains, the niggers didn't want to come with them, and they sold them to a speculator.

I asked if it were possible they would prefer to be sold to a trader, who might take them off and sell them to a cotton planter.

"O, yes, they had a great fear of the mountains ; they would rather, they said, be sent to a cotton farm, or a rice or sugar farm—anything else ; so we sold them to the first nigger speculator that come along." The old woman called out again, that she wished they had n't, for after all they was a great help to her, and it was very hard sometimes to do all the work she had to do, alone. " Those Yorkers did n't like slaves neither," she continued, coming into the room, " they said they could n't bear to have 'm do anything for 'em, they was so shacklin and lazy, but one of the gals

married a man who owned a heap of niggers, for
all that."

Their notions of geography were amusing. They
thought Virginia lay to the southward, and was a
cotton-growing State, and they supposed that one
reason their niggers were willing to be sold was that
their mother came from Virginia, and they had heard
her talk of it, and that they thought they might be
sold to go back there upon a cotton farm. New York,
they thought, lay west of Georgia, and between them
and Texas. They asked about Indiana, and said that
I must have passed through it coming from Texas,
confusing it, probably, with Louisiana; and they asked
if New York were not the country the Yankees came
from—"the people that used to come peddling." They
supposed also that New York had a much warmer
climate than Georgia. The younger man informed me
that "the United States had lately annexed a new
country called Nebrisky. It was large enough to make
thirteen States, and they had had a great commotion
as to whether it should be Free or Slave States. The
people here all wanted it to be Slave States, because
they might want to move out there, and a fellow
might get a nigger and have to sell him. If a man
moved into a Free State, he'd have to sell his niggers;
if he didn't, they'd be free as soon as he took
'em in. He didn't think that was right; a man
ought to be able to take his property wherever he
pleased."

I replied that it would be a great deal better place

for non-slaveholders to move to, if slaves were excluded, to which he made no reply.

We had for supper cold corn-bread, cold bacon, and
hot coffee. The old woman remarked she had got so
warm she could n't eat anything, but she drank much
coffee. I was a good deal fatigued; about eight o'clock
I intimated that I would like to go to bed. The old
man lighted a candle, for until then we had been sitting by the firelight in the chimney, and after groaning
aloud for the space of ten minutes, began to read in a
very slow, monotonous manner, spelling out the hard
words, from the Bible. After continuing this exercise
for half an hour, he took a hymn-book, read two lines
and commenced to sing, and thus went on reading and
singing, the other two joining him at the second verse,
when we all rose. Thirteen verses were sung, and
then, after blowing out the candle, he kneeled for
prayer. He prayed with great fervor, much assisted by
the ejaculatory responses of his wife, for more than
half an hour. When we rose, the old woman took a
single clean sheet from a chest, spread it on one of the
beds, and told me that I could take that one. I began
to undress, and she slipped out-of-doors till I was
under the counterpane. The young man climbed into
the loft, and the two old people took the other bed.
There was no window at all in the house; they closed
both doors and left a considerable fire burning on the
hearth. There did not, however, appear to be any
want of ventilation, the logs and roof being sufficiently
open. It was the first time, with only one exception,

in more than a month that I had been furnished with a
clean sheet. (The luxury of two sheets I have never
had in a private house since crossing the Mississippi),
and I slept better than I have done before for weeks.

When I came to breakfast, the old woman was much
disappointed that I declined coffee. She had thought I
would like it sweet, and had taken pains to boil in
some sweetenin' (molasses) on my account; she said
she did not think I could have strength to travel such
hot weather without it. I replied that I thought that
I had found that in hot weather, after a little while, its
effect was rather debilitating. "Perhaps it was so,"
she said, "and that was the reason she felt so weak
and sleepy in the afternoon. They did n't have no
coffee for dinner, and she had thought she ought to
have it, because in the afternoon she was always so
tired and sleepy she could hardly drag about till supper time, and at supper she always drank a lot of coffee
just to keep from going to sleep till after prayers. She
didn't feel as though she could live without coffee."

She had taken much pains otherwise to get a good
breakfast—thick griddle-cakes of Indian meal, which
I could really praise with a good conscience. This
greatly elevated her, and she told me in a confidential
whisper, "there were none of her neighbors ever had
anything nice, not even for company, because they
did n't any of 'em know how to cook beyond the
common."

Molasses they always used as if in the plural number (like oats), urging me to take "them molasses—

but perhaps I would n't like them with my bacon."

My horse was well cared for, voluntarily, by the hired man; cleaned and fed generously with corn, fodder, hay, and sheaf oats. Charge for all, including two of the notable Indian slap-jacks, which I carried away in my haversack, sixty-two and a half cents. When I wanted to wash I was directed to "the spring," the old woman having the wash basin in use. In fact, she was mixing the cakes in it.

TENNESSEE COPPER MINING

I have been visiting the mining region, which I approached through the pretty valley of the ———, where, for the first time in this journey, I met with hemlocks and laurels growing in great perfection.

The first discovery of ore was made ten years ago, soon after which specimens were taken to New York, but no mining was done, and nothing was known of it here, until a New York company bought a tract of land three years ago, and immediately commenced operations. New veins were soon found and new companies formed, and the excitement continues, new discoveries being made up to this time. At the public house were ten or twelve gentlemen of wealth, who had come to sell or buy copper land, or to learn "the signs" that they might look for them on their own land elsewhere.

The mines in operation at present are owned almost entirely in New York and London. The miners employed are mostly white North Carolinians, who are paid twenty to twenty-five dollars a month, when digging perpendicular shafts, and twenty-five to thirty dollars when working horizontally. There are here, however, several hundred Cornish men ("London miners," a native told me), and more are constantly coming. They are engaged in Cornwall, and have their expenses out paid, and forty dollars a month wages. They are said, at these wages, to be much more profitably employed than the natives. Two, whom I found at work together, one hundred and fifty feet from the surface, told me that they had been here about six weeks, and were well pleased. They each got forty dollars a month; in England, they had earned respectively but three or four pounds. Board costs here at the boarding-houses seven dollars a month, but they thought that a man living "in a cottage" by himself could live cheaper than in England. Cornbread (though Cornish men) they had not yet eaten, and they did not believe that they should ever come to it. They must have wheaten bread. The only thing they much missed was ale; the people here did not know what it was, but drank whiskey. They would rather have one draught of Cornish swipes than a gallon of this whiskey.

Some of the miners, including some of the Cornish men, had been getting ready a pole, which they were to erect, and hoist a flag upon, on the Fourth of July. I heard a report the day before I reached the mines, that the Englishmen at the mines were going to hoist the English flag and hurrah for the Queen on the Fourth

18

of July. The country people were much excited by this report, and on the third I met a great many of them, armed with rifles, coming in " to see about it " I could not persuade them that the Englishmen were intending in good faith to celebrate the day, so strong was their belief in the continued hostility of the English people to American independence.

There were few settlers here when the mines were discovered. At present, the population is reported to be many thousand. If so, it must be remarkably scattered, for there is nothing like a village; the only houses, with two or three exceptions, being small log cabins. I stopped at what is considered the best public house. When I asked for a bed, I was pointed to a room in which there were seven beds, and told that I could take my pick. Two gentlemen immediately called out to inform me which of the beds they had used the night before, hoping that I would respect their claim to hold them. All the beds had been slept in by others without change of sheet. Being the first to withdraw from the bar-room, I had my choice, and found one straw bed among them, which, of course, I appropriated. Fortunately, I had no bed-fellow ; the other beds were mostly doubly occupied.

At a public house, a few nights before, I heard the landlord, while conducting two men to their sleeping-room, observe, that he supposed that they would like to sleep both in the same bed, as they came together, and I afterwards saw them together in a feather bed, notwithstanding there were several vacant beds in the

same room. It was almost the hottest night I ever
experienced out of the East Indies, and I sweltered
upon the floor.

A SMART YANKEE

Everybody at the mines took me for either a shrewd
speculator, or a mineralogist who had come to make
examinations for a speculator. I was several times
stopped and asked if I did not wish to look at a good
piece of mineral land, and often requested to give my
opinion of specimens, nor could I make myself believed
when I said I knew nothing about the matter. After
I returned from visiting some of the mines, there was
a room full of people at the public house. One asked
me if I would tell them what I thought about those I
had seen I assured him that I was not in the least
able to judge of their value, probably not half so much
so as he was himself. He laughed, and another,
laughing, asked, "What do you carry in that thing at
your side?" and everybody smiled.

"In this pouch, do you mean?"

"Yes, if it's no offence—no offence meant, no offence
taken, you know."

"Certainly not; I'll tell you exactly what I've got
in it." I opened it and looking in, as it were, read the
contents, "a pair of gloves, a knife, a corkscrew, a
fleam, a toothbrush, a box of tapers, and a ball of
twine." All laughed aloud, being quite sure in their
minds that the pouch contained a blow-pipe, tests, and
specimens of ore, and that I was a very knowing fellow, who could keep his own counsel.

July 5.—Last evening I rode several miles, constantly saying to myself as I passed the miserable huts, "that, I can't put up with," and still going on to try further for something better, until, just as it was getting dark, I came to some larger cabins, one of which had creepers trained over a porch, for which sign of taste I selected it. It was occupied by a family, possessing a number of negro servants, and living in more comfort than I have seen for some time. My horse being brought out in the morning covered with mire, I asked the negro if he would not clean him. He picked up a piece of corn cob and began scraping him. "Had n't he got any currycomb or card?" I asked, but he did not know what I meant, and laughed when I explained it to him, as you would laugh at some little article of pure foppery.

I passed through Murphy to-day, a pretty, shady town, surrounded by lovely scenery. I was a little surprised at the sight of a pillory and stocks, and to learn that a white man had been recently stripped, whipped, and branded with a red hot iron for some petty crime, by the officers of the law, in the presence of my informant, and of all of the inhabitants who could be called together to witness this solemn testimony of the legislative barbarism of their State.

While I stopped under a tree near a house as a heavy rain cloud was passing, a white man came out, and after greeting me with a single word, began calling : " Duke, Clary, Tom, Joe," etc., finally collecting seven little negroes and three white children ; "Just

look a here! here's a reg'lar nigger dog; have it to
ketch niggers when they run away, or don't behave."
(He got a piece of bread and threw it to Jude.)
"There! did you see that! See what teeth she's got,
she'd just snap a nigger's leg off. If you don't mind
I'll get one—you Jule, if I hear you crying any more,
I'll get this gentleman to send me one. See how
strong its jaws be; he says all he's got to do when a
nigger don't behave, is just to say the word, and it'll
snap a nigger's head right off, just as easy as you'd
take a chicken's head off with an axe." (The niggers
look with dismay at Jude, who is watching them very
closely expecting some more bread. The white children laugh foolishly)

July 6 —I have to-day crossed the Tomahila mountain, having spent the night at an unusually comfortable
house, known throughout all the country as "Walker's,"
situated at its western base. Apparently it is a house
which the wealthy planters from the low country make
a halting station on their journey to certain sulphur
springs further north and east. There were plenty of
negroes, under unusually good government, and the
table supply was abundant and various. Yet everything was greasy; even what we call simple dishes,
such as boiled rice and toast, were served soaking in a
sauce of melted fat. I gave the stable-boy a dollar for
thoroughly cleaning my horse, but rode away with less
than usual scrutiny of the harness, and when I came
to climb a steep pitch of the mountain, discovered that

the rascal had unbuckled and kept the preventer-girth.

The road, which is excellent, and which was built by aid of a State appropriation, follows for some distance, the slopes of a water-course, and then, tack and tack, up a steep mountain-side, until, at about twelve miles from Walker's, a small plateau and clearing is reached, on which stands a cabin occupied by a man, who, as he told me, gets his living by turning bed-posts of maple, which grows here abundantly and is scarce below.

After leaving this place, the road descends into a shallow valley in which flows the Tomahila River, a stream some twenty yards across, then follows for several miles along the crest of a deep, dark gorge, at the bottom of which the river roars in frequent cascades, and then mounts another high ridge. From the summit there is a grand prospect to the eastward. Directly below is a deep valley, surrounded on all sides by a succession of mountain peaks. With the exception of one bald prominence towering up on the left, these are all, notwithstanding their great height, densely wooded. Those directly opposite are some forty miles distant, and are among the highest elevations on the continent.

While I was resting my horse and looking at these distant summits, some thunder clouds drifted around and collected before them, and then floated forward, hovering over the minor peaks and pouring copious showers upon them. The thunder grew constantly more threatening, and I began to descend hastily. A zigzag road has been made with great labor, so that by travelling two miles upon a descending slope, never more rapidly than at the rate of perhaps six feet in one hundred, you accomplished with entire ease what would be, in a direct course down the steep side of the mountain, not more than a thousand feet. The entire distance to the valley is six miles.

A little boy on a mule, carrying a mail-bag, here overtook me. He said that he carried the mail from Ashville to Murphy, one hundred and fourteen miles, travelling each way once a week. He starts from Ashville Monday morning and returns there Saturday night, rests on Sunday, but during the week travels an average of nearly forty miles a day on a mule's back. Last winter, he said, the snow was up to the mule's shoulders on the mountain, but he did not fail to accomplish his stated journey every day. When I asked him how old he was, he said, "he believed that he should be about fifteen in three or four months." He had two mules, but only changed from one to the other on alternate weeks. He was paid $5 a month and board.

Speaking of mountains, he asked if I "had ever been on Old Balsam?" He had; he was up on the top of it one morning at sunrise. I asked how he could sleep there,—was there a cabin? No, but he had been coon hunting with some fellows all night, and toward daylight they got to running a wild-cat, for they had a dog that would kill any wild-cat if it could catch it. They did not succeed, however, and just at sunrise they gave it up and found themselves close to the top of Old Balsam. Then he had to go down the mountain and get up his mule, and ride forty miles with the mule before he could go to sleep. It was as much as he could do to keep awake that day.

Hearing that I belonged in New York, he asked if I knew a man there by the name of Poillon. Yes, I did; he lived a little way out of New York City, though—in the country. "The man I mean lives in New York centre—right in the village itself," he replied. I knew that there was a man of that name, I said. "Well, he went from Ashville." "Yes, perhaps so." "Oh he did, he went from there two year ago. Do you know a man there by the name of Ogee?"

"No."

"There was a man in Ashville, came from somewhere in that country—Charleston, I believe 't was—by that name."

"Charleston is not very near New York."

"Aint it? well, 't was Charleston he said, I believe; Charleston or New York, or some place out there."

Another man near Waynesville in this region, asked me if I knew Mr. White, of New York. I did not. "Why, he belongs in New York."

"Very likely, but New York is a large place. There are probably a hundred people of the name of White there, but I don't happen to know one of them."

"Reckon you 'd know this man if he came from there,

for he's a man of talent; must be one of the first men; I never see a man who knew so much about all sorts of things, and who could explain everything out to you, as well as he. Expect he must have come from some other place. I thought he said he was raised in New York, too."

"Very possibly he was, but I know but very few indeed of all the men of talent in New York. You don't consider how many people there are there."

" It's a right smart business place, I know; it must be. You know Mr. ——, don't you?"

"Who is he?"

" Why, the little man that keeps store in Waynesville; reckon you know him, he goes to New York every spring to buy goods; seen him there, haint you? "

"I don't think that I have; you see, there are seven hundred thousand people in New York, and there are thousands and tens of thousands whom I never saw. It would be impossible for me to see one in a thousand of the people who come there every year. In fact, though I have lived in New York some years, I have but very few acquaintances there, not nearly as many as you have in this county probably."

"Such a big place; I suppose there's some people been living there all their lives that don't know each other, and never spoke to one another once yet in their lives, aint there?"

" Certainly—thousands of them."

" 'T 'aint so here; people's more friendly, this country."

END OF VOLUME I.

CPSIA information can be obtained
at www.ICGtesting.com
Printed in the USA
LVHW082143060921
697168LV00022B/502

9 780353 052932